Educational Policy for School Administrators

Educational Policy for School Administrators

PATRICIA F. FIRST

University of Oklahoma

Allyn and Bacon

Boston London Toronto Sydney Tokyo Singapore

Series Editor: Ray Short
Series Editorial Assistant: Jo Ellen Caffrey
Production Administrator: Annette Joseph
Production Coordinator: Holly Crawford
Editorial-Production Service: Laura Cleveland, WordCrafters Editorial
  Services, Inc.
Cover Administrator: Linda K. Dickinson
Manufacturing Buyer: Megan Cochran

Copyright ©1992 by Allyn and Bacon
A Division of Simon & Schuster, Inc.
160 Gould Street
Needham Heights, MA 02194

Library of Congress Cataloging-in-Publication Data

First, Patricia F.
   Educational policy for school administrators / by Patricia F.
   First.
       p.   cm.
   Includes bibliographical references and index.
   ISBN 0-205-13390-8
   1. Education and state–United States. 2. School management and
organization. I. Title.
LC89.F57 1992
379.73–dc20   91–37992
                                                   CIP

Printed in the United States of America

10 9 8 7 6 5 4 3 2 1   97 96 95 94 93 92

To Ben C. Hubbard—
Professor, Mentor, Friend

Contents

SECTION FOUR

Local Government and Education Policy   **209**

School Boards: The Great Responsibility

Contributing Authors

Ira Bogotch, Assistant Professor of Educational Administration, Department of Educational Leadership and Foundations, University of New Orleans, New Orleans, Louisiana

Caroline B. Cody, Associate Professor and Chair, Department of Educational Leadership and Foundations, University of New Orleans, New Orleans, Louisiana

G. Robb Cooper, Assistant Professor of Educational Administration and School Business Management, Northern Illinois University, DeKalb, Illinois, and Of Counsel, Scariano Kula, Ellch & Himes, Chicago, Illinois

Joan L. Curcio, Associate Professor of Educational Administration, Department of Educational Leadership, University of Florida, Gainesville, Florida

Gordon A. Donaldson, Jr., Associate Professor of Educational Administration, College of Education, University of Maine, Orono, Maine

Patricia F. First, Professor, Department of Educational Leadership and Policy Studies, University of Oklahoma, Norman, Oklahoma

Thomas E. Glass, Professor of Educational Administration, Department of Leadership and Educational Policy Studies, Northern Illinois University, DeKalb, Illinois

Steven S. Goldberg, Associate Professor and Coordinator, Educational Leadership Program, Beaver College, Glenside, Pennsylvania

H. C. Hudgins, Jr., Professor and Chair, Department of Educational Administration and Supervision, East Carolina University, Greenville, North Carolina

John Maddaus, Assistant Professor, College of Education, University of Maine, Orono, Maine

Charles McCormick, Assistant Superintendent for Business Affairs, DeKalb Community Unit School District #428, DeKalb, Illinois

James Meza, Jr., Visiting Associate Professor of Educational Administration, Department of Educational Leadership and Foundations, and Administrator of the Accelerated Schools Project, College of Education, University of New Orleans, New Orleans, Louisiana

Jeffrey E. Mirel, Associate Professor, Foundations Faculty, Department of Leadership and Educational Policy Studies, Northern Illinois University, DeKalb, Illinois

Louis F. Miron, Assistant Professor of Educational Administration, Department of Educational Leadership and Foundations, and Director, Urban Educational Laboratory, College of Education, University of New Orleans, New Orleans, Louisiana

Sally Bulkley Pancrazio, Professor and Chair, Department of Educational Administration and Foundations, Illinois State University, Normal, Illinois

Russell J. Quaglia, Associate Professor of Educational Administration, College of Education, University of Maine, Orono, Maine

Lawrence F. Rossow, Professor and Chair, Department of Educational Leadership and Policy Studies, University of Oklahoma, Norman, Oklahoma

Charles Russo, Assistant Professor of Educational Administration, Division of Administration, Policy, and Urban Education, Fordham University, New York, New York

Rosemary A. Salesi, Professor of Reading and Language Arts, College of Education, University of Maine, Orono, Maine

Robert J. Shoop, Professor of Educational Administration, College of Education, Kansas State University, Manhattan, Kansas

Edward P. St. John, Associate Professor of Educational Administration, Department of Educational Leadership and Foundations, University of New Orleans, New Orleans, Louisiana

Preface and Acknowledgments

As a professor of educational administration, I am in daily contact with aspiring and present educational administrators in my classrooms, in the schools, and in government agencies. I admire them greatly. Their perseverance, creativity, and leadership can, and do, make a difference in the education and the lives of our nation's children.

This book is designed to improve understanding of the policy-related roles of these educational administrators. The book opens with a discussion of what policy means for the administrator and then moves to discussion about educational policy making at the federal, state, and local levels. At the end of each section, contributing authors illustrate policy-making procedures and issues and the roles of the educational administrator. I am indebted to these authors, whose names are listed on the contributing authors' pages, for the thoughtful pieces that enliven and illuminate the ideas discussed throughout this book. Their time, expertise, and friendship in being part of this project are gratefully acknowledged.

Other thanks to friends and colleagues are also due. During the writing of this book I was privileged to have been a member of three fine faculties in educational administration. From each the friendship and colleagueship, the support and the intellectual exchange have contributed to the success of this and other projects and to the joy of being a professor of educational administration. My thanks to David Carr, Robb Cooper, Ron Everett, Fred Frank, Tom Glass, Jim Heald, H. C. Hudgins, Ray Lows, Muriel Mackett, Jeri Nowakowski, Chuck Sloan, and Al Thurman, all of whom were with me at Northern Illinois University; to Gordon Donaldson, Russ Quaglia, John Skehan, and Jerry Work, my colleagues at the University of Maine; and to my colleagues at the University of New Orleans, Ira Bogotch, Caroline Cody, Dick Elliott, Jim Meza, Lou Miron, Ed St. John, and Bob Wimpellberg.

To Amy Cates, Melissa Savage, and Tracy Sanborn of the University of Maine, warm thank-yous for the care and professionalism with which this material was processed from beginning to end through many changes and drafts. To Louise Dieterle, grateful acknowledgment of her generous contribution of assistance and encouragement. Thank-yous are also due to the reviewers whose comments contributed greatly to the finished product: Dale Hayes, Professor Emeritus, University of Nebraska-Lincoln, and William Silky, State University of New York at Oswego.

Policy: What It Is and How to Study It

Making, Implementing, and Analyzing Educational Policy: What This Means for the School Administrator

In every transitional age one must let go the finishing, and look on beauty bare. The incompleteness, the groping, fits our age. (May, 1985, p. 201)

The Administrator's Policy-Related Role

School administrators are policy makers, policy implementors, consumers of policy research, and perhaps more than other educators, they are the victims of the confusing milieu of educational policy making. Victims or those perceived as victims cannot readily exert leadership in their field, and much of the literature to date denies the real and potential leadership of school administrators at all levels of the educational governance system. The by now tiresome manager versus leader debate denies the complexity of the political world of the school administrator and does not acknowledge the subtle and incremental leadership exerted daily in U.S. school systems.

It is the contention in this book that more attention to the policy-related roles will both highlight the leadership already being exhibited by school administrators and assist them in exerting more and stronger leadership throughout the educational system. The policy-related roles—policy maker, policy implementor, policy analyzer and evaluator, consumer of policy research—have, until recently, been largely ignored in the academic preparation of school administrators. The emphasis in educational administration preparation has been on management skills, and in the case of the potential superintendent of schools, on the chief executive relationship between the superintendent and the school board. An increased emphasis on the study of

1

educational policy followed the tremendous impact of the abrupt shift in federal policy when President Reagan initiated the "New Federalism." This shift, plus the avalanche of commission reports, beginning with *A Nation at Risk* (1983), highlighted the need to study policy-making processes, policy decisions, and policy makers.

In the 1980s, the main action in educational policy making moved to the state level, but the pressure was greatest on the school administrators at the local level who were struggling with the implementation problems inherent in hastily conceived state reform packages. There was frantic state activity in response to the commission reports, with governors in the forefront of initiating educational change and legislators active in areas they used to leave to state boards of education. Poor policy making, characterized by impulsive action based on incomplete data, frequently set the stage for long-range problems. At the same time, local school superintendents saw reform issues pushed to the local level for further policy analysis as well as implementation. Expertise for this task was at times lacking.

That expertise is often still lacking and it is still needed because policy is never static. It is continually growing and evolving and policy language is forever in need of reformulation. Even after the present debates have rested in their historical niche, the need for understanding and practicing the intricacies of policy making at all governmental levels will remain important. The sections in this book address both the understanding and the practice of the administrator's policy-related roles. The emphasis throughout the book remains on the integration of theory and practice. One cannot survive without the other.

The Legacy of the 1980s

In 1980 President Reagan ushered in the "New Federalism," an era in which there was an abrupt shift in the balance of power among the intergovernmental layers of governance. "Federalism" refers to the balance between state and federal power in the governance system. In keeping with the conservative belief in a government that is close to the people, President Reagan started shifting power from the federal level back to the state level. In education, this shift took the initial form of the consolidation of previously discreet federal categorical programs into block grants to the states. In parallel moves, this shift in power was accomplished in other fields and within other federal agencies.

This era in educational history is discussed in the sections on federal governance, but for now its effect on the administrator's policy-related position is the important point. For as power and discretion shifted to the states at the same time that there began to be a ground swell of public criticism of the nation's schools, the pressure on the educational administrator began to build. This pressure increased and intensified through the 1980s, as state after state passed massive educational reform packages, some containing hundreds of new mandates, many without increased money for the accomplishment of these mandates. The movement included calls for accountability, which brought pressure from "above" upon the head of the educational administrator and calls for teacher power and better school-site management, which brought pressure from "below" upon the educational administrator.

The Use of the Policy-Related Framework

The 1990s began with no indication that the pressure will ease or that the administrator's job will become more "manageable." Virtually everyone, all the governmental institutions and the citizenry in all of its manifestations as parents, students, teachers, community members, interest group members, and governing board members expects more and demands more of public education. As the field has struggled to meet these varied expectations, a variety of work roles have been proposed and promoted for the educational administrator, including manager, instructional leader, staff developer, adult educator, and counselor/facilitator/group leader. From a theoretical perspective, the educational administrator is seen as leader, facilitator, hierarchical linkpin, and visionary.

The view that educational administration is a policy-related field does not compete with any of these characterizations, all of which can be seen as valid and/or important depending upon time, place, and circumstances. Rather, the policy-related view of the school administrator can be a framework of understanding placed around the countless roles and tasks that fill an administrator's day. To think of or discuss the role as policy related may not be to do anything differently (or, of course, it may, as all thoughtful consideration and discussion may, bring change), but it may bring a new understanding of the role, the "why I am doing this" to accompany the "how to get this done."

Policy drives the educational system. Although a direction or directive may not always be labeled as "a policy," the administrator's days are driven by national, state, and local educational policies and increasingly by international policies as well. When the school principal attends a staffing for a special education student, he or she is implementing national policy regarding how children with special needs are to be treated in the public schools of the nation. When the superintendent of schools serves on a state-level committee to refine the state's assessment instruments, the superintendent is making policy at the state level. When the assistant superintendent for instruction interprets the district's report card to the press and the community, he or she is analyzing policy while explaining it. When the principal is empowered to implement a new program for the community's latchkey children, a program in which all affected had the opportunity to participate in the planning, the principal is the recipient of well-made policy. When a "good," organized principal is working six nights a week as well as weekends to get the job done, he or she is the victim of unreasonable burden under mismade policy. In all of these examples, the educational administrator can and should be taking a leadership stance in the policy-making process.

Leading in Troubled Times

From Drucker (1980, 1986) to Naisbett (1982) to May (1985) to Toffler (1990), writers in a variety of fields have told us we are living in turbulent times, or as many put it, transitional or troubled times. Although this may be small consolation for the administrator trying to lead via his or her policy-making roles, it is worth examining and understanding what makes our times so difficult. And, besides, it is always helpful to know that we are not the only ones who think so.

Rollo May (1985) writes that "in all transitional periods there is a confusion as to what the new meaning . . . is going to be. Our period is especially difficult since we are in the very midst of that confusion" (p. 191). May is writing about the arts as he compares our period to the great transitions such as the death of Hellenism and the birth of the Roman culture and the end of the medieval era and the birth of the Renaissance. But his point applies to our era broadly, and the educator may feel he speaks directly to him or her when he writes that our period is especially difficult. "At this moment, we are in the midst of a new cultural transition with its attendant difficulties and confusion" (p. 191).

In these troubled times, educational administrators are expected to assume leadership in an enterprise with endless responsibilities to both individuals and society. They must, therefore, emerge as leaders who are aware of society's trends and issues and who have a sense of vision to usher schools into the future (First, 1988). It is the contention here that viewing and understanding the educational administrator's role as policy related can assist him or her in seeing beyond the daily administrative role to the leadership role in education, that crucial enterprise that remains the great opportunity for countless numbers of people. Educational administrators are societal leaders in charge of a priceless public good. They operationalize this leadership through the execution of their policy-related roles.

The Paradigm Shift and Educational Issues

In *Leaders,* Bennis and Nanus (1985) write, "The fact is that as difficult, frustrating and fearful as these times are, they are also interesting, catalytic and crucial.... A new paradigm is being born" (p. 13). Bennis and Nanus write that this new paradigm is a major turning point in history, "where some new height of vision is sought, where some fundamental redefinitions are required, where our table of values will have to be reviewed" (p. 13). In describing the dimensions of the new paradigm, Bennis and Nanus refer to John Naisbitt's *Megatrends* (1982). The changes described are:

From:	*Industrial Society*	To:	*Information Society*
	Force Technology		High Tech/High Touch
	National Economy		World Economy
	Short Term		Long Term
	Centralization		Decentralization
	Institutional Help		Self-Help
	Representative Democracy		Participatory Democracy
	Hierarchies		Networking
	North		South
	Either/Or		Multiple Option

As the world view shifts to the new paradigm complex, societal and educational issues are generated. Although these societal issues are addressed simultaneously in multiple and stratified policy-forming entities, it is the practicing administrator who is held responsible by the public for the success or failure of the school's response to the issues caused by each change. The briefly stated nine issues that follow serve as examples of how the paradigm shift generates educational policy options. These issues are not exhaustive of those impacting schools, but they are symbolic of the paradigm shift necessitating a massive reexamination of our educational policy.

1. Models for Restructuring Education

Traditional education appears to be on a collision course with social and economic forces that already are straining their capacity to serve all who must or need to be served. Some reformers question fundamental assumptions upon which we currently organize schools. They call for new relationships within and among schools and their encompassing systems. Although some suggestions at first seem too visionary for practical application, administrators must be aware of their universe of reform options. Practicing administrators need to be knowledgeable about these new ideas, to grasp their potential and their problems, and to be open to and experiment with new concepts, with variety in approaches to reform and with grass-roots initiatives.

2. State versus Local Control

Issues involved in state versus local control have taken on new meaning as local school officials have become more involved in designing and implementing policies and programs resulting from the reform movements and as they are asked to produce better student-achievement gains. States are seeking to strengthen the link between state policy and local practice with a byproduct of the 1980s reforms being more curricular control at the state level. Finding and appropriating money for the reforms has been and will continue to be a state problem. Also, research on effective schools identified the individual school as the effective unit of reform (Edmonds, 1982; Lezotte and Bancroft, 1985). Although the apparent conflict has not yet been resolved, policy change continues to be initiated both from the state and the district level. Clearly, to function in such a confusing milieu administrators need to know more about the politics of education, educational policy analysis, and the governance of the educational system. In assuming responsible leadership positions, they will need to be able to assess the validity and viability of proposed reforms, but, in a larger sense, initiate and lead efforts for creating and managing better educational institutions.

3. Growing Respect for Education's Economic Impact

State legislators and other policy leaders recognize that education plays a strong role in a state's economy, welfare, and technological development. While this recognition has brought criticism of the schools, hasty reform, and some interference, the attention received, regardless of its negativism, can be turned to the benefit of schooling by astute administrators. As an example, superintendents and principals have taken advantage of the public's interest in the reform movement to forge, coordinate, and solidify increasingly important ties between public education and the private sector. Such coalitions can do much to lobby for increased funding, which obviously continues to be a major issue. The climate of interest in education also has become conducive to meaningful school-funding formula reforms in the 1990s.

4. Choice and Change

The only real block to reform may be adherence to the outmoded belief that there is only one way to achieve it. Openness to varied strategies for change need to be emphasized by educational administrators. Everhart (1982) writes that "we may inquire about the extent to which state controlled public schooling (the dominant form of legitimate public education) constitutes a predominant orthodoxy about the nature of formal education, the acceptance of which limits our conception of education and the forms it may take" (p. 18).

The times call for our educational leaders to be flexible in considering new structures, vouchers, magnet schools, and other mechanisms of choice or privatization. Educational leaders need to display a respectful, responsible, and caring attitude toward flexibility regarding people and organizational structure and toward the willingness to share power. We must subscribe to the commitment that educational administrators are leaders and as leaders they must be visionary. As Bennis and Nanus (1985) so succinctly put it, "Managers do things right. Leaders do the right thing" (p. 21).

5. Empowerment

Empowerment is a concept that has emerged in both the public and private sectors. In government, this may mean control being exercised through mediating structures. In education, specifically, this may mean the preparation of professionals through such structures as administrators' academies. For schools of education, it means sending educational administrators into the field, empowered with the skills and knowledge necessary to be visionary leaders who can make, influence, implement, and evaluate policy. For educational governance, empowerment is not really new. The state has, throughout history, governed education through the mediating structure of the local school board. The day is past when the public acknowledged that all educational expertise resided in the trained professional. District superintendents of the future must be educated to negotiate the delicate balance of providing leadership to, while truly sharing power with, local school boards. Principals must learn collegial leadership and leave behind the last vestiges of the patriarchal model.

In the private sector, the concept of empowerment has led to important knowledge about how human potential can be tapped. People's talents are best unleashed when high-level administrators act with energy not only to set the tone and direction of the company, but also to develop vehicles and opportunities for workers to participate creatively in all levels of the organization (Kanter, 1983). Creative superintendents and principals will apply these business concepts to schooling. The school leaders of the future will "empower others to translate intention into reality and sustain it" (Bennis and Nanus, 1985, p. 80).

6. Polarization

Constituencies of a school tend to agree less today on common purpose and education (Ravitch, 1983). Each concentrates on issues important to the members of its group. School administrators need to strive to create a mechanism and a climate so that common dreams and goals of parents, students, teachers, taxpayers, and minorities can be reestablished. At the same time, administrators need to generate respect for diverse methods of meeting those goals.

7. Education as a Public Good

Public education is believed generally to have a public relations problem. Seventy-eight percent of adults have no direct tie to public schools (Bakalis, 1985). But public relations, in the marketing sense, is only a piece of this problem. Educational leaders need to do their part in rekindling the idea, very old and very basic to U.S. society, that a public education free and available to all is a commonweal. The support of education for all, for the future benefit of all, is a value that must be shared, both by professionals and the public.

Linked to this problem is a wave of anti-intellectualism running through the United States. Administrators must be cognizant of this theme as it is a subtle block to true educational reform. In a truly stimulating educational environment, students question and argue. They change. But parents and citizens often do not want their children to change, particularly when change is at a rate beyond, or in a direction outside, their personal tolerance limits. The administrative challenge is twofold: to provide stimulating educational environments and to engender the support of education for all.

8. Minorities

Although minority groups are growing and multiplying in the United States, the reformers with policy powers too often ignore their special needs. For example, education has yet to deal satisfactorily with the problems of teaching in many languages and with the problems of the urban poor. For instance, many administrators and school boards tried for far too long to ignore the problem of educating homeless children. Of equal importance is the problem of recruiting minorities into the field of educational administration itself, which is still predominantly white. According to Feistritzer (1988), superintendents are 97 percent white and principals are 90 percent white. To be effective, education must provide for all the road to the better life so many of us already enjoy. Within the educational administration field, the issues surrounding these problems and their potential solutions should be thoroughly examined even though many present administrators are predominantly from settings that do not yet have populations with special needs. What is happening in our "neighbor's" district should also be of concern to us.

9. Effective Schools

Research results converged in the 1980s to tell others what we in educational administration have always believed: That upon the shoulders of a school principal rests the responsibility for change, success, and the climate in which exciting and meaningful education occurs. In programs of educational administration, the emphasis is now on educating principals to be instructional leaders and superintendents to provide principals with the freedom and resources needed to make education thrive in the schools. Now we need to add education for the policy-related roles of these administrators so they are able to effect needed changes at all levels of the governance system. Effective schools need support from all the governmental layers.

The impact of each of the preceding issues is felt in the daily work of educational administrators. For each of these areas, and for many others, policy has been made and continues to be made at all levels of the educational governance system. In the midst of such massive shifts, educational administrators truly hear "the sound and discord of cultures grinding together" (May, 1985, p. 201).

The Reports

A Torrent of Criticism

In education, the general societal shift of power to the states was combined with an avalanche of commission reports critical of the country's educational system. These began with *A Nation At Risk,* the report of the National Commission on Excellence in Education in 1983. This blockbuster report began a long, intense period of national attention on education at all levels that reached its peak when President Bush and the governors agreed on national goals for education in 1990. During the eighties, report followed report. To illustrate the rapidity with which these reports flooded the public consciousness, Tables 1.1 and 1.2 present information about nine major reports released between 1982 and 1984. As Townsel (1986) points out, the contents of those reports provided the basis for numerous federal and state policies during the 1980s, yet they were used by policy makers

TABLE 1.1   • *Profile of Reports*

TITLE	ACADEMIC PREPARATION FOR COLLEGE	ACTION FOR EXCELLENCE	AMERICA'S COMPETITIVE CHALLENGE	HIGH SCHOOL
	What Students Need to Know and Be Able to Do	*A Comprehensive Plan to Improve Our Nation's Schools*	*The Need for a National Response*	*A Report on Secondary Education in America*
Sponsor/ Author	Education Equality Project-The College Board	Task Force on Education for Economic Growth Education Commission of the States	Business-Higher Education Forum	Ernest L. Boyer The Carnegie Foundation for the Advancement of Teaching
Chair(s)	Not Identified	Governor James Hunt, Jr.	R. Anderson David S. Saxon	Ernest L. Boyer
Representation of Task Force Members	200 high school and college teachers as members of various College Board committees and council	41 members: governors, legislators, CEO's, state and local school boards, and labor	16 members: business and higher education	28 members: state and local level educators, higher education, and business
Data Bases Utilized	Data collected from 1400 people through questionnaires and meetings, also judgements and recommendations	Task Force consensus on problems and recommendations	Past surveys and contemporary expertise	Field studies of 15 public high schools, data from High School and Beyond (NCES) and A Study of Schooling (Goodlad)
Time Frame of Study	3 years	1 year	1 year	3 years
Date of Release	May 1981	May 1981	April 1983	September 1983

Source: From A. H. Townsel, Some commentary on contemporary reforms: Ambivalent samaritans or education reactionaries? *Thresholds in Education, 12*(2), 29–33. Copyright © 1986 by The Thresholds in Education Foundation. Reprinted by permission.

without sufficient attention to defining the problems or the methodologies to be used to set, study, and achieve reform goals. For instance, the needs of urban youth and of urban school systems to keep these youth in school were often in conflict with a problem definition based on declining test scores. Thus, in many states reforms were begun that ignored the goal of equity. "In rapid-fire succession states engaged in massive reforms of their systems of public education

MAKING THE GRADE	A NATION AT RISK	THE PAIDEIA PROPOSAL	A PLACE CALLED SCHOOL	A STUDY OF HIGH SCHOOLS
	The Imperative for Educational Reform	*An Education Manifesto*	*Prospectus for the Future*	
Twentieth Century Fund Task Force on Federal Elementary and Secondary Education Policy	The National Commission on Excellence in Education-US Department of Education	Mortimer J. Adler on behalf of the Paideia Group	John I. Goodlad	National Association of Secondary School Principals and the Commission of Educational Issues of the National Association of Independent Schools
Robert Wood	David P. Gardner	Mortimer J. Adler	Ralph W. Tyler	Theodore R. Sizer
11 members: state departments, local school level, and higher education	18 members: governor, legislators, States Boards, local school level, higher education and professional associations	22 members: National, state and local level educators	6 members: National, state, and local level	Study team of educators and educational researchers
Background paper Paper by Paul E. Peterson utilizing existing data	Commissioned papers, public oral and written comment existing analyses, and descriptions of notable programs	Primarily philosophical	Questionnaires and observations in 38	Field studies of 14 public and private high schools
15 years	15 years	1 year	8 years	3 years
May 1981	April 1981	September 1982	September 1983	January 1984

TABLE 1.2 • Critical Areas of Recommendations from the Nine Major Reports

	ACADEMIC PREPARATION FOR COLLEGE	ACTION FOR EXCELLENCE	AMERICA'S COMPETITIVE CHALLENGE
	The College Board	*Education Commission of the States*	*Business Higher Education Forum*
School Organization and Management		✓	✓
Curriculum	✓	✓	✓
Students and Learning	✓	✓	✓
Quality and Equality	✓	✓	
Teachers and Teaching	✓	✓	✓
Postsecondary Education	✓	✓	✓
Leadership			
Local Role	✓	✓	✓
State Role	✓	✓	✓
Federal Role		✓	✓
Business & Industry		✓	✓
Research		✓	✓

Source: From A. H. Townsel, Some commentary on contemporary reforms: Ambivalent samaritans or education reactionaries? *Thresholds in Education, 12*(2), 29–33. Copyright © 1986 by The Thresholds in Education Foundation. Reprinted by permission.
✓ Indicates that the report discusses this theme.

which frequently ignored two decades of progress made toward equity" (Townsel, 1986, p. 29).

These nine reports are only a sample of the flood of reports and recommendations that continued through the 1980s. School administrators were swept up in a virtual whirlwind of change. Thus, the need arose to concentrate on the policy-making roles of the school administrator because where and how educational policy was being made became questions of immediate concern. The need to study policy-making processes, policy decisions, and policy makers became crucial as administrators coped with the implementation problems inherent in hastily conceived state reform packages; for example, the 1985 Illinois reform package contained 149 different measures without the accompanying funds to make them effective. The pressure again landed on school administrators.

Burden on the Schools

The burden on the schools grew heavier. The enormous number of tasks schools were expected to perform increased. Figure 1.1 presents a sample list of the tasks schools are expected to do. It is obvious from reading such a list that the school administrator needs to set priorities and, in order to do so, policy-related skills are needed. Expertise is needed for making, analyzing, implementing, and evaluating all of

HIGH SCHOOL	MAKING THE GRADE	A NATION AT RISK	THE PAIDEIA PROPOSAL	A PLACE CALLED SCHOOL	A STUDY OF HIGH SCHOOLS
Ernest L. Boyer	*The Twentieth Century Fund*	*Commission of Excellence*	*Mortimer J. Adler*	*John I. Goodlad*	*Theodore Sizer*
✓	✓	✓		✓	✓
✓	✓	✓	✓	✓	✓
✓	✓	✓	✓	✓	✓
✓	✓	✓	✓	✓	✓
✓	✓	✓	✓	✓	✓
✓		✓		✓	
✓	✓	✓		✓	
✓	✓	✓		✓	
✓	✓	✓			
✓	✓	✓			
	✓	✓		✓	

FIGURE 1.1 • *The Burden of the Schools*

Teach good nutrition habits . . . train students in pulmonary-coronary resuscitation . . . give specialized instruction to those with hearing, visual, and neurological impairments . . . treat people with emotional disturbance . . . train those with mental retardation . . . teach the gifted . . . do eye testing . . . give inoculations . . . teach first-aid procedures . . . provide pregnancy counseling . . . assist in disease prevention . . . inculcate morals, ethics, and values . . . prevention of drug, alcohol, and tobacco abuse . . . help students develop political know-how . . . develop civic responsibility . . . provide sex and AIDS education . . . maintain birth information and age-certification data . . . provide instruction in good health care . . . teach driver training . . . promote civil rights and racial tolerance . . . foster integration . . . teach the principles of free enterprise . . . assist in career planning . . . provide career information . . . detect and report child abuse . . . teach telephone manners and etiquette . . . eradicate head lice, scabies, and other diseases . . . assist in charity fund raising . . . provide vocational training . . . build economic awareness . . . serve hot lunches and breakfasts . . . dispense surplus milk . . . do job placement . . . stress bicycle safety and pedestrian safety . . . promote physical fitness . . . assist bilingual language development . . . counsel delinquents . . . foster metric education . . . provide transportation . . . teach consumer education . . . counsel students with problems, including fear of war and crime . . . follow due process procedures . . . protect student privacy . . . teach humanness and individual responsibility . . . eliminate sex discrimination . . . develop an appreciation of other people and other cultures . . . promote the uses of information . . . develop the ability to reason . . . build patriotism and loyalty to the ideas of democracy . . . promote an understanding of the heritage of our country . . . build respect for the worth and dignity of the individual . . . develop skills for an entry into a specific field of work . . . teach management of money, property, and resources . . . develop curiosity and a thirst for learning . . . develop skills in the use of leisure time . . . teach pride in work . . . build a feeling of self-worth, of self-respect . . . avoid religion—and teach reading, writing, arithmetic, and computer literacy.

this policy, both new and old. It has become clear that at both the state and local levels this expertise is too often lacking.

Specialists were making all this new policy, but often in isolation from each other and in isolation from the educators who would be implementing the policies. Sometimes each individual policy was valuable but the cumulative whole became a tremendous burden. It became clear that there was a need for generalists who could assess the significance of the specialists' knowledge. These generalists could then convey their assessments to lay citizens (lay policy makers such as members of state and local boards of education). This is a policy analyst's role, but it is also the role and duty of the school administrator operating in his or her policy-related capacity. Given this need, this role, it is time for school administrators to become as interested in the processes by which policies or general directions are set for the schools as they are in how things are done in the schools.

Policy Defined

Policy can be simply defined as a vision of where we want to go and guidelines for getting there. Sandell (1977) described policy analysis as a "set of procedures for inventing, anticipating, exploring, comparing, and articulating the alternatives available for achieving certain objectives. It is a method of managing . . . collecting and organizing . . . information. It is an effort to ease the consternation that stems from seeking better ways to ordain the process of decision making" (p. 48). Decision making is what the administrator does. This view of policy analysis encompasses a process view of a policy-related method that leads to sounder decisions.

A "working" definition of *policy* may be helpful at this point. Figure 1.2 presents the working definition of policy and a policy statement used by the Illinois State Board of Education in its policy-development cycle. The crucial points to note are the references to policy as long term, involving leadership, and giving direction to subsequent decisions such as the allocation of resources. Note that in this working definition it is also pointed out that policy statements may require the subsequent development of procedural statements such as guidelines, rules, and regulations. It is the confusion between policy and procedural statements that often creates chaos for the educational administrator.

It is important that we agree that policy is wide, rather than narrow, long term rather than short term, and that it involves leadership. The leader is needed to paint the vision that becomes the policy statements.

FIGURE 1.2 • *Policy: A Working Definition*

What Is Policy? A Working Definition:

In general, *policy making* involves decisions intended to have wide rather than narrow influences on people and operations, and which are intended to have more than a short-range impact. In somewhat less general terms, *policy making* has the following three characteristics:

1. Policy making involves the strategic function of leadership and guidance.
2. Policy making shapes and clarifies substantive goals and major objectives.
3. Policy making gives direction to the development and operations of programs, influencing or determining the allocation of resources vis-à-vis competing demands.

A *policy statement* can be defined as having the following characteristics:

1. A clear intent to provide general direction (statement of position) rather than specific orders (statement of procedure);
2. Application to a well-defined population;
3. The (usual) absence of a specific reference to time;
4. Addressing an area over which the policy-making body has authority or particular influence.

Statements of policy, by design and by definition, are intended to have relatively long-term effects. They may require the development of procedural statements (e.g., guidelines, rules, and regulations) that assist the respondent in the implementation of the policy.

Source: Illinois State Board of Education, *The State Board of Education Policies and Procedures Handbook.* Springfield: Illinois State Board of Education.

It may be helpful here to briefly consider some other terms. In its broad sense, a policy-development process is an attempt at systematically anticipating and improving the future. Policy analysis is the process of identifying the issues inherent in, or related to, a policy statement. There are many definitions of these terms. "It must be noted that no one definition of policy should be glibly accepted" (Musial, 1986, p. 3). Musial goes on to point out that not all definitions are equal in their consequences for policy analysis: "Each definition calls for its own data, sources, and methods and each produces unique outcomes. Explicitly or tacitly, each different definition has an enormous impact on the processes and products of policy analysis. What constitutes a better definition is of course a matter of values; thus, the selection of a particular definition involves a value choice" (p. 3).

No matter how we define policy, policy-development processes, or policy analysis, knowledge and its purveyors can enhance public policy, and analyses, planning, and forecasting can improve public decision making. This may be an unfashionable view, a bit Pollyannaish in the face of mountains of poor decision making during the 1980s decade of educational reform. Some, in fact, call it a "myth" of policy analysis (Fischer, 1987). However, we can improve educational policy making, although it may be necessary to "let go the finishing" (May, 1985, p. 201) and be content with incompleteness.

A Basic Policy Issue: Compulsory Education

We so take for granted that children must go to school that it is easy to forget that this was once a controversial notion, one seen as infringing on parental rights and the primacy of the family unit. It is worth revisiting this battle briefly for it illustrates the notion of policy as broad with long-term effects. Also, the tug-of-war between parental and state rights, which was at the heart of the compulsory schooling debate in the 1920s, is an issue of the 1990s in the form of home schooling.

Pierce v. *the Society of Sisters* (1925) is the landmark Supreme Court decision that established the basic constitutional framework within which the states regulate schooling. The decision was called the Pierce Compromise because it gave the states unquestioned power to compel attendance at a school; however, it also established that the states cannot employ that power to eliminate all educational choices.

Such far-reaching national policy emerges often from such a Supreme Court decision. In the specifics of this case, the State of Oregon had passed a law requiring children to attend public school. The issue at hand involved antipathy toward immigrants who often chose private schools as a route to preserving their religions and cultures. In the 1922 referendum campaign in Oregon, a Ku Klux Klansman was quoted as saying, "Somehow these mongrel hordes must be Americanized; failing that, deportation is the only remedy" (Yudof, Kirp, van Geel, and Levin, 1987, p. 11).

In settling this specific dispute within one state, the Supreme Court supported the states in requiring children to attend school and preserved for posterity choice and options within that requirement. But policy changes and grows. It accumulates incrementally, one policy made leading to more policy questions. The *Pierce* decision opened new areas of controversy, some litigated and continuously refined to this day. For instance, to what extent can the states regulate the private schools? How can the states regulate and still not interfere with the religious rights of these schools? How is home schooling regulated? This is a problem of great concern in the early nineties and raises again some very basic questions about the state's responsibility, as critics of home schooling say that the very loose regulation in some of the states amounts to an abrogation of responsibility to the affected children. Others see the issue as one of parental rights and/or religious freedom.

There are different kinds of interpretations to explain the phenomenon of compulsory education (Yudof, Kirp, van Geel, and Levin, 1987, p. 11). For our purposes, it is an example of looking for the roots of some of the policy questions that are on the agenda today. Understanding the policy issues of the past can help us in our policy making today.

Why the Administrator Should Care

The administrator should care about policy making and his or her policy-related roles because he or she has a unique contribution to make in the policy arena. Close to the scene, the superintendent or the principal may be the only one with certain pieces of information needed to improve public policy making. One of the themes of this book is that educators at all levels do have an opportunity to set, or at least to influence, educational policy making. "Furthermore, it might be argued that educators have an obligation to help shape educational policy, for without engaging in this policy making role with diligence, educators in effect proclaim that they are less than professionals in their own field. Not to be involved in policy setting is to abdicate leadership in education to others" (Gooler, 1986, p. 37).

Participating in the educational policy development processes is important to the democratic notion of self-government. The ability of citizens to assert control over educational institutions through elections and other participatory means is the heart of democratic legitimacy (Yudof, Kirp, van Geel, and Levin, 1987, p. 11). Regarding educational policy, elections are seldom the means available, except at the local level where some school board members are elected. But administrators can impact the educational policy development processes in the various ways discussed in these pages, and thus help shape the goals of government.

The goals of government in the educational realm have varied through the decades from efficiency to equity to quality. Societal forces have determined which of these goals is paramount at any one time, and their rotation can most easily be seen in state policy making. Underlying all of these goals has been the continuing theme of choice (Marshall, Mitchell, and Wirt, 1990). In the 1990s, choice has emerged as a major goal itself.

One of the reasons these interweaving goals can be seen most clearly at the state level is because states have the power in education. The governance of education is a state rather than a federal responsibility because of the Tenth Amendment to the U.S. Constitution, which reads: "The powers not delegated to the United States by the Constitution, nor prohibited by it to the States, are reserved to the States respectively, or to the people." Nevertheless, the federal government is involved in education in many ways justified under the General Welfare Clause of the Constitution and under other Amendments, particularly the First, Fourth, and Fourteenth. The provisions of many federal statutes also involve the federal government in educational affairs. These will be discussed in the chapters on federal policy making.

But in the main, the states have the power. All states except Hawaii have chosen to disburse that power by delegating authority to local boards of education. In so doing, states have not surrendered their prerogatives regarding education. In creating local school districts, the states have merely determined the machinery by which the state function shall be performed. Legally, local districts and local boards of education could be abolished tomorrow. The political realities, however, are quite different. As many states have discovered through the years, merely consolidating school districts is politically divisive if not impossible. The emotions of citizens in many communities have been aroused over the prospect of losing their local school district, and/or the symbols that represent it such as the high school basketball team. As states have debated educational plans in the 1990s, the possibilities of eliminating local school districts as we know them have been debated.

We see throughout this book that educational policy making at all levels of the governance system in intertwined with policy making at all the other levels. Accordingly, although the book sections are divided by level of governance, educational policy making at any level will not be treated as an isolated entity. Stressed here is the interplay of the governance system, the law, policy making, and educational practice, particularly the practice of educational administration.

Contributions

We need to be aware that history is ignored at our peril in the making and analyzing of educational policy. The first contribution, from Jeffrey E. Mirel, stresses the interplay of history and educational policy through exploration of the recurring problem of national teacher shortages.

In the next contribution, John Maddaus analyzes the politics of parental choice, particularly the ideological rationales involved and the powers of the various governmental layers as they converse over these issues.

In the final contribution in Section One, Steven Goldberg discusses policy in the arena of special education. In analyzing due process, the IEP, and why legalization may have failed, we can see how policies generate unanticipated consequences and how policies can be thwarted at the implementation level.

As these authors explore these current policy issues from their respective viewpoints, the enormous complexity of educational policy making is demonstrated.

JEFFREY E. MIREL

History and Educational Policy: Some Reflections on National Teacher Shortages

In the area of policy studies, history is a victim of its own success. History is so deeply ingrained in the policy-making process that most policy makers and policy analysts simply take it for granted. During the Reagan administration, for example, advocates of bilingual education denounced as a return to the discriminatory practices of the past plans by U.S. Secretary of Education William Bennett to alter federal bilingual guidelines. In response to these critics, Bennett also claimed historical precedent, arguing that the proposed policy change would restore traditional power to local districts, power that had previously been usurped by the federal government (Fiske, 1985; Lyons, 1985). Clearly, a sense of history was central to both of these stands. In fact, it is often difficult to tell where historical consciousness ends and where policy positions begin.

Unfortunately, that historical consciousness is often based on an inaccurate or even distorted knowledge of the past. Careful historical research frequently seems to be an afterthought in the policy process. Probably nowhere is that more apparent than in the area of educational policy. Over the last two decades, we have seen a great deal of excitement over such programs as open classrooms, career education, effective schools, and "back to basics," programs that policy makers seem to really believe are "new and innovative." In one form or another, these "innovations" merely represent a recycling of old ideas, and educational historians watch school leaders embrace them as panacea with considerable cynicism (Perkinson, 1977). In U.S. education, it seems that those who cannot remember the past compel our children to repeat it.

Given the situation, it is not surprising that a great deal of the recent literature on "applied history," the linking of history to policy studies, centers on justifying the ways of historians to policy analysts (Neustadt and May, 1986). In that vein, my purpose here is to present some of the main approaches historians take in analyzing policy and to demonstrate how a historical perspective can illuminate a specific educational policy issue that has a striking parallel in the past: the impending national teacher shortage.

An earlier version of this work appeared in *Thresholds in Education, 12*(2), May 1986.

The arguments historians use to justify the inclusion of their discipline in policy analysis generally fall into two broad categories: (1) history provides a "natural laboratory" for testing policy questions, and (2) history alone can demonstrate if there has been change or lack of change over time (Mandelbaum, 1977; Grob, 1979; McCurley, 1979; Resnick, 1981; Stearns, 1982; Tyack and Hansot, 1982; Graham, 1985). As Tyack and Hansot (1982) note, the first of these arguments rests on the idea "that most significant human *problems* have a long history," and historical study offers us the chance to see how others have tried to solve them. History then becomes a laboratory in which these solutions can be analyzed. "This kind of historical experimentation," Tyack and Hansot argue, "has at least two advantages: it is cheap (no small matter when funds are short); and it does not use live guinea pigs (usually poor people)."

This type of "laboratory research" is ideal for answering several interrelated policy questions. What are the historical precedents for a given change or reform? What analogies and judgments can be made when considering present situations and past conditions? And what have been the outcomes of efforts to solve particular problems in the past (Nuestadt and May, 1986)?

If that general approach to policy analysis is akin to work in a laboratory, the other, seeking changes over time, is probably best compared to the process of navigation. Much as navigators determine their physical location in relation to where they have been and where they wish to go, historians plot the position and direction of events and trends through time. This approach is based on the belief that human action has meaning as it relates to past and future events. Here historical and policy analysis almost indistinguishably merge. As McCurley (1979) argues, "The policy process represents the means by which governments try to resolve issues. More importantly, policies are the institutional mechanisms which allow governments to effect and/or ameliorate change in society. The policy process thus exhibits two traits of specific interest to historians: continuity and change over time." Indeed, any definition that describes policy as a course or pattern of action implicitly demands analysis over time—historical analysis (Anderson, 1979).

This approach to policy studies can provide answers to a very different set of questions from those raised in the historical "laboratory." Given the conditions before and after the implementation of a policy, how well have the policy goals been realized? What are the relationships between ends and means? Are specific policies examples of incremental or fundamental change? What new problems have new policies created? And, perhaps most significantly, are things better or worse because of particular policies (Mirel, 1990)?

Although I have described these two approaches to historical policy analysis separately, in fact, historians use both as complementary tools in their research. In applying them, historians have access to the storehouse of human policy failures and successes. Such knowledge can be vital to policy analysis. As Wildavsky (1979) argues, "Analysis aims to bring information to bear on current decisions that do have future consequences. Taking these consequences into account (acting now to do better later) is the soul of analysis. Because prediction comes at a premium, however, analysis uses history—what has been tried in the past, how past patterns have led to present problems, where past obligations limit future commitments—as a source of both limits and possibilities."

A current educational issue that is especially appropriate for historical analysis is the growing national teacher shortage. What has occurred was the confluence of several demographic and social trends that made the 1970s and 1980s strikingly parallel to the 1930s and 1940s. As in the 1970s, the national birthrate throughout most of the 1930s was dropping. Consequently, in both periods, elementary school enrollments and the number of teaching positions also declined. The financial crisis in education in the 1970s, although not as severe as in the Great Depression, had several similar consequences for teachers. Faced with declining enrollments and taxpayer revolts, school districts in both eras fired teachers and increased class sizes. As a result of these trends, in the 1930s as well as the 1970s, there were far more teachers than there were jobs. Not surprisingly, in both periods, enrollments in colleges of education and other teacher-training institutions plummeted as young people sought more marketable careers (Church and Sedlak, 1976; Tyack, Lowe, and Hansot, 1984; Mirel, 1984; Lenz, 1985; Saunders, 1985; Salholz, 1985).

The situation began to change in the early part of both the 1940s and 1980s. As in 1945, school districts in 1985, particularly major urban ones, announced serious difficulties in filling teaching positions. By 1942, the Depression era oversupply of teachers had vanished, and many of the teachers who had clung to their jobs during the hard times began leaving the classroom either for military service or, more frequently, for better paying jobs in defense plants. Similarly, by 1980, most of the surplus teachers in the 1970s had left the profession, and many teachers trained in math and science abandoned the schools for higher salaries and greater status in private industry. In both periods, the number of available teachers also declined rapidly because of an increasing number of retirements. Following World War II, many older teachers, who had put off retirement for patriotic reasons during the war, began to leave the profession. Today, experts project that, over the ten years between 1985 and 1995, 30 percent of the teachers in the schools will retire (Kandel, 1948; Lenz, 1985). Finally, both eras witnessed substantial increases in the birthrate with the postwar baby boom and now with the babies of the baby boomers (Church and Sedlak, 1976; "Mini-Baby Boom," 1985). William Bennett predicted that "elementary school enrollments will increase annually through the early 1990s." Unfortunately, Bennett warned, the number of available teachers is expected to remain constant (quoted in "Mini-Baby Boom," 1985).

The post-World War II years are, then, an ideal laboratory in which to analyze how educational policy makers dealt with a very "contemporary" problem. Yet to deal with the past as if it is a precise analog of the present is to be ahistorical. A number of differences between the eras must be taken into account if this type of historical analysis is to be useful. First, the roles of both the state and federal governments in education were far more limited in the 1940s than they were in 1985. Today, we expect the state and/or federal government to take a major role in resolving almost every educational problem. Second, except in several large urban school systems, teachers' unions played only a minor part in educational politics and policy making during the 1940s. In postwar years, teachers' organizations had little or no say about the adoption or implementation of policy. Today, teachers' unions are a powerful factor in educational politics. Third, because teaching was one of the few occupations open to women in the postwar years, public school officials could routinely count on a sizeable number of talented and ambitious women to fill vacant faculty positions. The successes of the women's movement in the 1970s has enabled many women who previously would have been teachers to seek higher status, better paying jobs. Fourth, we do, however, have a far larger pool of college-educated individuals today than we did in the immediate postwar years. These individuals could be easily retrained as teachers if they chose to enter the profession. And finally, it does not appear that the current baby boom or teacher shortage will be as large as those of the past. Each of these factors indicates a major change over time and each must be taken into account in any thorough analysis of the teacher shortage, then and now.

With these factors in mind, how can we use historical research to chart the course of current policy on the teacher shortage? One area that is ripe for investigation is the debate over the educational requirements for entry into the teaching profession. During the postwar years, states and local districts tried to increase the supply of teachers by issuing thousands of emergency certificates to individuals who did not meet the standard requirements of teacher certification. Fifty thousand such certificates were issued in 1946 alone ("Labor Bureau Says," 1946). As late as 1963, as many as 100,000 teachers holding emergency certificates were still teaching, often in urban districts (Drachler, 1977). In response to the current shortage, some states and districts are repeating that "solution." In 1985, Los Angeles, which had suffered a chronic lack of teachers for several years, "invoked an emergency section of the state law to hire over 1,250 teachers who lacked teaching credentials. New Jersey now allows college graduates to earn their certification on the job" (Salholz, 1985).

Leaders of the nation's teachers' unions, such as Albert Shanker and Mary Hatwood Futrell, vehemently denounced these policies. They saw such actions as further examples of the contempt in which the teaching profession is held and as a movement to weaken already lax standards for entry into the field. Almost invariably, they invoked the specter of postwar emergency certification, claiming that the policy loosed a flood of incompetent teachers upon the schools and contributed to the decline of U.S. education. They contended that if we pursued such a course again the quality of the public schools would deteriorate even more (Shanker, 1985; Salholz, 1985).

But will it? Noah (1985) notes that Albert Shanker, who entered the profession during the postwar teacher shortage, "didn't have to get his teaching credit before teaching in the New York schools, and [Shanker] speculates that his fellow "permanent substitutes" would rank in the top 25% of teachers today." Except for the dig at Shanker, Noah's argument proves nothing unless it becomes the starting point for historical inquiry. Investigation into the educational backgrounds and the careers of teachers who were granted emergency certificates in the postwar years is the only way we can assess the quality of the teachers who entered the profession under these circumstances. Additional historical investigation can reveal how students fared with these teachers. By comparing the educational outcomes of classes taught by teachers with and without emergency certificates, we can gain important insights into the impact these policies had on student performance. Without these kinds of studies, the claims and counter-claims about the effects of emergency certification are mere rhetoric.

Such projects represent only a small portion of the possibilities for historical inquiry into the certification aspect of the teacher shortage. Other work, for example, could focus on such areas as higher education and could investigate whether there were postwar changes in the process of teacher certification. Particular attention might be paid to extension courses, in-service programs, and other nontraditional avenues to certification offered by colleges of education during the postwar years. Since colleges of education are once again on the front lines of this crisis, knowledge about how they handled this problem forty years ago could be invaluable for guiding current policy decisions.

Coinciding with that research might be studies into the relationship between colleges of education and state departments of education during these years. Since both state and federal governments will be deeply involved in this issue in the next few years, whatever insights we could draw from the state/college interaction of the postwar period could be useful in forecasting the consequences of an increased governmental role in the certification process. Right now, one of the most widely cited recommendations for dealing with the shortage are state and federal scholarship programs for prospective teachers. Would such programs increase "outside" influence on the certification process? What state and federal strings will be attached? Could such strings harm efforts by teachers for greater control of entry into the profession? While the historical analogies we draw in this area may not be precise, the parallels may be close enough to provide some telling answers to these questions.

Of equal importance to research into certification is inquiry into how the few strong teachers' unions of the 1940s responded to the crisis. Most of these unions were located in urban areas such as Atlanta, Chicago, Cleveland, Detroit, and New York, which bore the brunt of the teacher shortages. Many of these unions experienced dramatic growth in membership and power during this period. With more jobs available than there were teachers to fill them, organized teachers found themselves able to win major concessions from local school boards. It is not surprising that the first successful teachers' strike in the nation occurred in 1947 and amid the worsening shortage (Eaton, 1975).

The growth of union power during the postwar years suggests that during the coming shortage, teachers' unions may wield even greater influence than they do today. The call by Albert Shanker (1985) for a national "bar exam" for teachers is not merely a response to concerns about lower professional standards during the shortage. It is also the first test of union strength in a political and educational environment that is changing because of the shortage. How the teachers' unions will reach for power and how they will act if they gain it is another aspect of the policy process that can be illuminated by historical research. We need to know a great deal more about the development of the large urban teachers' unions during the 1940s and 1950s. How did they use the undersupply of teachers to their advantage? What concessions other than salary increases did they wrest from local school boards? How did their policy agenda change as their power and influence grew? What policy precedents were set during these years? Was there an anti-union "backlash"?

As this sample analysis shows, even when strong historical parallels exist, the issues that demand careful research are numerous. But it is only through close historical investigation of those issues that politicians and educational leaders can attain the measure of insight and predictability needed for making effective policy.

If history is so powerful a tool for policy analysis, why hasn't it been central to the study of public policy? There are several reasons. First, policy analysts and historians approach their tasks from very different perspectives. Analysts seek knowledge that is immediately useful, while historians often seek knowledge that is relevant only to their discipline. At their worst, these positions lead to analysis that is merely expedient and to history that, in Tolstoy's words, answers questions that nobody asked. Yet as we have seen, historical investigation of policy issues can both sharpen the questions posed by policy analysts and produce fruitful historical research. For a lasting marriage between these fields, both sides need to work toward a middle group that respects relevant historical inquiry.

A second more critical problem is that historical research is often exceedingly slow, while policy analysts often find time at a premium. Analysts struggling with worsening human problems cannot wait for definitive historical works before making decisions. Yet historians, like other social scientists, get nervous when they are asked to go beyond their data and make recommendations based on incomplete research.

This dilemma, however, may be more apparent than real. If most policy changes are indeed incremental, then historians who specialize in the history of particular policies or institutions probably could use their knowledge to provide quick and accurate assessments of new proposals. Also, historians often undertake research into areas that, at the time, seem irrelevant to policy questions and yet, when completed, prove to be extremely timely. A good example of that situation is research into the history of religion in U.S. education that began, unnoticed, in the mid-1970s and emerged on the cutting edge of educational policy debates in the 1980s (see, for example, Brereton, 1981; Perko, 1983). And, of course, historians can anticipate policy issues that will become "hot" and plan their research accordingly. Scholars who begin working now on histories of the dropout problem will find their studies increasingly important to the national debate that we will surely have on that issue.

The final, and perhaps most troubling, problem is the historians' fear that policy makers and policy analysts may not be interested in accurate historical research at all. Ronald Reagan is only the most visible, not the only, politician who distorted history for political purposes. Historical findings of politicians from both sides of the political spectrum are often merely weapons of political warfare. And, as in any war, truth is often the first casualty (Bromwich, 1985; Decter, 1985).

The great variety of historical interpretations offers at least a partial solution to that problem. Politicians and analysts can choose between well-crafted liberal, conservative, or radical studies of most major events and trends. While the interpretations may differ, the canons of historical scholarship, the ground rules for scholarly debate, will remain intact.

But historians who enter the policy process allied to one political faction or another almost inevitably will face a more troubling problem. Where does one draw the line between historical interpretation and political expediency? How much subtlety can one sacrifice in the political use of one's work before it is stripped of substance? In short, how can one maintain professional integrity while playing a political role? Perhaps the only answer lies in Wildavsky's challenge, that the true goal of policy analysis is not the exercise of power, but rather speaking truth to power.

References

Anderson, J. (1979). *Public policy making.* New York: Holt, Rinehart & Winston.

Brereton, V. L. (1981). Fundamentalist Protestant bible Colleges, 1882–1940. Unpublished doctoral dissertation, Columbia University.

Bromwich, D. (1985). Reagan's contempt for history. *Dissent, 32,* 265–268.

Church, R., & Sedlak, M. (1976). *Education in the United States: An interpretive history.* New York: Macmillan.

Decter, M. (1985). Bitburg: Who forgot what? *Commentary, 80,* 21–26.

Drachler, N. (1977). Education and politics in large cities: 1950–1970. In J. Scribner (Ed.), *The politics of education.* Chicago: University of Chicago Press.

Eaton, W. E. (1975). *The American federation of teachers.* Carbondale, IL: Southern Illinois University Press.

Fiske, E. B. (1985, September 26). Education department seeking to alter bilingual efforts. *The New York Times,* pp. 1, 16.

Graham, P. A. (1985, January 30). Cautionary admonitions from our educational past. *Education Week,* pp. 24, 19.

Grob, G. N. (1979). Reflections on the history of social policy in America. *Reviews in American History,* 293–306.

Kandel, I. (1948). *The impact of the war on American education.* Chapel Hill: University of North Carolina Press.

Labor bureau says teacher shortage in nation over 160,000. (1946, October 21). *The Detroit Teacher,* p. 2.

Lenz, L. (1985, August 14). Teacher lag by '90? *The Chicago Sun-Times,* p. 16.

Lyons, J. J. (1985, October 23). Bilingual-policy initiative "doesn't make sense." *Education Week,* p. 15.

Mandelbaum, S. (1977). The past in service to future. *Journal of Social History, 11,* 193–205.

Mini-baby boom expected to increase school roles this fall. (1985, August 23). *The Honolulu Advertiser,* p. A-18.

Mirel, J. E. (1990, August). What history can teach us about school decentralization. *Educational Excellence Network News and Views, 9,* 40–47.

Mirel, J. E. (1984). Politics and public education in the great depression: Detroit 1929–40. Unpublished doctoral dissertation, University of Michigan.

McCurley, J., III. (1979). The historian's role in the making of public policy. *Social Science History, 3,* 205.

Noah, T. (1985, June 24). Albert Shanker, statesman. *The New Republic,* pp. 17–19.

Nuestadt, R. E., & May, E. R. (1986). *Thinking in time: The uses of history for decision makers.* New York: The Free Press.

Perkinson, H. J. (1977). *The imperfect panacea: American faith in education, 1865–1976.* New York: Random House.

Perko, M. (1983). By the bowles of God's mercy: Protestant and Catholic responses to educational developments in Cincinnati, 1830–55. *Journal of the Midwest History of Education Society, 11,* 15–33.

Resnick, D. (1981). Educational policy and the applied historian: Testing, competency, and standards. *Journal of Social History, 14,* 539–559.

Salholz, E. (1985, September 9). Help wanted: Teachers. *Newsweek,* p. 99.

Saunders, D. (1985, September 8). The glut's over–teacher shortage looms. *The Chicago Sun-Times,* p. 76.

Shanker, A. (1985, January). Albert Shanker proposes the creation of a national examination for beginning teachers. Speech to the National Press Club, Washington, DC.

Stearns, P. N. (1982). History and policy analysis: Toward maturity. *The Public Historian, 4,* 5–29.

Tyack, D., & Hansot, E. (1982). A usable past: Using history in educational policy. In A. Lieberman & M. W. McLaughlin (Eds.), *Policy making in education.* Chicago: University of Chicago Press.

Tyack, D., Lowe, R., & Hansot, E. (1984). *Public schools in hard times: The great depression and recent years.* Cambridge, MA: Harvard University Press.

Wildavsky, A. (1979). *Speaking truth to power: The art and craft of policy analysis.* Boston: Little, Brown.

JOHN MADDAUS

The Politics of Parental Choice

Parental choice of school is a concept that underlies a large number of very diverse programs and policy proposals (magnet schools, alternative education programs, vocational schools, vouchers, tuition tax credits, etc.), and that has drawn support as well as opposition from a range of ideological positions. Some of these programs and policies have been clearly identified with the parental choice concept, while others, although they embody some significant degree of choice, have been considered or implemented for entirely different purposes. If one accepts a broad definition of parental choice programs as including all those programs that, in fact, offer parents (and, especially at the secondary level, students themselves, whether or not their parents are involved) options among schools or programs, then numerous government units at all levels of the U.S. political system (federal, state, and local) have at one time or another considered and implemented some form of policy involving parental choice. A given governmental unit will consider an explicit parental choice policy only if certain conditions are present. The most important conditions, and the ones considered at length here, are the ideologies supporting and opposing the concept of choice, and the powers, resources, and existing programs of the governmental unit.

Ideological Development

In the decade of the 1980s, the concept of parental choice was most clearly identified politically with the conservative wing of the Republican Party, and especially with the Reagan administration. Conservative ideological support for parental choice can be traced to the free-market economist Milton Friedman, who introduced the concept of education vouchers in his 1962 book, *Capitalism and Freedom.*

Basically, Friedman's position is that free markets stimulate competition, forcing producers to make a better product and providing a variety of products to meet the needs and preferences of diverse consumers. A competitive marketplace rewards both the enterprising producer and the discriminating consumer. Government monopolies, on the other hand, are inefficient and costly, stifling the creativity of producers and generating a homogeneous product often insensitive to consumer preferences. This analysis underlay efforts in the 1980s in the United States and even more visibly in Great Britain to "privatize" a wide range of government services. The Soviet Union and other eastern European countries are now beginning to move in the same direction.

Friedman has consistently sought to apply the same theory of free-market economics to education, arguing that public schools are in fact government monopolies subject to all the problems inherent in any government monopoly. In a 1973 *New York Times Magazine* article, he pointed out that Americans would never accept having to buy their groceries at a single, government-owned and operated store in their neighborhood, and asked why it made any more sense to "buy" our children's educational services that way. He accepted that public interest required that government *finance* education in order to ensure that it was available to all, but he emphasized that this did *not* require that government *provide* education. Rather, he argued, government should give parents the money, in the form of a voucher, with which to purchase services from any provider they wished.

Ironically, the two most sustained efforts to initiate education vouchers in the 1970s owe less to the conservative ideology of Milton Friedman than to the liberal philosophies of two groups of academics in Cambridge, Massachusetts, and Berkeley, California. The Cambridge-based Center for the Study of Public Policy (CSPP) adopted the voucher concept in a 1970 report funded by the federal government's antipoverty agency, the Office of Economic Opportunity (OEO). Christopher Jencks, author of *Inequality: A Reassessment of the Effect of Family and Schooling in America*, was the head of CSPP at that time. In its reports to OEO, CSPP argued for vouchers on the grounds that the political mechanisms that supposedly make public schools accountable to their clients are clumsy and ineffective, and thus that parents can only take responsibility for their children's educations if they are able to take individual action. Furthermore, affluent parents retain control by means of residential mobility or private school enrollment, whereas low- to moderate-income parents lack such alternatives. Finally, CSPP argued that an unrestricted voucher could reinforce the advantages of the affluent, so in true liberal fashion it argued for various restrictions on how the voucher could be used. In summary, CSPP's case is based on a conception of government-sponsored empowerment of the poor.

CSPP's regulated voucher model was the basis for an OEO-sponsored voucher demonstration project in San Jose, California, from 1972 to 1977 (see "Federal Powers"). About the time this experiment was coming to an end, John Coons and Stephen Sugarman, two law professors at the University of California at Berkeley, undertook an effort to put their own version of the regulated voucher on the general election ballot in California. They had previously been involved in the landmark *Serrano* decision, in which the California Supreme Court overturned California's school aid practices on constitutional grounds, on the basis that these practices favored children attending school in wealthy districts. In *Education by Choice: The Case for Family Control,* Coons and Sugarman argue that parents—as the people who are closest to their children, know them best, and are most likely to have their interests at heart—should have the final decision regarding where they attend school. But their statewide voucher initiative failed to generate much enthusiasm among parents (or anyone else, for that matter) and fell short of enough signatures to qualify for the ballot (Catterall, 1982).

While both conservatives and liberals have been advocates for the parental choice concept, opposition to the concept has come primarily from public school educators and from moderate and liberal politicians, especially those within the Democratic Party. The critique of parental choice is based on the long-standing ideologies of public (common) schooling, representative government, and local control. Defenders of public schooling have often viewed parental choice as an attack on the main institution of society that promotes equality of opportunity. Public education, its defenders say, is based on the idea that a common school attended by all of the people will promote upward mobility based on merit, not privilege. Vouchers, they argue, would result in a two-tiered system of education based on social class, with public schools becoming a dumping ground for the poor. Defenders also claim that public education will promote democracy by teaching civic values and understanding of diversity, whereas allowing parents to make their own choices could result in reinforcing their narrow parochial views. The concepts of representative government and local control ensure parents the opportunity to influence their children's educations through influencing their local school boards.

Government Powers

Units at each level of government have initiated parental choice programs based on a variety of different powers exercised by those units. The following review of efforts by federal, state, and local governments to promote parental choice describes the major powers at each level that have been utilized to promote parental choice of school as well as representative examples of programs relying on those powers. The reader should keep in mind that something that is a state power in one state may be exercised by local governments in another state. Furthermore, since local school systems are creations of state governments, the exercise of powers in any given state between state and local levels may change from one point in time to another by a simple act of the state legislature. While the various powers of federal and state government are relatively stable in our federal system of government, changes do occur, as when President Reagan attempted to redirect some powers, including determining program priorities in education, from the federal government to the states.

Federal Powers

The primary power of the federal government over local school systems is the power to give or withhold money and to regulate the use of the money given (and of local monies) in a multitude of ways. Depending on what programs one is willing to accept under the heading of parental choice, the federal government has either funded parental choice programs for decades or has never funded a parental choice program (except as a demonstration project). Vocational, special education, and voluntary school desegregation programs (e.g., magnet schools) all offer some enrollment options that parents may control or at least influence if they so desire. However, the major effort by a president to introduce the concept of choice into a categorical aid program—President Reagan's proposal to "voucherize" the Chapter 1 ECIA compensatory education program—was rejected by Congress in 1985–86.

The earliest explicit attempt by the federal government to introduce the parental choice concept into education was the public school voucher demonstration project conducted in the Alum Rock Unified School District of San Jose, California, in 1972–77. Begun by the Nixon administration, the Alum Rock project is an example of the federal government's program development, evaluation, and dissemination function. However, the findings contained in the reports of the program evaluation conducted by the Rand Corporation did little to encourage adoption of parental choice. With the change in administrations in Washington in 1977, this effort to introduce vouchers was shelved.

Another federal power with implications for parental choice of school is the power to levy and collect income taxes. To some people, tax credits for private school tuition are simply a matter of tax fairness, based on the argument that private school parents are paying for two school systems, only one of which they actually use. Others argue, however, that tuition tax credits offer an incentive to parents to take children out of public schools and enroll them in private schools. Which view is more accurate would depend on the size of the credit and whether it was refundable to parents with little or no federal income tax liability. In any case, the efforts of religious groups, several members of Congress, and President Reagan to write a tuition tax credit into federal income tax law failed on several occasions in the 1970s and early 1980s (Catterall, 1983).

Despite repeated failures in recent years by the Reagan and Bush administration to win congressional approval for parental choice programs, key people in both administrations have kept the parental choice issue visible in the national media through the use of what some have referred to as the "bully pulpit." William Bennett, especially during his tenure as U.S. Secretary of Education, was extremely adept at keeping the concept of choice (along with the other two of his "3 Cs," content and character) before the public. One of President Reagan's last official acts (January 10, 1989) was to convene a White House Conference on Choice, at which he passed the torch to President-elect Bush (Paulu, 1989). Bush in turn made sure that choice was one of the issues placed before his much-publicized "education summit" with the nation's governors in September 1989. Secretary of Education Lauro Cavazos conducted a series of regional meetings in places across the country where choice programs have been implemented in order to promote the concept. The federal courts, in the exercise of their powers to interpret the U.S. Constitution, have also dealt with choice of schools on a number of occasions. Most of the federal court cases dealing with parental choice of school have dealt with actions of state governments and local school boards, and therefore will be discussed in the next section.

State Powers

Consistent with the Tenth Amendment to the U.S. Constitution, which states that powers not explicitly assigned to the federal government are reserved for the states and the people, the states historically have had primary responsibility for and power over education.

The school systems that we take so much for granted today were created by the educational reformers of the nineteenth century. People such as Horace Mann and Henry Barnard, although their influence spread far beyond their home states, exercised what limited power they had primarily at the state level. In creating systems of public education, these reformers and their successors overcame the formerly widespread belief that parents had the right to determine whether as well as where their children attended school. Public school systems absorbed private schools in many communities, and compulsory attendance and residency laws were passed in state after state. In most states, counties or independent school districts were given authority over education. In most cases, this reform movement's efforts had the effect of reducing parental choice in education.

In Maine and Vermont, however, state policy makers in the late nineteenth and early twentieth centuries created an anomaly in U.S. education, the student whose entire school tuition was paid for out of public funds. Under state law, towns were responsible for education, but they had the option of paying tuition to a private school or to a public school in another town rather than building and maintaining their own public schools. In some such cases, the students and their parents had choices among two or more schools. Thus, the practice of town tuitioning in Maine and Vermont is probably the earliest form of state-supported parental choice of school in the United States (Maddaus and Mirochnik, 1991).

Other options in education depended on the wording and judicial interpretation of compulsory attendance laws. In many cities and states, Catholics opted to form their own schools rather than send their children to public schools that they regarded as hostile to their religious beliefs. In 1920, the State of Oregon passed a compulsory attendance law that required all students to attend public schools. This law was eventually overturned by the U.S. Supreme Court, which ruled in *Pierce* v. *Society of Sisters* (1925) that parents should have the right to determine which schools their children should attend, while permitting some regulation of such schools by the state. Parents and private schools have subsequently sought to limit state regulation of private schools and expand opportunities for home schooling. In the case of *Wisconsin* v. *Yoder* (1972), Amish parents won the right to end their children's formal schooling entirely after eighth grade.

Along with a state's interest in ensuring that students attend school goes the state responsibility to help fund education. Several states over the past thirty years have sought to extend financial aid to private, including sectarian, schools for a variety of purposes. A series of court decisions has permitted some forms of state aid, such as transportation and secular textbooks, while prohibiting other forms of state aid, such as building construction and teachers' salaries. Such cases may have a direct effect on parental choice by altering costs of and access to private education. In a variation on the tuition tax credit proposal with respect to federal income taxes, Minnesota adopted an education tax deduction to its state income tax. This deduction, covering tuition, transportation, and textbooks for both private and public schools, was upheld by the U.S. Supreme Court in *Mueller* v. *Allen* (1983).

Some states have also used the power of the purse to promote parental choice of school within public education. The most notable instance of this is the law, recently passed by Minnesota and several other states, requiring school districts to allow students to transfer to other districts, with their state aid following them. While some states have long-standing practices of allowing students to attend school in other districts by superintendents' agreement (which parents can request), open enrollment laws transfer the power to make this decision to the parents. Another traditional variation on interdistrict transfer has allowed parents to enroll children outside their district of residence by paying tuition, usually equal to the receiving school's per pupil expenditures. The Minnesota law and others like it eliminate such tuition payments.

States may also promote parental choice of school within school districts. This has been attempted most frequently with respect to desegregation cases in which states may provide categorical aid for magnet schools and/or transportation aid to help cover busing costs. States may also provide technical assistance to school districts setting up magnet schools and voluntary transfer plans.

Local Powers

While local school districts are legally the creations of state government, local school boards do have varying amounts of leeway to develop their own policies within the constraints imposed by state (and federal) law. In some states, for example, local districts have broad autonomy to determine curriculum content and instructional methods. Usually such policies are decided at the district level and apply uniformly throughout the district. But this does not have to be the case. Beginning in the 1960s, teachers and parents in many communities have created innovative schools (known variously as alternative schools, free schools, or street academies) to better meet the needs of children. Such schools may reflect different philosophies of education, may focus on children with distinctive learning styles or subject interests, or may be aimed at children who are potential or actual school dropouts. Some of these new schools were created by or absorbed into public school systems as relatively autonomous but publicly funded programs. In addition, some local districts have created schools-within-schools programs, including ungraded classrooms and a variety of other curriculum options.

Magnet schools are a special case of schools that offer a variation of some kind from the standard district curriculum. Such schools enable local districts to meet desegregation guidelines by offering educational alternatives thought to be attractive to white parents from outside the schools' predominantly minority neighborhoods. The first magnet schools were created when several alternative schools already

in existence in Minneapolis were written into a court-ordered desegregation plan in 1972. These schools had attracted racially mixed
student bodies, and the school district committed itself to monitoring
enrollment by race in the future (see McMillan, 1980).

Generally, school districts with more than one school at a given
level have the power to set up policies determining which students will
attend which schools. In most cases, this determination is based on
locally drawn attendance areas assigning students to "neighborhood"
schools. However, assignments are also made on the basis of race, first
to segregate children of different races from each other, then, in accordance with *Brown* v. *Board of Education* (1954) and subsequent decisions, to bring students of different races together. A plan adopted in
Cambridge, Massachusetts, eliminated attendance area boundaries
entirely and replaced them with a controlled choice system of school
enrollment that allows parents to express their preferences for particular schools while ensuring racial balance.

Local districts in some states also have the power to establish
policies relating to home schooling. Since many families opting for
home schooling have done so for religious reasons, this has involved
school boards in difficult issues relating to religious freedom and child
welfare.

This brief overview of parental choice of school has focused on two
considerations affecting decisions regarding parental choice programs:
the ideological rationales and the powers of various levels of government. Other conditions include whether a given program is viewed as a
choice program, and thus whether ideological issues related to choice
are invoked; the constellation of interest groups advocating and opposing a particular policy; and the decision-making process within the
governmental unit, including the priorities and skills of key government officials. The concept of parental choice remains a controversial
one. The implications of parental choices for both parents and administrators are discussed separately in Section Four.

References

Brown v. Board of Educ. of Topeka, 347 U.S. 483, 74 S. Ct. 686, 98 L. Ed. 873
    (1954).
Catterall, J. S. (1982). The politics of education vouchers. *Dissertation Ab-
    stracts International, 43,* 1041-A. (University Microfilms No. 8220436).
Catterall, J. S. (1983). *Tuition tax credits: Fact and fiction.* Bloomington, IN:
    Phi Delta Kappa Educational Foundation.
Center for the Study of Public Policy (1970, December). *Education vouchers: A
    report on financing elementary education grants to parents* (OEO grant
    CG8542). Cambridge, MA: Author.

Coons, J. E., & Sugarman, S. D. (1978). *Education by choice: The case for family control.* Berkeley: University of California Press.

Friedman, M. (1962). *Capitalism and freedom.* Chicago: University of Chicago Press.

Friedman, M. (1973, September 23). The voucher idea: Selling schooling like groceries. *The New York Times Magazine,* pp. 22–23, 65, 67, 69–72.

Jencks, C. (1972). *Inequality: A reassessment of the effect of family and schooling in America.* New York: Basic Books.

Maddaus, J., & Mirochnik, D. (1991). *Parental choice options in Maine.* Orono: College of Education, University of Maine, Occasional Papers Series.

McMillan, C. B. (1980). *Magnet schools: An approach to voluntary desegregation.* Bloomington, IN: Phi Delta Kappa Educational Foundation.

Mueller v. Allen, U.S., 103 S. Ct. 3062, 77 L. Ed. 2nd 721 (1983).

Paulu, N. (1989, October). *Improving schools and empowering parents: Choice in American education.* Washington, DC: US Government Printing Office.

Pierce v. Society of Sisters, 268 U.S. 510, 45 S. Ct. 510, 69 L. Ed. 1070 (1925).

Serrano v. Priest, 226 Cal. Rptr. 584 (Dist. Ct. App. 1986).

Wisconsin v. Yoder, 406 U.S. 205, 92 S. Ct. 1526, 32 L. Ed. 2nd 15 (1972).

STEVEN S. GOLDBERG

Federal Special Education Policy: Why Legalization May Have Failed

Congress passed the Education for All Handicapped Children Act (PL 94–142) in 1975 to delineate and fund educational rights for students with disabilities. For the first time, a statute provided that parents may challenge educators' decisions about their child's school program. By imposing a legal mandate for resolving school-based disputes, Congress intended for parents and students – as well as administrators – to have a fair and satisfactory way to advocate for the programs they sought. But despite the negative experiences of school officials and parents in several states that had previously passed similar requirements, Congress did not anticipate the resistance that would occur when this law was introduced to the schools. This essay describes the intent of the legal model and its shortcomings, which have led most states and the federal government to encourage alternatives to litigation in order to avoid the "legalization of special education" (Goldberg, 1989; Neal and Kirp, 1985).

Why Use a Legal Model?

Historically, the due process hearing, an unbiased tribunal, has been used to guarantee accuracy in fact finding and to provide fairness for those who seek government benefits. At the very least, the government must provide notice to the parties affected by the decision and an opportunity to provide evidence regarding the benefit sought, as well as a written decision drafted by an unbiased hearing officer. In special education, the legal model grants parents the ability to challenge any aspect of a current or proposed special education program. The program, subject to challenge, is the individualized education program (IEP), by now well known to parents and school officials, which must be developed for each child with disabilities in a school district. This document sets forth long- and short-term goals, services offered, and methods to be used for instruction. When a proposed IEP is challenged, a number of procedural protections for enforcing a right to education are triggered. Basically, parents must be notified in writing of any proposed alteration in their child's classification or placement and the reasons for it. When a disagreement arises, either parents or school administrators may request a hearing to be presided over by an impartial hearing officer. This is the crux of the adversarial system imposed by Congress (Goldberg, 1982).

By passing PL 94–142, Congress assumed that a legal system would result in appropriate programs. Yet, the adversarial method is not the best method for resolving disputes in education. Indeed, the nature of the legal system undermines efficient and collegial dispute resolution, because it undermines relationships and takes time to develop a final result. While lawyers are trained to resolve conflict through law, educators are comfortable in a culture of conflict. Research on the legal implementation of special education has shown that school personnel, in response to the legal mandate, develop "coping behaviors" for dealing with angry parents. State and federal mandates in an area where educators had previously dealt informally with parents are considered an uninvited and unnecessary intrusion into the educational process. Even though administrators are frequently dedicated and work long hours, attending to program development may become a secondary concern to dealing with what they consider to be attacks on their schools (Weatherly and Lipsky, 1978).

Thus, relations–which need to be improved–have become strained. School personnel routinize their behaviors to keep parents at a distance, as well as to control access to available benefits. The policy required by law is delivered in a manner the lawmakers did not intend. Educators resist change in large measure because they are placed in the roles of defendants, rather than in their traditional self-defined roles as advocates on behalf of children with special needs.

Moreover, school officials "dread" having their actions reviewed by courts; consequently, most school districts of any size have set up subunits whose employees specialize in administering the special education legal requirements. There persons are expected to settle disputes quickly and insulate other school officials.

There are other problems that have led to a failure of the legal model. For example, the law will not work if it is not used by its intended beneficiaries. Some research shows that the legal right to a hearing is not exercised and has had little impact on the education system. But perhaps the most critical obstacle to change is the way the law has been imposed, which has doomed it to failure. This is a key implementation problem. When omnibus federal programs are imposed by Washington, they will not work. Local school personnel will resist outside intervention. Moreover, social programs have the best chance of success when their drafters seek "small wins"–relatively small programs whose intentions are easy to clarify and implement. Change programs that are not proposed by motivated people who work within the system will not produce long-standing change (McLaughlin,

1990; Beer, Eisenstat, and Spector, 1990; Firestone and Corbett, 1988; Weick, 1984).

What Are the Lessons of Research?

The research documents serious concerns with legalization. In a pioneering Pennsylvania study of due process procedures, Kuriloff (1985) argued that justice cannot be assessed in special education hearings because professionals cannot agree on standards necessary to establish the accuracy of hearing decisions. Instead, he suggested that a person's ability to influence administrative hearings by effectively using due process elements may be a reasonable substitute for accuracy in a decision. Kuriloff called this "objective justice." He demonstrated that, for the first five years of Pennsylvania hearings, due process enabled parents who used its elements effectively—those who knew how to play the system—to influence the course of a decision more than those who used it less effectively, and in that sense promoted justice. Of course, persons must have access to the system in order to obtain its benefits.

In addition to promoting objective justice or procedures, the legal system also must promote a sense of fairness of "subjective justice" in participants. A second Pennsylvania study (Goldberg and Kuriloff, 1991a) was designed to discover how parents and school officials perceived special education hearings. In particular, the research sought to learn if parents and school officials believed that they were accorded the rights they were supposed to receive under PL 94–142, and if they believed their hearings were fair in that they had been allowed to participate fully and had had all the reasons for the decisions explained to them. Additionally, the study sought to determine if they believed that the outcomes of their hearings were accurate reflections of the quality of the evidence presented. Most importantly, Did each set of parties believe they had been treated fairly in an overall sense? Were they satisfied with the decisions of the hearing officers? Finally, this work sought to discover how the parents' and school administrators' perceptions varied as a function of having won or lost the case.

At the prehearing level, most parents believed that they were notified about their rights in a timely fashion, but that schools had not explained their children's records adequately. Reflecting on their experience in the hearings, a majority of the parents believed that hearing officers explained their actions fully, but only a bare majority of parents thought they had been accorded their rights. Still fewer thought that the hearings were fair or that the results were accurate. It is not surprising, then, that a large majority of the parents reported being dissatisfied with the overall experience. On every measure, school officials perceived the hearings as fairer and more satisfactory than did parents. (Of course, they tended to win more often than parents.) Finally, parents and school officials both felt more fairly treated when they prevailed than when they lost.

Hearings, then, promoted "objective justice" because they allowed participants who used due process elements more effectively to win more often than those who used them less effectively. Yet, they undermined "subjective justice" (the individual sense of fair treatment). Since parents are more likely to have a greater emotional investment in the outcome than school officials, these findings support an emerging hypothesis in the procedural justice literature that in matters of major importance, people judge fairness by winning more than by obtaining procedural safeguards.

What Are the Implications of Failed Legalization?

These findings have implications for research and practice. First, experimental studies on procedural justice that do not take peoples' emotional or financial "stakes" into account may draw false conclusions about the relationship between procedures and perceived fairness. Instead, future research should focus on the ways of measuring the relationship of procedures and objective justice in the legal system and on assessing the effects of alternative forms of dispute resolution on subjective experiences of fairness. Scholars have discussed and are examining several of the most promising of the alternative models, including negotiation, conciliation, arbitration, and mediation (Kolb and Rubin, 1989). For example, some data show that the opportunity for mediation has been favorably received where it has been tried (Singer, 1990). On the other hand, a preliminary analysis of New Jersey's mediation program (Goldberg and Kuriloff, 1991b) seems to find mixed results, somewhat similar to the Pennsylvania due process studies described. Participants may only be happy when they win. If that is so, these alternatives have failed because justice requires fair procedures and a sense of fairness, regardless of outcome; a win is a pleasing, but not necessary, element for justice to have been applied. When the shortcomings of the legal system itself are considered with the resistance owing to flowed program implementation, legalization seems to be inappropriate for resolving educational questions. Perhaps the best system is ultimately one where all parties' concerns are freely and openly expressed in a nonlegal forum within schools (Handler,

1986). In this way school administrators and parents might avoid the pitfalls of unwelcome litigation and promote trust among those who are responsible for educating children.

References

Beer, M., Eisenstat, R., & Spector, B. (1990). Why change programs don't produce change. *Harvard Business Review, 68,* 158–166.

Firestone, W., & Corbett, H. (1988). Planned organizational change. In J. Boyan (Ed.), *Handbook on research in educational administration.* New York: Longwood.

Goldberg, S. (1989). The failure of legalization in education: Mediation and the Education for all Handicapped Children Act of 1975. *Journal of Law and Education, 18,* 441–454.

Goldberg, S. (1982). *Special education law.* New York: Plenum.

Goldberg, S., & Kuriloff, P. (in press). Parents and school officials evaluate the fairness of PL 94–142 hearings. *Exceptional Children.*

Goldberg, S., & Kuriloff, P. (1991b). Evaluation of mediation in special education. Unpublished manuscript.

Handler, J. (1986). *The conditions of discretion.* New York: Russell Sage Foundation.

Kolb, D., & Rubin, J. (1989). *Research into mediation.* Washington, DC: National Institute for Dispute Resolution.

Kuriloff, P. (1985). Is justice served by due process? *Law and Contemporary Problems, 48,* 89–118.

McLaughlin, M. (1990). The Rand change agent study revisited: Macro perspectives and micro realities. *Educational Researcher, 19,* 11–16.

Neal, D., & Kirp, D. (1985). The allure of legalization reconsidered: The case of special education. *Law and Contemporary Problems, 48,* 63–87.

Singer, L. (1990). *Settling disputes.* Boulder, CO: Westview Press.

Weatherly, R., & Lipsky, M. (1978). Street level bureaucrats and institutional innovation: Implementing special education reform. *Harvard Educational Review, 47,* 171–197.

Weick, K. (1984). Small wins: Redefining the scale of social problems. *American Psychologist, 39,* 40–49.

SECTION ONE REFERENCES

Bakalis, M. J. (1985). *Report of the Illinois Project for School Reform.* Evanston, IL: Author.

Bennis, W., & Nanus, B. (1985). *Leaders: The strategies for taking charge.* New York: Harper & Row.

Drucker, P. F. (1980). *Managing in turbulent times.* New York: Harper & Row.

Drucker, P. F. (1986). *The frontiers of management.* New York: E. P. Dutton.

Edmonds, R. R. (1982). "Program of school improvement: An overview." *Educational Leadership, 46*(10), 4–11.

Everhart, R. B. (Ed.). (1982). *The public school monopoly.* Cambridge, MA: Ballinger.

Feistritzer, C. E. (1988). *Profile of school administrators in the U.S.* Washington, DC: National Center for Education Information.

First, P. F. (1988). "Issues affecting the preparation of educational administration as the societal paradigm shifts." *The AASA Professor, 10*(3), 9.

Fischer, F. (1987). Policy expertise and the "New Class": A critique of the neoconservative thesis. In F. Fischer & J. Forester (Eds.), *Confronting values in policy analysis: The politics of criteria* (pp. 94–126). Newbury Park, CA: Sage.

Gooler, D. D. (1986). Educating educators for their policy making roles. *Thresholds in education, 12*(2), 37–40.

Kanter, R. M. (1983). *The change masters: Innovation for productivity in the American corporation.* New York: Simon & Schuster.

LeFotte, L. W., & Bancroft, B. A. (1985). "Growing use of the effective schools model for school improvement." *Educational Leadership, 42*(6), 23–27.

Marshall, C., Mitchell, D., & Wirt, F. (1989). *Culture and Education Policy in the United States.* New York: Palmer Press.

May, R. (1985). *My quest for beauty.* San Francisco: Saybrook.

Musial, D. (1986). "First principles and policy development: A perspective from educational foundations." *Thresholds in Education, 12*(2), 2–4.

Naisbitt (1982). *Megatrends.* New York: Warner.

National Commission on Excellence in Education. (1983). *A nation at risk: The imperative for educational reform.* Washington, DC: US Government Printing Office.

Pierce v. Society of Sisters of the Holy Names of Jesus and Mary, 268 U.S. 510, 45S.CT. 571 (1925).

Ravitch, D. (1983). *The troubled crusade: American education 1945–1980.* New York: Basic Books.

Sandell, S. (1977, March). Does your board need its own policy analyst? *The American School Board Journal,* 48–49.

Toffler, A. (1990). *Power shift.* New York: Bantam.

Townsel, A. H. (1986). Some commentary on contemporary reforms: Ambivalent samaritans or education reactionaries? *Thresholds in Education, 12*(2), 29–33.

Yudof, M. G., Kirp, D. L., van Geel, T., & Levin, B. (1987). *Educational policy and the law.* Berkeley, CA: McCutchan.

The Federal Government and Educational Policy

The Wavering Role

It is perfectly true that that government is best which governs least.
It is equally true that that government is best which provides most—
Walter Lippmann, "The Red Herring," *A Preface to Politics* (1914)

Education as a National Concern

Educational administrators live a love-hate relationship with the federal government. We love the money (and want more of it) but we hate the strings that accompany it (and continually demand their loosening or elimination). Federal requirements, particularly of the evaluative and record-keeping type, provide a convenient scapegoat for many disgruntled accusations.

Even the governors, during the discussions, manipulations, and processes that resulted in the National Education Goals of 1990, echoed these essentially contradictory sentiments. The governors asked for more real federal support, that is, money, to assist in the achievement of the goals and simultaneously requested a lessening of federal mandates and requirements that might hinder the flexibility of the governors and the educational governance systems in the states in attaining the goals. Of course, this approach-avoidance behavior is duplicated in many fields and between and among many layers of governance. But in the field of education, the federal government is particularly vulnerable to criticism because of a word missing from the Constitution. Nowhere is the word "education" to be found in the document that embodies our freedoms.

Education and the Constitution

Since education is not mentioned in the Constitution, the powers and responsibilities for educating the citizens fall to the states under the wording of the Tenth Amendment to the Constitution, which reads,

"The powers not delegated to the United States by the Constitution, nor prohibited by it to the States, are reserved to the States respectively, or to the people." So education is a state function, but we all know that in many ways, both large and small, the federal government influences and directs education. How is this allowed under the Constitution?

One way the federal government gets into the act is through the wording of the General Welfare Clause of the Constitution. The General Welfare Clause of the federal Constitution, Article I, Section 8, authorizes Congress "to lay and collect Taxes, Duties, Imposts and Excises, to pay the Debts and provide for the common Defence and the general Welfare of the United States." Since the general welfare has been construed broadly, it includes educational matters.

Other clauses in the U.S. Constitution affect educational matters. Article 1, Section 10 prevents the states from passing any law impairing the obligation of contracts and thus affects such matters as collective bargaining in the schools.

The separation of church and state is of course a constitutional matter, as is the matter of free speech. The First Amendment states that "Congress shall make no law respecting an establishment of religion, or prohibiting the free exercise thereof; or abridging the freedom of speech, or of the press; or the right of the people peaceably to assemble, and to petition the Government for a redress of grievances."

The school administrator takes actions nearly daily that are governed by Fourth Amendment protections such as unreasonable searches and seizures and when an action is governed by probable cause. The Fourth Amendment reads: "The right of the people to be secure in their persons, houses, papers and effects, against unreasonable searches and seizures, shall not be violated, and no warrants shall issue, but upon probable cause, supported by oath or affirmation, and particularly describing the place to be searched, and the persons or things to be seized."

In the Fourteenth Amendment we find two clauses particularly important to the functions of school administrators. These are the Due Process and the Equal Protection Clauses. The Fourteenth Amendment states that "all persons born or naturalized in the United States, and subject to the jurisdiction thereof, are citizens of the United States and of the State wherein they reside. No State shall make or enforce any law which shall abridge the privileges or immunities of citizens of the United States; nor shall any State deprive any person of life, liberty, or property, without due process of law; nor deny to any person within its jurisdiction the equal protection of the laws."

The Equal Protection Clause needs to be considered by educational administrators especially in relation to questions of access to schools and to programs. Many groups have pressed the educational enterprise for equal access—blacks, women, people of limited English-speaking ability, and the handicapped, for instance. In the late 1980s and early 1990s, advocates for the homeless were pressuring schools to provide the equal access to which these children were entitled under the Fourteenth Amendment.

The Due Process Clause needs to be especially remembered by school administrators in their everyday dealings with students and teachers. Due process means fairness. The extension of Constitutional fairness to within the walls of school buildings began with the landmark *Tinker* case (1969).

Federal Educational History

In some forms, the federal involvement with education has a long history. At the end of this section is a brief historical overview of federal programs for education and related activities from 1787 to 1988.

The federal share of funding for public elementary and secondary schools has never been large. At its height of under 10 percent around 1980, we can see in Figure 2.1 that it decreased slightly but steadily in the 1980s. But the federal dollars had an impact bigger than those percentages would indicate because federal policy sends that money to the states and localities by the means of categorical funding.

Categorical Funding

First via the U.S. Office of Education and then through the U.S. Department of Education, the federal government has concentrated its aid to the schools through categorical funding. This is funding earmarked for special programs for special populations rather than money given in an unrestricted manner to another level of educational governance.

Wirt and Kirst (1989, p. 357) classify federal modes of affecting public education into six basic categories:

1. *General aid:* Provide no-strings aid to state and local education agencies or such minimal earmarks as teacher salaries. A modified form of general aid was proposed by President Reagan in 1981. He consolidated numerous categories into a single bloc grant for local education purposes. No general-aid bill has ever been approved by the Congress.

FIGURE 2.1 • *Sources of Revenue for Public Elementary and Secondary Schools: 1969–70 to 1986–87*

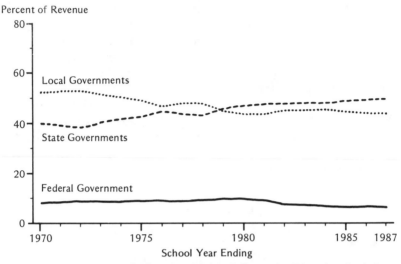

Source: U.S. Department of Education, National Center for Education Statistics, *Statistics of State School Systems, Revenues and Expenditures for Public Elementary and Secondary Education,* and Common Core of Data surveys.

2. *Stimulate through differential funding:* Earmark categories of aid, provide financial incentives through matching grants, fund demonstration projects, and purchase specific services. This is the approach of Elementary and Secondary Education Act (ESEA).
3. *Regulate:* Legally specify behavior, impose standards, certify and license, and enforce accountability procedures. The bilingual regulations proposed by the Carter administration (and rescinded by President Reagan) are a good example.
4. *Discover knowledge and make it available:* Have research performed; gather and make other statistical data available. The National Science Foundation performs the first function and the National Center for Education Statistics the second.
5. *Provide services:* Furnish technical assistance and consultants in specialized areas or subjects. For example, the Office of Civil Rights will advise school districts that are designing voluntary desegregation plans.
6. *Exert moral suasion:* Develop vision and question assumptions through publications and speeches by top officials. Thus President Reagan's Secretary of Education William Bennett advocated three Cs—content, character, and choice—in numerous speeches

and articles in the popular media. This mode of federal influence is termed "the bully pulpit" by the press.

Federalism

Ours is an intergovernmental system, and in education we can see clear powers at the federal, state, and local levels, with shifting influences and overlapping responsibilities clouding the scene. This shifting and overlapping causes problems for the administrator seeking to influence policy. Who is really making what decisions where and when is always a question. The term *federalism* refers to the balance of power between the national and state governments. Campbell, Cunningham, Nystrand, and Usdan (1985) write that we have moved from dual federalism, where there is separation of power between the state and national governments, to a shift of power more and more to the national government. We now have national federalism although they write that there has been some recent slowing of this trend.

Some feel, particularly because of the omission of a direct reference to education in the Constitution, that the state level of government has a claim to being closer to the people and thus, by "rights," should be more influential in education. Elmore wrote in 1986 that "the federal and state governments are in fact but different agents and trustees of the people" (p. 171). Further, he wrote, "Neither federal nor state government has a claim to being 'closer' to the people, since both take their authority directly from the people" (p. 171).

Shifting Power

Power related to educational governance shifted among the layers of government during the period from 1950 to 1987. Both the federal and state levels of governance were winners of power during this time period, despite the shifts in power between the two. The local level of educational governance clearly lost influence during this time period (Wirt and Kirst, 1989). For the school administrator, this indicates a need to be attuned to, and knowledgeable about, the policy making occurring at these more powerful levels, even though day-to-day life seems governed still by the local governance entities.

Federal, but "Visible" in the State

For the school administrator seeking to sort out which level of governance is doing what, where, and when, some of the outreach programs of the federal government can be confusing. For instance, the Regional

Educational Laboratories are federal entities situated in national geographic regions that provide services to and through state agencies, regional service centers, and local educational agencies. The network of Regional Educational Laboratories came into being in 1965, as the result of recommendations of an educational reform task force, for the purpose of knowledge diffusion.

In 1990, funding for the labs was the second largest item in the budget request of the Office of Educational Research and Improvement (OERI), part of the U.S. Department of Education fiscal 1990–$17.8 million out of a total of $51 million. During the Reagan administration, senior department officials wanted to eliminate the program, but were unable to do so because of its strong support in Congress.

The laboratories were originally intended to serve as knowledge brokers between researchers, who would develop improved educational practices and methods, and the teachers and school administrators, who would use them in the nation's schools and classrooms. Part of the labs' work was to disseminate the information and provide local educators with training and technical assistance in its application. Twenty labs were originally established, with no boundaries for delivering their services. In 1972, the labs came under the control of the newly created National Institute of Education (NIE), which later became OERI.

In 1985, with calls from the education reform movement for increased accountability for tax funds invested, the labs were directed to devote a significant portion of their budgets to delivering services "with and through" such agencies as state education departments rather than directly to local school districts. Their number was reduced to nine.

In addition to the regional laboratories, there are also regional research centers, the Educational Resources Information Centers (ERIC), and the National Diffusion Network. It is indeed a complex federal service-delivery system the school administrator must keep track of.

The Shifting Federal Influence

One thing for school administrators to remember is that the federal involvement in education is not a steady source of influence. The federal interest in the educational enterprise waxes and wanes with that of the country and often depends on events outside education's sphere. The Russian launching of Sputnik, for instance, in the 1950s sparked an educational reform movement led from the federal level and fueled by the nation's desire to catch up to the Russians in the space race. Similarly, in 1983 the publication of *A Nation at Risk* by the National Commission on Excellence in Education portrayed the country as vulnerable due to an inadequate educational system and thus was launched the "decade of reform" of the 1980s.

In what might be called the era of federal intervention, the following major legislation came from the federal level: the National Defense Act of 1958, which was a response to the Russian-launched Sputnik satellite; the Civil Rights Act of 1964, which outlawed discrimination in all federally aided programs; the Economic Opportunity Act of 1964, which began programs like the Job Corps; the Elementary and Secondary Education Act of 1965; and other federal aid to both public and private education such as the G.I. Bill, the National Defense Education Act, the National Science Foundation Act, and the National School Lunch Act.

Wirt and Kirst (1989) summarize three stages in the federal role in education from 1965 to 1988. The years 1965 to 1972 included large-scale federal involvement in targeted programs intended to assist previously neglected populations. During this period, federal aid peaked at 9 percent of total school expenditures.

An example of these large-scale targeted programs is Title I of the Elementary and Secondary Education Act (ESEA) for the educationally deprived. In the responsibilities assigned to each governance level, its plan reflected the legal framework of the federal system. Responsibilities of the federal government included establishing the rules under which the program is to operate, distributing grants to state education agencies, and ensuring that state agencies properly administer the funds. The responsibilities of state government included explaining requirements to local school districts, approving local applications, distributing grants to LEAs, and administering the program (monitoring and auditing). The responsibilities of local government included designing programs and providing services. Title IX of the Education Amendments of 1972, which deals with sex equity in education, is another example of an equity claim cycle of initiation or initial constitutionalization of the equity claim, incorporation into legislatively guaranteed entitlement or enactment of nondiscrimination standards, implementation concerns, and subsequent rounds of constitutional litigation.

The years 1973 to 1980 marked a time of consolidation and increased regulatory effectiveness. The federal percentage of the budget stabilized, and state and local instrumentalities adjusted to the federal objectives. During the years 1980 to 1988, there was a gradual devolution of responsibility to states and localities with an attendant decline in the federal budget share to the 1988 level of 6 percent. Federal innovative techniques shifted from categorical programming to exhortation and persuasion, called by some leadership from the "bully pulpit."

This change was a planned one, in keeping with the Reagan administration's plan to disassemble the federal government establishment by reducing the size and scope of federal expenditures in education, reducing federal control and monitoring in the field of education, accomplishing a transfer of responsibility for education from the federal to the state and local levels, eliminating the Department of Education, and removing educational policy from a position of priority on the federal agenda. These were major policy changes. The resultant upheaval generated fear and confusion through all the layers of educational governance and contributed heavily to the administrators' feeling of being helpless while educational policy was made elsewhere.

State-level educational administrators were equally anxious and confused as major federal policy changes altered the way state education agencies had been doing business. The Education Consolidation and Improvement Act (ECIA) of 1981 established the bloc grant program, which consolidated twenty-eight separate federal programs into one bloc grant. Some discreet federal-state hierarchies began to crumble. Thus, the policy-related relationships among the federal, state, and local educational policy actors had to be reconfigured. Familiar communication channels were altered and administrators felt threatened. But in such times of change, power is also shifting and educators at all levels do have an opportunity to set, or at least to influence, educational policy making.

Several factors contributed to the successful restructuring of national education policy in the 1980s. These included the ideological convictions and persuasive talents of President Reagan himself; a recognition (or growing belief) by influential interest groups that education alone could not solve social problems; a substantial decline in the power of education interest groups as the field became increasing splintered and involved in internal power struggles; an appeal to "popular" feelings regarding race, religion, and federal control; and the perceived burden of some federal initiatives tied to fundamental social change [Title IX, (Gender Equity); P.L. 94–141, (Special Education); and P.L. 94–482 (Vocational Education)].

Emphasis on some of the educational policy positions of the Reagan administration continued under the Bush administration in the 1990s. These issues included:

1. *Institutional competition:* Breaking the monopoly of the public school to stimulate excellent performance.
2. *Individual competition:* Recognizing excellence to stimulate excellence.
3. *Performance standards:* Increasing minimum standards for teachers and students.
4. *Focus on content:* Emphasis on basics to ensure performance in critical instructional areas.
5. *Parental choice:* Parental control over what, where, and how their children will learn.
6. *Character:* Strengthening traditional values in schools. (Clark and Astuto, 1988)

Despite the federal reversion, however, the U.S. outlays for education from the federal, state, and local governance levels combined continued to rise after 1982. Total outlays for fiscal years 1979–1986 are shown in Figure 2.2.

The 1980s ended and the 1990s opened with a president who stated his desire to be the "Education President" and a Secretary of Education, Lauro Cavazos, putting less "bully" into the pulpit. Their strategy involved inviting all fifty governors to an historic Education Summit, only the third such summit in U.S. history devoted to a single policy area and the subsequent development of highly publicized edu-

FIGURE 2.2 • *U.S. Outlays for Education: Fiscal Years 1979–1986*

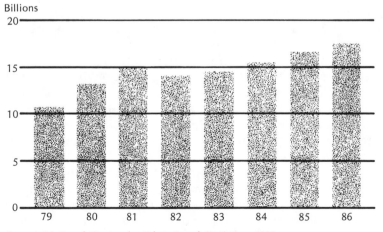

Source: National Center for Educational Statistics, 1989.

cation goals. These goals are presented and discussed later in this section.

The Federal Role

Federal Role in the 1990s

Hill (1990) suggests that the federal focus in the 1990s should be aimed at helping entire urban school systems to solve their own problems. Hill notes that past federal programs directed efforts at students, whereas the focus is shifting to helping schools and districts help students. This shift could provide more policy input linkages and opportunities for school administrators. Past programs, such as Title I/Chapter 1, the Education Act for All Handicapped Children Act, and the bilingual education initiatives had other features in common in addition to the focus on helping students. For instance, they were authorized to fund services in nearly all school districts; they were designed to correct inequities in the distribution of resources to the students and schools within districts; they were targeted at specific groups previously neglected in society; there were procedures to ensure that the services would be delivered directly to the students in these groups; and, very significantly, these massive federal programs were built on the assumption that local educators could deliver the services with sufficient funds and motivation to do so.

Hill cites demographic statistics and the condition of urban education today to build a case for the targeting of federal education resources in the 1990s toward the large urban school systems. Hill writes that "federal resources are needed to help urban school districts initiate the very difficult (and therefore inevitably long and frustrating) struggle for across the board improvement" (p. 400). In helping urban school districts to solve their own problems, the federal government could concentrate on stimulating and assisting local planning and consensus-building processes; helping with teacher recruitment, training, and pay; and promoting improved instruction in urban secondary schools (Hill, 1990).

That a focus on urban schools is urgently needed in the 1990s is hardly debatable. In broader terms, however, there is some agreement that there remains a federal role. Generally agreed upon components of that role are to identify national priorities in education, do something about the national priorities through legislation and appropriations, support research on education, and deal with issues of equity and equal opportunity.

President Bush's 1991 budget for educational research and statistics reflected an interest in the support for the research component of the federal role. Perhaps to deflect the anticipated demands for additional revenues to support the governors' national goals, the president's advisors emphasized the unique role of the federal government in research and statistics. Secretary of Education Lauro Cavazos testified, "It is these relatively small investments [research and statistics] that can have the greatest impact on education reform in the long run" (1990).

Also included in the 1991 research and statistics budget were new initiatives that help define what Bush meant when supporting this component of the federal role and what his administration saw, in 1990, as areas in great need of federal support:

- A request for $5 million to fund research on dropout prevention. Funds would be available for short- and long-term research as well as for creation of an additional national center on dropout prevention.
- A second request for $3 million to evaluate reform initiatives at the state and local level. The Office of Educational Research and Improvement (OERI) hoped to be able to fund as many as twelve evaluations with this money.
- There was a request for $20 million to conduct research and evaluation programs necessary to support the achievement of the national goals generated by the Education Summit. Such money could result in a major increase in research opportunities if it is channeled toward basic and applied research necessary to design strategies for achieving increased math and science achievement, for example.
- Finally, the research budget included a $25 million proposal for using excellent principals to train and mentor prospective ones. Here was an opportunity for policy-oriented principals to truly make a difference.

We can see the fourth component of the federal role, issues of equity and equal opportunity, displayed in Table 2.1, which shows spending for major federal programs for elementary and secondary education in 1988. Note the number of items and the large percentage of the money that is related to these issues.

TABLE 2.1 • *Major Federal Programs for Elementary and Secondary Education, 1988 (in thousands of dollars)*

Basic grants for the disadvantaged (ECIA Chapter 1)	$4,336,543
Education for the handicapped	1,869,019
Vocational education	888,243
Impact aid	708,476
Special programs	
1. Improving school programs	
(a) State bloc grants (ECIA Chapter 2)	478,700
(b) Secretary's discretionary fund:	
(1) Inexpensive book distribution	7,659
(2) Arts in education	3,315
(3) Law-related education	3,830
(4) National diffusion network	10,244
(5) Other discretionary programs	4,691
2. Drug-free schools and communities	229,776
3. Teacher training and improvement	131,727
4. Magnet schools assistance	71,805
5. Education of homeless children and youth	4,787
6. Women's educational equity	3,351
7. Training and advisory services	23,456
8. Follow through	7,133
9. Dropout prevention demonstrations	23,935
10. Workplace literacy	9,574
11. Star schools using educational television	19,148
Education research and statistics	202,615
Bilingual education	146,573
Adult education	124,462
Indian education	66,326

Source: U.S. Department of Education, 1988.

The Nation's Mood and Influence

"The public education system in the United States is an instrumentality for carrying out a function that society has determined to be a desirable one—the education of all the people" (Reutter, 1985, p. 1). But how much and what kind of support society is willing to put behind that function changes as the mood of the nation changes.

The Mood in the Early 1980s

A Nation at Risk (1983), the report of the National Commission on Excellence in Education, was the right report for the right time. The nation was tired of massive federal "fix" programs that were not showing enough results fast enough for the "quick-fix" age. And, as has been discussed, the president and the nation were in accord that the federal educational establishment had become too intrusive.

The wording of *A Nation at Risk* also reflected the deeply held beliefs of the American people that public education was a visible symbol and embodiment of our jointly held democratic values with such language as the following: "A high level of shared education is essential to a free, democratic society and to the fostering of a common culture, especially in a country that prides itself on pluralism and individual freedom. For our country to function citizens must be able to reach some common understandings on complex issues, often on short notice and on the basis of conflicting or incomplete evidence."

Chubb and Moe (1990) have since presented research that supports their argument that the very projection of these democratic beliefs into the political environment of schooling can be detrimental to the very excellence that the National Commission was trying to engender. They write that public schools are captives of democratic politics.

Another tactic of the National Commission on Excellence in Education was resorting to a call to competition with other countries. This strategy had sparked cycles of education reform in the past, for instance in the Sputnik era when calls for competition in the space "race" motivated a reform movement that generated many programs and much federal financial support. The Commission noted that "learning is the indispensable investment required for success in the 'information age' we are entering." In its report on the report, the American Association of School Administrators (1983) emphasized this line with more blunt language. "Our national prosperity and even our national defense depend on an educated citizenry" (p. 1).

A Nation at Risk ended with a stirring call to patriotism: "It is their America, and the America of all of us, that is at risk; it is to each of us that this imperative is addressed. It is by our willingness to take up the challenge, and our resolve to see it through, that America's place in the world will be either secured or forfeited. Americans have succeeded before and so we shall again."

And so began the "decade of reform." State legislatures responded to the call with the massive reform packages that today's school administrators are struggling to implement and evaluate.

The "Education President" Calls a Summit

This reform drama reached peak national political intensity in the fall of 1989 when President Bush's call to the governors to convene in Charlottesville, Virginia, in 1990 for a "summit" on education. Only the third time in our history that a president has convened such a meeting on one policy issue, the symbolism of the event perhaps overshadowed the national goals for education that were the product of the actual meeting. Theodore Roosevelt called such a session to discuss environmental issues. Franklin D. Roosevelt held a summit with the governors on what to do about the Depression.

The National Education Goals

As of 1990 we had national education goals, six big ones, accompanied by twenty-one objectives, and we had ten years to reach them. The six goals read as follows:

1. By the year 2000, all children in the United States will start school ready to learn.
2. By the year 2000, the high school graduation rate will increase to at least 90 percent.
3. By the year 2000, U.S. students will leave grades four, eight, and twelve having demonstrated competency over challenging subject matter, including English, mathematics, science, history and geography, and every school in the United States will ensure that all students learn to use their minds well, so they may be prepared for responsible citizenship, further learning, and productive employment in our modern economy.
4. By the year 2000, U.S. students will be first in the world in science and mathematics achievement.
5. By the year 2000, every adult American will be literate and possess the knowledge and skills necessary to compete in a global economy and exercise the rights and responsibilities to citizenship.
6. By the year 2000, every school in the United States will be free of drugs and violence and offer a disciplined environment conducive to learning.

The six goals with their twenty-one objectives are displayed in Figure 2.3. It might be instructive to remember, however, that influential groups have, with great fanfare, been setting national goals for education since at least 1893 when, under the leadership of Harvard University's president, the Committee of 10 concentrated on curriculum goals. There were other attempts at national goals during this century such as The Cardinal Principles of Secondary Education by a commission of the National Education Association in 1918, and the

FIGURE 2.3 • *National Goals for Education*

Readiness

Goal 1: By the year 2000, all children in America will start school ready to learn.

Objectives: All disadvantaged children will have access to high quality and developmentally appropriate preschool programs that help prepare children for school.

Every parent in America will be a child's first teacher and devote time each day helping his or her preschool children learn; parents will have access to the training and support they need.

Children will receive the nutrition and health care needed to arrive at school with healthy minds and bodies, and the number of low-birthweight babies will be significantly reduced through enhanced prenatal health systems.

School Completion

Goal 2: By the year 2000, the high school graduation rate will increase to at least 90 percent.

Objectives: The nation must dramatically reduce its dropout rate and 75 percent of those students who drop out will successfully complete a high school degree or its equivalent.

The gap in high school graduation rates between American students from minority backgrounds and their nonminority counterparts will be eliminated.

Student Achievement and Citizenship

Goal 3: By the year 2000, American students will leave grades four, eight, and twelve having demonstrated competency in challenging subject matter including English, mathematics, science, history, and geography, and every school in America will ensure that all students learn to use their minds well, so they may be prepared for responsible citizenship, further learning, and productive employment in our modern economy.

Objectives: The academic performance of elementary and secondary students will increase significantly in every quartile, and the distribution of minority students in each level will more closely reflect the student population as a whole. .

The percentage of students who demonstrate the ability to reason, solve problems, apply knowledge, and write and communicate effectively will increase substantially.

All students will be involved in activities that promote and demonstrate good citizenship, community service, and personal responsibility.

Continued

FIGURE 2.3 • *Continued*

The percentage of students who are competent in more than one language will substantially increase.

All students will be knowledgeable about the cultural diversity of this nation and about the world community.

Mathematics and Science

Goal 4: By the year 2000, U.S. students will be first in the world in mathematics and science achievement.

Objectives: Math and science education will be strengthened throughout the system, including special emphasis in the early grades.

The number of teachers with a substantive background in mathematics and science will increase by 50 percent.

The number of U.S. graduate and undergraduate students, especially women and minorities, who complete degrees in mathematics, science, and engineering will increase significantly.

Adult Literacy and Lifelong Learning

Goal 5: By the year 2000, every adult American will be literate and will possess the skills necessary to compete in a global economy and exercise the rights and responsibilities of citizenship.

Objectives: Every major American business will be involved in strengthening the connection between education and work.

All workers will have the opportunity to acquire the knowledge and skills needed to adapt to constantly emerging new technologies, new work methods, and new markets through public and private vocational, technical, workplace, or other innovative programs.

The number of quality programs that are designed to serve more effectively the needs of the growing number of part-time and midcareer students will increase significantly.

We will substantially increase the proportion of those qualified students, especially minorities, who enter college; who complete at least two years; and who complete their degree programs.

The proportion of college graduates who demonstrate an advanced ability to think critically, communicate effectively, and solve problems in areas such as the natural sciences, the social sciences, and the humanities will increase substantially.

Safe, Disciplined, and Drug-Free Schools

Goal 6: By the year 2000, every school in America will be free of drugs and violence and will offer a disciplined environment conducive to learning.

Objectives: Every school will implement a firm and fair policy on use, possession, and distribution of drugs and alcohol.

Parents, businesses, and community organizations will work together to ensure that schools are a safe haven for all children.

Every school district will develop a comprehensive K–12 drug and alcohol prevention education program. Drug and alcohol curriculum should be taught as an integral part of health education. In addition, community-based teams should be organized to provide students and teachers with needed support.

Source: U.S. Department of Education.

Ten Imperative Needs of Youth from the National Association of Secondary School Principals in 1944. Congress took a crack at setting national education goals in 1929 when it authorized a national survey of secondary education and in 1958 with the National Defense Education Act. And in 1983, backed by its report, *A Nation at Risk,* the National Commission on Excellence in Education called for strengthening high school graduation requirements and began a decade-long reform movement.

In all of these efforts and in others not mentioned, improvement in education was tied to larger societal issues. So it is with the 1990 national goals. But what is new is that the governors and the president, those most visible leaders of the larger society, took a turn at leadership in educational goal setting. Although their sustained attention to those matters may be doubtful and their efforts dismissed by some as mere symbolism, one can as easily hope that the very symbolism of their positions might be enough to galvanize efforts behind national goals for educational improvement.

There were obvious problems with these goals. For one, they may have been unreachable; but as long as progress is applauded, we should be able to accept the "goals-as-vision" definition. Other problems remain, such as how to pay for the changes needed to reach the goals, how to measure progress toward the goals, and who should be responsible for such oversight.

As of summer 1990, these questions were being hotly debated and, most likely, they will never be fully settled, but will continue to provoke controversy while, hopefully, work on the goals begins. Via access to state political process, that is, governors' staffs and other influentials, administrators have the opportunity, singly and in groups, to influence the continued refinement, implementation, and evaluation around these national goals.

Reading the six goal statements by themselves does not tell much of the story. In reading the entire text of the statement issued by the governors, one clearly sees the ties to business and the economic base upon which these goals were built. As administrators, we know that the business community at all levels has had increasing power in educational policy making. The opening paragraph sets the tone: "If the United States is to maintain a strong and responsible democracy and a prosperous and growing economy into the next century, it must be prepared to address and respond to major challenges at home and in the world. A well educated population is the key to our future."

What really happened in this goal setting procedure was the culmination of ten years of justifying public energy and expenditure on education in terms of its economic importance and the competitive needs of U.S. society in a world economy. It was clearly a triumph of the business-oriented view of the value of education. This is certainly not all bad, but neither is it all good.

The document lacked the language of the justness and rightness and goodness of education that some could hope for in a document that claimed leadership for our national educational enterprise for the coming decade. Our social problems were not addressed except in relation to economic needs. For instance, there were repeated references to the needs and achievements of minority and disadvantaged students, but not because addressing such concerns is a good in itself, but because of the ties of an educated citizenry to worldwide competitiveness. The language and tone of competitiveness ran throughout this document. There was no sign of the emerging paradigm of cooperation.

William Boyd wrote in the spring 1990 issue of the *Politics of Education Bulletin* that "the new national politics over the national goals have already begun." Boyd went on to write that this new level of pluralistic national politics was to be seen in the dispute over the composition and activities of the bipartisan panel created to oversee the implementation of the new goals. Boyd went on to ask a crucial question about these national goals and their relationship to national politics: "Are we really serious about the national performance goals for education that President Bush and the state governors have set" (p. 2)? Boyd's answer was discouraging. "Sadly, as a nation, we presently lack not only the commitment, but the societal learning conditions and the teaching force necessary to achieve these laudable goals (p. 2)." Boyd cited as some of the reasons for his pessimistic outlook the fact that the president was widely criticized for ignoring the link between poverty and school failure; the costs of making good on the goals are probably too high for politicians and the society to be prepared to pay; and our teaching force has acute shortcomings when it comes to math and science education.

The president and the governors agreed to ten full years of cooperative effort toward the achievement of these six goals and twenty-one objectives. They agreed to work with the Congress and education and business groups to institutionalize a process to address the problems already mentioned, to report regularly on progress toward meeting the goals, to oversee the development of new measures and indicators, and to revise goals and objectives if justified by subsequent research and development.

Were the president and the governors really serious about national goals? We have some evidence that they were, and some contrary evidence too. For instance, the president included the goals in his 1990 State of the Union address, but shortly after that, on February 26, he told the governors that while he strongly supported the goals, he was prepared only to "encourage the people of this country to support state and local initiatives." Perhaps it was time to remember that national leadership was needed during the civil rights era because state and local instrumentalities did not rise to the occasion and address necessary change. In 1990, we were still educationally a "nation at risk" in a changing world. There is no evidence that this time federal leadership was less needed in the face of stupendous challenge.

The issue of how much and what kind of federal support for these goals was forthcoming may help answer the question of whether or not Mr. Bush will be remembered as the "Education President." It is interesting to look at the president's goal-setting work with the governors in light of its symbolic significance to his wish of being known as the "Education President." By merely being held, the Charlottesville summit that began the process was an historic meeting.

If we think of our intergovernmental system of educational governance from an organizational point of view, the political and symbolic value of this meeting becomes clear. Politically, education is certainly an arena of scarce resources, and the governors were playing the political games of bargaining and coalition forming. In the summit aftermath of making and amending the goals, the governors faced the classic problem of Bolman and Deal's (1988) political frame: power unevenly distributed and so broadly dispersed that it is difficult to get anything done.

These six goals were huge, perhaps unattainable, and some of the twenty-one objectives were vague. Such goals left much room for the political maneuvering that took place as implementation began. For instance, in the background report on choice and restructuring, which was prepared after the fall 1989 summit, choice was noted as a powerful catalyst in educational reform both for its empowerment of parents and its potential to empower teachers, as teachers are given power to create the various programs that will give the parents true choice. Thus the theme of tying choice to school-site management, which Secretary Cavazos had been promoting, was strengthened.

In the background report on a competitive workforce, the governors mentioned "warranties" that would guarantee graduating vocational students adequate training for the workplace or retraining at the schools' expense. This was one of many signs that the strongest underlying value, even as the summit began, was education as the foundation for economic growth. Other justifications for educational improvement were never seriously considered. Throughout all the background reports, there was a call for federal money, but not for federal interference, and even for a loosening of any federal rules and regulations still in place which may reduce the flexibility of the governors in their restructuring efforts. But while the governors decried interference "from above," they spoke of much change "below" that may be seen as interference by those affected.

Although flexibility and local options were praised by the governors, a strong national theme was evident when the entire goal-setting process is considered. The very idea of national goals, national accountability, and national and international comparisons provided the foundation for the entire process. The governors called for more "clarity" in the federal role, although the functions mentioned were some of the traditional ones that many have agreed for years are best done at the federal level. There was support for basic research, serving as a clearinghouse, continuing to grade the states, disseminating information, and assuming responsibility for areas of special need.

Federal Policy Making

The Iron Triangle

One of the ways of explaining the making of federal educational policy is the iron-triangle theory. The three members of the triangle are the educational units of the executive branch, congressional committees, and interest groups (Guthrie and Reed, 1986). The idea of the iron triangle is used to explain the collaboration and, some say, co-option, that occurs once an idea for legislation is created and/or farther along in the process when a bill is introduced. Under this theory, in order for policy to be enacted all sides of the triangle must in some measure be in agreement. The term is used in somewhat of a derogatory sense in that it "violates" the purists' conception of separation of powers. Nevertheless, in actuality, the process of compromise and accommodation that takes place at all stages of policy development between and among the various members of an iron triangle is what eventually brings about new policy.

This concept of the iron triangle in policy making is really no different from the idea of inclusion or "ownership" that is recommended and practiced by many at the state and local levels. The basic idea is to bring in as many of those interested or affected by the potential policy as early as possible along the way. The more actors who "buy into" the process early on, the less likely that large-scale opposition eventually will be mounted. This is not to say that controversy is thus eliminated at any level of government, certainly not at the federal level, which is the focus of our discussion here. For instance, many more bills are defeated than make it through the enactment process. And many bills and other manifestations of policy must be suggested year after year for many years before the social context is right for enactment.

Once legislation is passed and the policy direction is set, policy is refined by the issuance of rules and regulations and/or nonregulatory guidelines. When policy is in place the question becomes one of the kinds of controls the federal level can use to ensure compliance.

Kind of Federal Controls

Once policy is made, the federal level exerts its influence and power through a variety of mechanisms. Some of these are (1) the law, via statute and regulation, and sometimes regulations are reinforced by other laws and regulations such as fortification by civil rights enforcement; (2) the courts with their great and growing control, for example in civil rights; (3) the distribution of money and in the federal way categorical funding constitutes control; (4) the establishment of federal offices in state agencies to administer the federal categorical programs such as vocational education, special education, education for the disadvantaged, and sex equity; (5) federal regional resource centers that are specifically designed to promote federal programs at state and local levels; (6) teacher training requirements for specific fields such as vocational education; (7) professional interest groups built by federal money to support the federal initiatives; and (8) lay special interest groups such as citizens' "advisory" committees for the support of the federal initiatives. Administrators can build links to all of these federal mechanisms to influence the making, notification, implementation, and evaluation of federal policy.

It can be seen that all of the levels of the intergovernmental system are intertwined in this enforcement of federal policy. Policy, as represented by legislation, regulations, guidelines, and informed agreements, holds the levels together. Delegated control allows the levels to work. The challenge of implementation is achieving a balance between enforcing policy and delegating control. Elmore (1979) writes that in trying to increase control with more specific legislation, tighter regulations and procedures, centralized authority, and closer monitoring of compliance, legislators increase complexity and in so doing actually threaten effective control.

There are variations in implementation when everyone agrees the policy is a good idea, and certainly there are variations in implementation when there is disagreement over the fundamental goals of a policy. What can go wrong when everyone agrees it is a great idea? There can be legitimate professional differences on the most effective way to address a problem on the operating level, incompatibility of other commitments of the implementation, variation in a sense of urgency, existing policies that slow or deflect implementation, disagreement over the assignment of professional responsibilities, and lack of resources to accomplish the policy objectives. And when everyone does not agree, they can express their resistance in a variety of ways, including diversion of resources, deflection of goals, and even outright resistance (Elmore, 1979).

Actors on the Federal Scene

The president, the Secretary of Education, and the Congress will be discussed here, but many other actors operate on the federal level. (The courts are discussed separately later.) Major political groups operating in federal educational policy making include major government actors such as politicians, educational politicians, school boards, and the courts; special interest groups including what Spring (1988) calls the Big Three of foundations, the corporate sector, and the teachers' unions; educational interest groups and single-interest groups; and the knowledge industry which includes the creators of knowledge such as funding agencies and researchers, the gatekeepers such as knowledge brokers and testing organizations, and the distributors of knowledge such as the publishing industry (Spring, 1988). All of these have their representatives at the federal level who attempt to influence all stages of policy making.

In addition to these major political groups, federal agencies other than the Department of Education are involved in federal policy making and policy implementation. Displayed in Figure 2.4 are the federal funds for education divided by implementing agency for fiscal year 1989.

FIGURE 2.4 • *Federal Funds for Education, by Agency: Fiscal Year 1989*

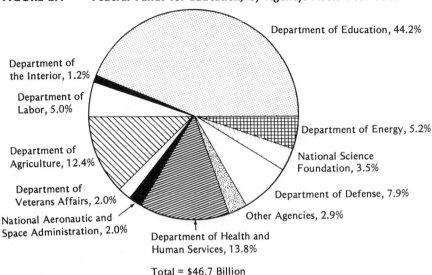

Department of Education, 44.2%

Department of the Interior, 1.2%

Department of Labor, 5.0%

Department of Agriculture, 12.4%

Department of Veterans Affairs, 2.0%

National Aeronautic and Space Administration, 2.0%

Department of Energy, 5.2%

National Science Foundation, 3.5%

Department of Defense, 7.9%

Other Agencies, 2.9%

Department of Health and Human Services, 13.8%

Total = $46.7 Billion

Source: U.S. Office of Management and Budget, Budget of the U.S. Government, Appendix, Fiscal Year 1990; and National Science Foundation, Federal Funds for Research and Development, Fiscal Years 1987, 1988, and 1989.

The President

Cronin (1989) presents a three-act version of leadership in the policy realm. In the first act, policy ideas are formulated; the policy ideas then spread and support for them is mobilized in the second act; and in the last act, where Cronin sees presidents operating, powerbrokers oversee the enactment and implementation of the policies. Cronin sees presidents as leaders in the third act only and, therefore, much other leadership is needed for national policy in education. Others must operate in the other acts to give the president something to work with. As Cronin puts it, "One myth about Presidents is that they act effectively at each of those stages. In practice, for constructive change to occur, there must be sustained, forceful, and creative leadership in each act by many people besides the Chief Executive" (Cronin, 1989, p. B1). If we accept that a variety of kinds of leadership from a variety of people is necessary at various phases of the policy-development process, then much leadership work and inspiration is necessary from others if President Bush, or any president, is to become known as the "Education President."

Some observers questioned the sincerity of President Bush's goal to be the "Education President," despite lines such as, "Education will be on my mind daily" (Bush, 1988). Charles McDowell of the *Richmond-Times Dispatch* called the education summit to which the president called the governors in 1989 "one more George Bush exercise in unfunded rhetoric."

Others question in general whether any president can really make a difference in education policy given that our nation has such a long and deep tradition of localism in education (Bakalis, 1988). Bakalis writes that "clearly there are limits as to what kind of direct impact a President can have on the nation's schools." Bakalis mentions Lyndon Johnson, whose Great Society program directed massive amounts of federal dollars and programs to the nation's schools, and in doing so believed that his most significant contribution as president would be judged to be in the field of education.

Now that there is a Cabinet-level post for educational leadership, the president makes an important policy decision when he or she appoints the Secretary of Education.

The Secretary of Education

The First Secretary and the Opening of the Department

The first Secretary of Education was Shirley M. Hufstedler, appointed by President Carter in 1980. Since in the same year Carter lost his re-election bid to Ronald Reagan, Secretary Hufstedler's tenure was far too short. She did, however, preside over an important milestone in educational governance, the birth of the department that established education as a federal concern.

The Education Department grew out of a 1976 campaign promise by then-presidential candidate Jimmy Carter to the National Education Association, among others. In the fall of 1979, the Carter administration and congressional supporters won the fight to remove education from the Department of Health, Education, and Welfare, and the doors of the Education Department opened the following May.

Supporters contended that a Cabinet-level agency would give education a louder voice in the government, eliminate some of the bureaucracy that existed under the mammoth Department of Health, Education, and Welfare, and provide a platform for new education initiatives. There was loud and sometimes bitter opposition to the creation of the department right into the mid-1980s. As the controversy died down and the department became an accepted part of the national landscape, it celebrated its tenth year of existence in 1990. At that event, some credited it with enormous successes such as the near-decade-long focus on education that followed the publication of *A Nation at Risk,* and others decried it as a "big, fat, nonevent" (Finn, 1990).

Secretary Bell and A Nation at Risk

President Reagan's first appointee to the post was Terrell H. Bell, a former Commissioner of Education in the HEW structure and an educational politician known to and knowledgeable about Washington. On August 26, 1981, Secretary Bell appointed the National Commission on Excellence in Education, the report of which, *A Nation at Risk,* released in 1983, shattered complacency about the state of U.S. education with its grim message about mediocrity in the schools. One of the most widely disseminated education documents in U.S. history, it has been printed millions of times and in a host of languages. Its influence is still generating activity at the state and local levels, and all school administrators are affected daily by its consequences. As an almost incidental side effect, the report "saved" the Education Department from being dismantled during the years of retrenchment under President Reagan. President Reagan had swept into office with promises to abolish the Education Department. His first budget augured sharp cuts in federal spending for schools and thus there seemed to be little prospect for a substantial audience for a report on education. But after release of the report, with the spotlight shining brightly on education, keeping a Cabinet-level Department of Education became politically acceptable, even politically wise.

The creation and work of the National Commission on Excellence in Education is a dramatic example of the influence of the blue-ribbon commissions and expert panels whose reports dominated the 1980s. That these reports stimulate discussion and debate is acknowledged. What is widely debated is whether or not the recommendations in the reports ever trickle down far enough to make any difference in the teaching and learning processes or in the functioning of schools. Wimpelberg and Ginsberg (1989) discuss the national commission approach to educational reform. They write: "First, commission reports seldom have much direct, sustained impact on schools and classrooms; second, they recur in perpetuum, nevertheless; and, third, commission advocates insist—in the face of apparent counter-evidence—that generic school improvement is a reasonably straightforward, specifiable, and achievable condition" (p. 13).

But there is no arguing that the commission reports dominated the educational political scene in the 1980s, so let us look more closely at the making of a bombshell report. There were eighteen members on the commission that created *A Nation at Risk*. These included two principals, a district superintendent, a "teacher of the year," four college and university presidents, a former governor, three individuals connected with state and local school boards, a parent, a retired corporate executive, a former commissioner of education, a Nobel-laureate chemist, a professor of physics, and a publisher of educational literature.

The staff included seven full- and part-time employees, numerous consultants, and the periodic assistance of other researchers at the National Institute of Education. Staff members produced a series of papers that summarized available information, laid out issues, and suggested directions for further research, based on the commission's charter. Those early outlines were followed by an intensive year of meetings, public hearings, commissioned papers, site visits, and discussions with education, corporate, and civic leaders. The schedule of a member of one of these national commissions can be strenuous. For instance, a trip to Chicago for the commissioners in June 1982 included a public hearing on college admissions and the school-to-college transition, a dinner discussion with twenty-nine corporate and community leaders, a breakfast meeting with twelve high school seniors and first-year college students, a site visit to two corporate-education programs, lunch with twenty-seven local college presidents and provosts, and a debriefing session.

The final report of this commission included five main emphases (see Figure 2.5). Despite the urgency of the language in the report, there was a reduction in federal funding and an obvious pulling back of the federal government's roles during the remainder of the 1980s. The burden of *A Nation at Risk* and the avalanche of reports that it spawned fell to the states and ultimately to the school administrators implementing the policies resulting from the reform reports.

And what do the commissioners who sat through the hearings, luncheons, and debriefings think of the subsequent federal retrenchment? According to an *Education Week* article in April 1988, two of them offered "biting appraisals" of what happened to federal funding after the publication of *A Nation at Risk*. "The obvious pulling back of the federal government's role is shocking and will be thought of as a self-inflicted, crippling wound in the future," said Gerald Holton, Professor of Physics and the History of Science at Harvard University. The nation needs an "Education Restoration Act," said William O. Baker, retired Chairman of the Board of Bell Telephone Laboratories, that is "federally sponsored and that involves a movement comparable to the space-age movement" of the 1950s and 1960s. The mobilization of our

FIGURE 2.5 • *Main Emphasis in* A Nation at Risk

A *Nation at Risk* stresses "excellence in education"; accountability; the need for a "Learning Society," in which education becomes a lifelong process; and a strong, public commitment to schooling.

Its 40 or so recommendations focused on five areas: stronger content; higher standards and expectations; more time for learning, more effectively used; better prepared, rewarded, and respected teachers; and responsible national, state, and local leadership.

These are the report's five overarching recommendations:

Content

"We recommend that state and local high-school graduation requirements be strengthened and that, at a minimum, all students seeking a diploma be required to lay the foundations in the Five New Basics by taking the following curriculum during their 4 years of high school: (a) 4 years of English; (b) 3 years of mathematics; (3) 3 years of science; (d) 3 years of social studies; and (e) one-half year of computer science. For the college-bound, 2 years of foreign language in high school are strongly recommended in addition to those taken earlier."

Standards and Expectations

"We recommend that schools, colleges, and universities adopt more rigorous and measurable standards, and high expectations, for academic performance and student conduct, and that 4-year colleges and universities raise their requirements for admission. This will help students do their best educationally with challenging materials in an environment that supports learning and authentic accomplishment."

Time

"We recommend that significantly more time be devoted to learning the New Basics. This will require more effective use of the existing school day, a longer school day, or a lengthened school year."

Teaching

"This recommendation consists of seven parts. Each is intended to improve the preparation of teachers or to make teaching a more rewarding and respected profession. Each of the seven stands on its own and should not be considered solely as an implementing recommendation."

Leadership and Fiscal Support

"We recommend that citizens across the nation hold educators and elected officials responsible for providing the leadership necessary to achieve these reforms, and that citizens provide the fiscal support and stability required to bring about the reforms we propose.

Source: U.S. Department of Education.

population is going to require a federal effort of unprecedented dimensions, and it could well be that it needs to be based around an independent agency that focuses particularly on science and mathematics, and just brings everything else along with it" (*Education Week,* 1988, p. 23).

The Master of the "Bully Pulpit"

Secretary Bell was followed by William J. Bennett, whose outrageous remarks kept education and educators in headlines and controversy. His cajoling, needling, and critical style came to be called leadership from the "bully pulpit." It has come to be a recognized style of leadership in which a prominent post is used for the purpose of "stirring things up."

An example of this kind of confrontation occurred at a Leadership Conference of the American Association of School Administrators (AASA) in 1987. Secretary Bennett talked about what he termed the "blob" of administrators that he maintained was diverting money away from instruction. "Yes, Virginia, there is a blob," the Secretary said, in response to a counterremark by AASA Executive Director Richard Miller that central office administration had increased only 0.3 percent since 1960. Bennett denied that his "blob" characterization referred to superintendents, principals, or teachers. Rather, he said, nonclassroom instructional personnel, which he claimed had increased in number by more than 400 percent in the last three decades, are the "heart of the blob."

Bennett acknowledged the hostility between himself and his audience, but said that the debate helped keep education in the limelight (an admitted goal of the "bully pulpit" technique). He went on to say, "I don't have anything against superintendents. I think every school district needs one. I do not think it needs, as I've seen in many places, a higher array of specialists of this, that, and the other" (*AASA Leadership News,* 1987, p. 3).

Later, under President Bush, Bennett became the nation's first Drug Czar, in which position he continued his bombastic style, sometimes still directing it toward education. Of the president's historic education summit with the governors he said, "There was the standard Democratic pap and Republican pap. And something that rhymes with pap. . . . Much of the discussion proceeded in a total absence of knowledge of what takes place in the schools."

The Quiet Secretary

Lauro F. Cavazos followed Bennett, and the contrast in styles could not have been greater. Critical voices were quickly raised about the appointment of Cavazos. Although the appointment was generally seen as a good political move, the new secretary's quiet style was so different from that of his predecessor that criticism came from the educational lobbying groups. Lobbyists generally like the attention that headlines bring education and the flamboyant style of Secretary Bennett had assured that kind of focus on educational issues. Secretary Cavazos, on the other hand, began his tenure at the Education Department in a quiet way. From the point of view of good policy-making processes, he laid positive groundwork from the beginning by reaching out to all the groups interested and involved in education, even some prominent Democrats. But this inclusive leadership style is not typical of Washington, and so it brought criticism that he might not be a savvy enough operator in the nation's capital to serve education well. The Secretary countered (some would say compensated) by filling some key appointments, such as his chief of staff, with experienced politicians. Secretary Cavazos resigned at the end of 1990. President Bush nominated Lamar Alexander, President of the University of Tennessee and former governor of Tennessee, to be the Secretary of Education to lead the nation's schools toward the national educational goals of the year 2000. Lamar Alexander earned a national reputation as one of the "education governors" of the 1980s. He implemented major education reforms in Tennessee, including a controversial merit pay plan for teachers.

The Wall Chart

Secretary Cavazos had continued use of the "Wall Chart," a comparison of the progress in the states on multiple measures of educational improvement. The Wall Chart, the first attempt to compare the state, was created in 1984 by then-Secretary of Education Terrell Bell. It has increasingly come under fire from educators and state officials, who contend that it compares unfairly and offers little guidance for improvement. Secretary Cavazos defended use of the chart while releasing the seventh annual Wall Chart in May 1990, but he was not pleased with the content. For instance, the chart indicated that, despite some gains by minorities, overall student performance on standardized college admission tests showed no improvement over the previous four years, and high school graduation rates had remained stable since 1987. Mr. Cavazos noted that this stagnation had occurred despite record levels of spending on education by districts, states, and the federal government. Secretary Cavazos told a press conference, "The latest Wall Chart makes it clear that as a nation we are still not committed to improving education for all Americans. Often I see indifference, complacency, and passivity, despite the need for immediate and radical school reform" (Rothman, 1990).

The Wall Chart may change or be replaced by measures more closely tied to the national goals for education that were established by the president and the governors in the spring of 1990. But at least through 1990, the Wall Chart compared state performance on the measures displayed in Figure 2.6.

Although its use is controversial, the Wall Chart is a manifestation of the federal data-gathering and analysis functions that have been generally accepted for some time. The need for a center for gathering data on the condition of U.S. education was a recognized need as early as the middle of the nineteenth century. It was needed to

FIGURE 2.6 • *Measures for State Comparisons Used in the Wall Chart*

Student Performance Measures
- ACT or SAT information
  - percentage of high school graduates taking the test
  - percentage of total scoring 26 and above for the ACT and 600 or above on either verbal or math for the SAT
- Graduation rate adjusted for migration and unclassified students
- Percentage of high school graduates scoring above a certain point on advanced placement exams

Resource Inputs Measures
- Percentage of total schools with advanced placement programs
- Average teacher salary
- Pupil/teacher ratio
- Current expenditures per pupil
- Expenditures for classroom teachers as a percentage of total current expenditures
- Federal funds as a percentage of school revenues

Characteristics Measures
- Per capita income
- Percentage of poverty, ages 5–17
- Minority percentage of enrollment
- Handicapped percentage of enrollment

State Reforms Measures
- Minimum competency test for graduation
- State interventions in academically bankrupt districts and year implemented
- Teacher or school incentives based on student performance
- Alternative teacher certification offered in the state
- State test to certify regular or permanent teachers
- State parental choice mechanisms

Source: U.S. Department of Education.

discern trends and directions and to help point out gaps to both educators and consumers of education. Recognizing this need, in 1866 the Thirty-ninth Congress established a Department of Education "for the purpose of collecting such statistics and facts as shall show the condition and progress of education in the several States and territories and of defusing such information respecting the organization and management of schools and school systems and methods of teaching as shall aid the people of the United States in the establishment and maintenance of efficient school systems and otherwise promote the cause of education throughout the country."

More recently, in the early 1950s the National Council for Chief State School Officers issued a call for uniform reporting categories for all state and territorial school systems so that data could be aggregated at the federal level to provide a picture of the condition of education both within and across the various states and territories. This call resulted in the publication of *A Common Core of State Educational Information* in 1953. This publication has been updated annually since then and provides the basis for nationally comparable statistics on education. The Wall Chart grew out of this history coupled with the call for accountability in the reform decade of the 1980s.

The Congress

The business of Congress is done in committees. Even when some sensational new scandal captures headlines, the behind-the-scenes business of the Congress is taking place at some rate, even if only by the staffers while the congresspeople are otherwise occupied. In this discussion we will address the functions of the committees most directly related to education.

The Committees

The committees of Congress do not fall into neatly categorized areas of responsibilities. Their functions overflow their organization charts, just as the academic disciplines overflow a university's neatly structured departments. And so, because of the necessities of time and space many of the committees that now and again meddle in educational affairs will not be considered here.

Two of the most powerful committees in the House are Appropriations and Budget—Appropriations because it controls the flow of money to programs authorized by other committees and Budget because its members can compete with the White House in establishing national priorities through a national budget. The House Budget

Committee is interesting for a reason other than its power. Its membership must rotate and no one is to serve more than two terms in ten years; thus it can be said to be symbolic of the "new" House where the stringent rules of seniority have loosened. The third powerful committee in the House is Ways and Means, which drafts bills dealing with taxes, fringe benefits, charitable giving, and Social Security.

Of the thirteen subcommittees of the Appropriations Committee, the one that deals directly with education is Labor, Health and Human Services, and Education. The Budget Committee is broken down into six Task Forces. Of the six, the Human Resources Task Force deals with education issues. Ways and Means is also broken down into six subcommittees. The Oversight Subcommittee has been charged to develop legislation to impose new taxes or restrictions on the business operations of tax-exempt organizations, including colleges and universities.

The committee that is visibly of great interest to educators is appropriately called Education and Labor. Of its eight subcommittees, three deal directly with education issues. The Subcommittees on Elementary, Secondary, and Vocational Education authorize the programs stated in their names as well as certain teacher training programs. The Subcommittee on Postsecondary Education authorizes higher education programs, library aid, and the arts and humanities endowments. The Subcommittee on Select Education authorizes education research conducted at the Department of Education and programs for the handicapped.

In addition to its standing committees, the House also can establish special, select, or ad hoc committees for specific investigation or oversight functions. One that was functioning in 1990, the Select Committee on Children, Youth, and Families, is of interest because of the national focus on the problems of families and youth. The Senate similarly addresses education issues via a committee and subcommittee structure.

The Congress, both House and Senate, use the expert panel or blue-ribbon approach to highlight the study of important policy issues. For instance, operating in 1990 was the National Commission on Children.

The Representatives' Think Tanks

Commissions such as those just mentioned create attention for an issue and occasionally their reports make a lasting impression on public policy as did *A Nation at Risk*. Less publicized, but with a continuing impact on public policy are the in-house think tanks of the

Republican and Democratic members of the House of Representatives. The most important, called "legislative service organizations," are the Republican Research Committee and the Democratic Study Group. The Democratic Study Group is the oldest (in operation since the late 1950s) and most prominent, but both foster awareness of issues among House members and both have the goal of influencing policy. The Democratic group has two dozen or so researchers studying policy issues with a budget of about $1 million. The Republican think tank has a much smaller budget and a staff of five. The role of both groups is to provide House members with material that will help them understand public policy issues. The Democratic group, for example, puts out a daily legislative update which members are said to rely on heavily—a lot of power for a group whose self-defined aim is to develop issues that will ultimately become policy and law. And what were these groups studying in 1990? Child care was high on the agenda, along with some foreign policy, defense, and tax issues.

Contributions

In the first contribution, H. C. Hudgins explores the role of the courts as policy makers. The courts' policy-making role has varied over time, but to today's administrators the perception is alive and well that the courts are aggressive in educational policy making. The analysis presented places the courts' role, both past and present, in a more balanced perspective.

In the next contribution, Charles Russo addresses the delicate area of religion and religious activities in the schools. Illustrated here is how Congress and the courts present school administrators with troublesome policy choices.

Robert Shoop then discusses how the courts can make fundamental policy decisions about the nature and direction of education in one decision. In this discussion of *Hazelwood* v. *Kuhlmeier,* we see that the Supreme Court may have interpreted the purpose of education in a way that may be limiting to the leadership of the school administrator in setting vision and goals for schooling.

Via the use of case studies, Edward P. St. John analyzes the question of who really decides educational policy and whether or not the educational practitioner can really influence public policy decisions at the federal level.

And in the final selection in this section, First and Cooper discuss a troublesome problem invoking the need for social and educational policy making. The access of homeless children to an education is an example of the need for the federal government to make educational policy to protect those whom state and local levels have denied service.

The section concludes with a listing that provides an historical overview of federal programs for education and related activities.

H. C. HUDGINS, JR.

Courts as Educational Policy Makers: An Historical Perspective

Introduction

As policy makers in education, courts are relatively young. The history of judicial intervention in educational policy making reveals that, rather than assuming responsibility for or taking credit for new directions in education, judges have played a reluctant role. This position may surprise critics of the courts, and school board members may doubt its validity, but it has merit when one examines the record. In fact, for approximately only 10 percent of our nation's history can the judiciary be properly characterized as activist initiators of educational change.

The initial basis of judicial noninterference may be readily explained by our country's early history. When the federal Constitution was written in 1787, public education as it later came to be known and as it is known today was largely nonexistent. What education existed grew out of the efforts of individuals banding together to operate and support schools. It was a number of decades after the drafting of the Constitution that states actually assumed responsibility for the education of their children. Just over a century ago, a state course resolved the question of the legality of taxing citizens to support secondary schools (*Stuart* v. *School District No. 1 of the Village of Kalamazoo*, 1874).

As public education first became available to the masses, it was state government, not federal government, that supported as well as controlled it. Through their legislatures, citizens gave considerable autonomy to local school boards for making decisions affecting the operation of local school systems. Thus was begun a partnership unique to public schools in America: state support for and local control of education. In no other country will one find the degree and kind of local control that exists in this nation's public school systems.

The one missing link to the partnership was the third level of government: the federal level. For many years, this level was essentially not involved with either the support or control of education. However, since the adoption of the Constitution, much has happened with respect to the balance of support and control of education at the

An earlier version of this work appeared in *Thresholds in Education*, 12(2), May 1986.

national, state, and local levels. This balance is reflected particularly in the judicial branch of the government, and it has considerable import in the kinds of decisions made that have resulted in educational policy. This is the central focus of this study—the courts as educational policy makers. For the purposes of convenience, three fairly well-defined stages of evolution of the courts as policy makers have occurred. They include the era of judicial noninterference, the era of judicial initiation, and the era of judicial indecisiveness.

Judicial Noninterference

This period encompasses by far the lengthiest of the three eras, covering the years from 1787 to 1950, or over three-fourths of the time our nation has been under the Constitution. It is characterized as an era in which education was ignored, for the most part, by the judiciary. With respect to elementary and secondary education, this noninterference was reflected by the very few cases upon which the Supreme Court acted. From 1787 to 1950, the nation's highest court heard fewer than two dozen cases, most of which were handed down in the latter third of this period. By contrast, the current Supreme Court typically hands down that many educational decisions in only two terms.

The earliest education cases based on the federal Constitution involved challenges to the First and Fourteenth Amendments. Those involving the First Amendment centered around a challenge to some fundamental rights claimed to have been violated, while those involving the Fourteenth Amendment were usually challenges of the legality of a statute. In neither instance was the fundamental right of boards of education as policy makers threatened (Hudgins, 1970).

The subject matter of the opinions of the Supreme Court during this period is as revealing as the few number of cases the justices heard. The justices revealed a hands-off attitude toward education. An example of this stance is an 1899 opinion. In it the justices ruled that it was legal for a rural county in Georgia to close an all-black school while keeping open an all-white school, despite the fact that the black students had access to no other school in the county (*Cumming* v. *Board of Education of Richmond City,* 1899). It upheld the legality of a Mississippi statute that classified students as white or colored, thus categorizing an oriental girl as colored (*Gong Lum* v. *Rice,* 1927).

During the time that the federal judiciary was staying out of school disputes, state courts also restrained themselves from hearing and acting on education controversies. Unless it could be shown that school board members had clearly abused their authority as policy makers or had acted arbitrarily, capriciously, or unreasonably, their action stood. Likewise, unless administrators had abused their positions as implementors of policy, their decisions were not questioned. A few examples are illustrative of the predominant thinking during this era. A Vermont court in 1859 upheld a school official who spanked children for misbehavior out of school and after school hours (*Lander* v. *Seaver*). A half-century later an Arkansas court refused to intervene in a principal's suspension of a student for having been intoxicated during the Christmas holidays (*Douglas* v. *Campbell,* 1909). In the 1940s, the search of a student believed to have stolen a coin was justified on the grounds that it was intended to establish the child's innocence (*Marlar* v. *Bill,* 1944). These cases support the notion that courts believed it best to leave education to the educators.

The last quarter-century of this period revealed a slight erosion of the hands-off attitude. Federal courts began to question the action of state legislators and even struck down some statutes. A Nebraska statute stipulating that children in the elementary grades could not study a foreign language was overturned (*Meyer* v. *Nebraska,* 1923), and twenty years later a statute requiring that children salute the flag also was overturned (*West Virginia School Board of Education* v. *Barnette,* 1943).

Similarly, state courts underwent an increase in litigation from 1925 to 1950. The courts made this possible by allowing persons to challenge state action under provision of the federal Bill of Rights. As originally drafted, the Bill of Rights was designed to curb the federal Congress. Thus, for many years a citizen could not bring suit against state action growing out of an alleged violation of a provision of the First Amendment. However, beginning in the mid-1920s and in a series of cases that followed, the Supreme Court began to assume a more assertive role in resolving education conflicts. The Court gradually made selected provisions of the Bill of Rights subject to the states as well as to Congress. The incorporation doctrine thus made it possible for citizens to challenge an alleged violation of their rights by both federal and state governments. At the outset, this increased involvement enabled the Supreme Court, with other courts following, to examine initially the legality of various kinds of religious practices in schools, based on state law, that were alleged to be a violation of the First Amendment. These practices included the flag salute (*West Virginia State Board of Education* v. *Barnette,* 1943), public financial support for transportation of children to nonpublic schools (*Everson* v. *Board of Education,* 1947), and for providing students with books (*Cochran* v. *Louisiana State Board of Education,* 1930).

A parallel development during this time was an increase in court litigation based on the language of the Fourteenth Amendment. At first, the Due Process Clause was frequently used as the basis for a court suit, and it was later followed by reliance on the Equal Protection Clause.

For almost 150 years the courts either refused or declined to become involved in educational policy making. Beginning in about 1925, however, local and state control of education began to be questioned as courts gave some indication of their assumption of an expanded role. When it ruled that Congress, by implication, may expend funds for education as a function of general welfare (*Helvering* v. *Davis,* 1937), the Supreme Court created an opportunity for citizens to view education in a much broader context, and, correspondingly, to transfer some of the control from states to the federal government. This control took the form of legislation with accompanying regulations, increased expenditures of federal funds for education, and the creation of additional questions inviting resolution by the courts.

Era of Judicial Initiation

Over a period of time, courts gradually began to exercise a closer and more frequent review of laws and policies related to education. Particularly at the federal level, courts began to weigh the merits of a statute or policy against a constitutional standard, as contrasted with obvious noninvolvement some decades earlier.

Selection of Earl Warren as Chief Justice of the United States helped initiate the era of judicial initiation in policy making. With the landmark desegregation decision (*Brown* v. *Board of Education of Topeka,* 1954) as a fulcrum, the Supreme Court made it clear that neither local boards of education nor state legislatures have authority over pupil assignment if race is at all a consideration; that became the province of federal courts. More than any other, this opinion ushered in an era of judicial activism affecting the civil rights of both teachers and students that set a new course for the courts. In short order, the Court struck down segregation in the listing of candidates on a ballot (*Anderson* v. *Mortin,* 1964), in interstate bus terminals (*Thomas* v. *Mississippi,* 1965), and in public parks (*Watson* v. *Memphis,* 1963), among other public places.

With respect to teachers, the Court overturned an earlier decision by invalidating a loyalty oath law in New York (*Keyishian* v. *Board of*

Regents, 1967) and expanded teachers' freedom of speech by upholding their rights to teach controversies (*Sweezy* v. *New Hampshire, by Wyman,* 1957).

In one of the most significant opinions during this era, the Court ruled for the first time that students, like teachers, have constitutional rights while at school (*Tinker* v. *Des Moines,* 1909). This decision laid the ground work for court expansion of student rights, including due process in disciplinary hearings (*Goss* v. *Lopez,* 1975) and recourse against school board members for violating the rights of students (*Wood* v. *Strickland,* 1975).

Lower courts overturned many school board policies and regulations by holding that students may refuse to salute the flag for a variety of reasons, determine the length of their hair so long as no disruption results, publish articles in the school newspaper without prior approval, participate in extraclass activities even though married, and make political statements through symbolic expression. The several hundred court opinions that decided in favor of students on these five issues represented direct challenges to the policy-making function of local boards of education. There was little question but that many board members resigned themselves to the reality of their decisions being reviewed and often overturned by courts.

Era of Judicial Indecisiveness

Approximately two decades after the *Brown* decision, Supreme Court decisions began to take a different direction. The justices began to retreat in their activism and instead started to look to the legislative branch of government for initiative in resolving educational problems. This stance reflected the thinking of Warren Burger, who had replaced Earl Warren as Chief Justice in 1969. The addition of Justice Blackmun in 1970 and Justices Powell and Rehnquist in 1972 gave him initial support. Although the philosophical cleavages of the justices have rearranged themselves since 1972, the Court did reveal a new direction through three key educational decisions in 1972–73. It held that a nontenured teacher has no right to procedural due process prior to renewal unless state statutes provide for it (*Board of Regents* v. *Roth,* 1972). It ruled that educational finance reform must be left to the states, not the federal courts, for education is not a fundamental right guaranteed by the federal Constitution (*San Antonio Independent School District* v. *Rodriguez,* 1973). It also declared that the *Brown* decision is limited to the southern states initially affected by it (*Keyes*

v. *School District #1 in Denver,* 1973). These three opinions signaled the Court's interest in reestablishing a more equitable balance of control among the three branches of government.

The Court continued its nonaggressive stance by ruling that corporal punishment does not violate the Eighth Amendment's prohibition against cruel and unusual punishment (*Ingraham* v. *Wright,* 1977) and academic dismissal of a student does not entitle one to due process under the Fourteenth Amendment (*Board of Curators of the University of Missouri* v. *Horowitz,* 1978). In these two opinions it is noted that the Court did not second guess the action of local school officials as initiators of policy and as makers of discretionary decisions.

The late 1970s also revealed the lack of a clear direction of the courts. The Supreme Court expanded the rights of teachers when it held that boards of education as collective bodies can be sued for a violation of individual civil rights (*Monell* v. *Department of Social Services,* 1978). But, in a very fragmented set of opinions, the justices declined to retain or destroy all elements of affirmative action (*Regents of the University of California* v. *Bakke,* 1978). They ruled one year later that physical facilities and programmatic considerations of an institution outweighed a handicapped student's rights (*Southeastern Community College* v. *Davis,* 1979).

For the first half-decade of the 1980s, the Court continued to chart a somewhat unpredictable, albeit restrained, course. It ruled that a child has a right to sue his or her local school board for unjustified removal of books from the library (*Island Trees Union Free School District* v. *Pico,* 1982), but it failed to state what might be acceptable guidelines for removal. It held that teachers may be required to perform nonmedical and noneducational services for special education students, particularly if those services related to a child's educational program (*Irving Independent School District* v. *Tatro,* 1984). Yet, the Court ruled that there are limits in requiring school boards to perform services to special education students (*Board of Education* v. *Rowley,* 1982).

Beginning in the mid-1980s and continuing through the remainder of the decade, the Supreme Court retreated from an activist stance. It deferred to school officials to make decisions regarding fundamental policy decisions affecting the rights of students balanced against administrative decision making. In three key cases, the Court supported school officials' autonomy in making decisions. It held that, although school officials are subject to the Fourth Amendment for purposes of searching students, they are not rigidly bound by it. That is, they need no warrant to search a student, and they need only reasonable suspicion, not probable cause, for initiating a search (*New Jersey* v. *T.L.O.,* 1985).

In the second case, the Court ruled that school officials may determine what is appropriate or inappropriate speech and discipline students who engage in lewd and offensive language (*Bethel School District No. 403* v. *Fraser,* 1986). This case is significant in that the Court, in limiting freedom of speech of students, determined that school officials may set the parameters of acceptable student speech, for student freedom of speech is subordinate to administrative autonomy.

In the third case, the Court ruled that school officials, not students, may determine what is appropriate or inappropriate content for a school-sponsored newspaper (*Hazelwood School District* v. *Kuhlmeier,* 1988). Taken together, these three cases clearly signaled a less activist role by the courts in determining educational policy.

When one reviews nearly two decades of court decisions (covering approximately 1970–1990), one notes a lack of clear and consistent judicial philosophy. In large measure, these twenty years reveal a fragmentation of philosophies that make one not very comfortable in predicting accurately how a court will rule on an issue. The net effect of judicial nonpredictability has not made it any easier for local school board members in dealing with policy issues.

The Present State

The present state of the judiciary is very much removed from the inaction of our country's earlier history, the period of judicial noninterference. It is also not so activist as the period of judicial intervention (1954–1972). The present period of uncertainty shows some indication of judicial restraint; its future course will likely be determined by the service of the nine members who constitute the Supreme Court. In the last five years, Chief Justice Burger and Associate Justices Brennan, Powell and Marshall retired from the Court. The upshot of these changes is that, given the philosophical bent of their replacements, the Court will likely head in a less activist, more conservative mode. The justices emphasizing judicial restraint are the younger members of the Court and will likely serve two to three decades. What well may happen is that policy making will become even less a function of the judiciary and increasingly a function of boards of education.

References

Anderson v. Martin, 375 U.S. 399 (1964).

Bethel School District No. 403 v. Fraser, 478 U.S. 675 (1986).

Board of Curators of the University of Missouri v. Horowitz, 435 U.S. 78 (1978).

Board of Education v. Rowley, 458 U.S. 176 (1982).

Board of Regents v. Roth, 408 U.S. 564 (1972).

Brown v. Board of Education of Topeka, 347 U.S. 483 (1954).

Cochran v. Louisiana State Board of Education, 281 U.S. 370 (1930). See also Board of Education of Centennial School District No. 1 v. Allen, 392 U.S. 236 (1968).

Cumming v. Board of Education of Richmond City, 175 U.S. 528 (1899).

Douglas v. Campbell, 89 Ark. 254, 116 S.W. 211 (1909).

Everson v. Board of Education, 330 U.S. 1 (1947).

Gong Lum v. Rice, 275 U.S. 78 (1927).

Goss v. Lopez, 419 U.S. 565 (1975).

Hazelwood School District v. Kuhlmeier, 484 U.S. 260 (1988).

Helvering v. Davis, 301 U.S. 619 (1937). See also U.S. v. Butler, 297 U.S. 1 (1936).

Hudgins, H. C. (1970) *The Warren Court and the public schools*. Danville, IL: Interstate Printers and Publishers, 1970.

Ingraham v. Wright, 430 U.S. 651 (1977).

Irving Independent School District v. Tatro, 468 U.S. 883 (1984).

Island Trees Union Free School District v. Pico, 102 S.Ct. 2799 (1982).

Keyes v. School District No. 1, Denver, 413 U.S. 189 (1973).

Keyishian v. Board of Regents, 385 U.S. 589 (1967).

Lander v. Seaver, 32 Vt. 114 (1859).

Marlar v. Bill, 181 Tenn. 100, 178 S.W. 2d 634 (1944).

Meyer v. Nebraska, 262 U.S. 390 (1923).

Monell v. Department of Social Services, 436 U.S. 658 (1978).

New Jersey v. T.L.O., 469 U.S. 325 (1985).

Regents of the University of California v. Bakke, 438 U.S. 265 (1978).

San Antonio Independent School District v. Rodriguez, 411 U.S. 1 (1973).

Southeastern Community College v. Davis, 442 U.S. 397 (1979).

Stuart v. School District No. 1 of the Village of Kalamazoo, 30 Mich. 69 (1874).

Sweezy v. New Hampshire, by Wyman, 354 U.S. 234 (1957).

Thomas v. Mississippi, 360 U.S. 524 (1965).

Tinker v. Des Moines, 393 U.S. 503 (1969).

Watson v. Memphis, 373 U.S. 526 (1963).

West Virginia State Board of Education v. Barnette, 319 U.S. 624 (1943). Overturned Minersville v. Gobitis, 310 U.S. 586 (1940).

Wood v. Strickland, 420 U.S. 308 (1975).

CHARLES RUSSO

The Courts, Religion, and the Public Schools

Among the many issues confronting public school administrators, few offer more potential difficulties than the place of religion and religious activities in the schools. Although a substantial line of cases beginning with the Supreme Court's 1948 ruling in *McCollum* (which declared unconstitutional a plan to permit religious teachers to conduct released-time classes in public schools) to the prayer and Bible reading cases of the early 1960s (*Engel* v. *Vitale*, 1962, and *Abington Township* v. *Schempp*, 1963) has kept organized prayer and religious activity out of the schools, the wall of separation between religion and public education appears to be in danger of collapse. In *Engel*, the New York Board of Regent's nondenominational prayer, which a local board ordered recited each day in class, was ruled a violation of the Establishment Clause. In the *Abington Township* case, the Supreme Court ruled that a Pennsylvania law that required ten Bible verses read without comment each day in school violated the Establishment Clause, even though children could be excused upon written request by parents.

Perhaps the most troublesome development in this area is the 1990 Equal Access Act (the Act). The Act, signed into law by President Reagan in 1984, provides that any public secondary school receiving federal financial assistance and that has a limited open forum cannot deny access to student groups based on the "religious, political, [or] philosophical" content of their speech, provided they wish to meet during noninstructional time. When the Supreme Court upheld the constitutionality of the Act in *Westside Community Schools* v. *Mergens* (1990), it may have opened a Pandora's Box since the Third Circuit has relied on this ruling in part to uphold the right of religious groups to use public school facilities for religious activities and the Second Circuit has the same issue before it as this piece is being written. In light of *Mergens*, this essay examines the place of religion and religious activity in the public schools in the 1990s.

In 1985, a group of high school students led by Bridgit Mergens (now Mayhew) at Omaha's Westside High School brought suit against the school district to permit them to organize a student Christian Bible study club in accordance with the Act. After making its way through the federal courts, the case reached the Supreme Court, which was faced with two issues: first, whether Westside's decision to permit the existence of non-curriculum-related groups created a limited open forum within the meaning of the Act and second, if it did, whether this violated the Establishment Clause.

Addressing the nature of the forum at Westside, the Court was confronted by the lack of a definition of a "non-curriculum-related student group." Even so, a majority of the Court agreed that this term is "best interpreted broadly to mean any student group that does not directly relate to the body of courses offered by the school." (Justice Marshall concurred in the judgment of the court but did not join its opinion. He wrote: "I agree with the majority that 'non-curriculum' must be construed broadly to 'prohibit schools from discriminating on the basis of the content of a student group's speech.'" Hence the Court rejected the school district's argument that it means "anything remotely related to abstract educational goals," for it reasoned that this would eviscerate the Act. Moreover, given the presence of the large number of non-curriculum-related groups present at the school, the Court found the existence of a limited open forum and precluded the exclusion of the prayer club.

Turning to the constitutional question, a plurality examined the Act under the ubiquitous *Lemon* v. *Kurtzman* (1971) test. Applying *Lemon*, the plurality's analysis of the Act failed to find a secular legislative intent, a desire to advance or inhibit the spread of religion, or an excessive entanglement between government and religion and so upheld the constitutionality of the Equal Access Act.

Between the time that *Lemon* was decided and the Court's ruling in *Mergens*, at least 28 Supreme Court cases, generating more than 100 opinions, have addressed the establishment of religion in and out of elementary and secondary schools. There were only three unanimous rulings and in two of these more than one opinion was filed; the third was a memorandum decision handed down without an opinion (Underwood, 1989).

In light of *Mergens*, administrators have a variety of options to consider when approached by students who wish to introduce organized religious activity into the public schools.

First, consistent with the Court's broad understanding of non-curriculum-related groups, schools can permit access to any and all groups who wish to organize. While this might open the schools up to a variety of religious and philosophical perspectives, it is fraught with practical difficulty. Not only would the schools be subject to a charge of impermissably advancing religion, but the potential for internecine conflict between and among school groups who hold antithetical opinions could lead to even greater difficulties and conflict within the school communities.

Second, do not have any school-sponsored groups and turn over the responsibility for school clubs to outside organizations such as the local Parent/Teachers Association (PTA). In this way, the schools would not be responsible for giving their approval or disapproval to which groups organize and so would arguably not be subject to the dictates of the Equal Access Act. However, while groups such as the PTA may not officially be part of the school district, they may well be sufficiently closely related to the schools that such an approach might not withstand a legal challenge.

Third, narrow the focus of school activities to permit only curriculum-related clubs while imposing a moratorium on non-curriculum-related activities. However, this might mean the exclusion of a wide variety of traditional and popular activities. For example, language clubs are most likely to be found clearly curriculum related and could be permitted, but what about the chess and photography clubs? And, what about student thespians? Would participation in school plays be limited to those students receiving academic credit for their involvement? Parents (and students) would be understandably upset over the loss of traditional extracurricular activities.

Although it may be argued that to exclude all clubs for a set period (one year, for example) might provide a cooling off period during which interest in prayer clubs and religious activity might die down, this risks throwing "the baby out with the bath water." Moreover, once student interest in traditional extracurricular activities has dwindled, it may be difficult to rekindle that interest and students would thereby be deprived of a wide variety of enrichment activities. And, would the freeze on these activities deprive students (especially in single-parent families and families where both parents are employed full time outside of the home) of some place to go after school, making them even more vulnerable to the many temptations confronting teenagers today?

One draconian possibility exists. Since the Act comes into play only in those schools receiving federal financial assistance, a school district can reject federal aid. However, in a time of decreasing financial support for public education, it is not likely that many schools can or would even be willing to consider this alternative.

In light of the Supreme Court's decision to permit organized student prayer in the schools, the religious use of the public school facilities by nonschool groups seems to be a logical extension of the relationship between religion and public education. The leading case to date is *Gregoire* v. *Centennial School District,* wherein a divided Third Circuit upheld the right of a religious group to rent public school facilities for worship and to distribute religious literature in conjunction with these services. In *Gregoire,* apparently the first case to rely even in part on *Mergens* (it was handed down five weeks after *Mergens*), the Third Circuit ruled that although a public school is not required to make its facilities available to outside groups, once it does, it is subject to questions over equal access and cannot deny access to a group over the religious content of its speech. Although the Supreme Court's refusal to grant *certiorari* in *Gregoire* is of no significant precedential value, it may signal the emergence of a trend as other suits involving applications by religious groups to use school facilities are currently under way in the federal courts (*Toby Travis* v. *Oswego-Appalachian School District* and *Lamb's Chapel* v. *Center Moriches Union Free School District*).

The policy options available to school administrators confronted by outside groups seeking to use public school facilities for religious activities are similar to those under *Mergens.* However, unlike *Mergens,* there does not appear to be any middle ground; that is, once a school is made available to outside groups, there can be no distinction based on the religious content of a group's speech or activities. Thus, it will be difficult to deny access to religious organizations.

Administrators seem to be faced with only two options. First, limit the use of school facilities to only those activities that are clearly school related and do not permit any nonschool groups access to the facilities. Unfortunately, this risks the loss of good will in the community as charitable and civic organizations may rely on the nominal rental costs or free use of school facilities to conduct their fund raisers and other activities. In addition, many of the same questions associated with limiting student groups to curriculum-related activities may be applied to school-related use of the facilities. For example, is a school play in which student participants do not receive academic credit sufficiently school related to withstand a challenge brought by a religious group seeking access? Second, allow all groups access, but this also presents many of the same difficulties considered under *Mergens.*

The wall separating religion and public education appears to be weakening as sectarian religious activity is being permitted to make its way into the schools. At present there are no clear guidelines that can be offered to prevent this gradual encroachment other than to follow the sparse advice offered by *Mergens* and its progeny. One thing is certain: As the relationship between religion and the public schools continues to evolve, there will be more litigation and, hopefully, some specific guidance from the courts.

References

Abington Township v. Schempp, 374 U.S. 203 (1963).

Engel v. Vitale, 370 U.S. 421 (1962).

Equal Access Act, 20 U.S.C. Section 4071 et seq. (1990).

Gregoire v. Centennial School District, 907 F.2d 1366 (3rd Cir. 1990).–U.S.–, 111 S.Ct., 253, (1990).

Lamb's Chapel v. Center Moriches Union Free School District, 736 F.Supp. 1247 (E.D.N.Y., 1990).

Lemon v. Kurtzman, 403 U.S. 602 (1971).

People of the State of Illinois ex. rel. McCollum v. Board of Education and School District Number 71, Champaign County, 333 U.S. 203 (1948).

Toby Travis v. Owego-Appalachian School District, 90-CV-90 (N.D.N.Y., July 5, 1990).

Underwood, J. (1989, November 9). Establishment of religion in primary and secondary schools. *55 Education Law Reporter*, 807.

Westside Community Schools v. Mergens, 110 S.Ct. 2356 (1990).

ROBERT J. SHOOP

School Districts Should Use Caution When Making Policy Decisions in Response to *Hazelwood* v. *Kuhlmeier*

The establishment of policy is one way in which people exert control, influence, or power over each other. Policy development at the school district level is often significantly influenced by U.S. Supreme Court decisions.

In the 1988 case of *Hazelwood* v. *Kuhlmeier,* the U.S. Supreme Court ruled that the First Amendment does not prevent educators from exercising editorial control over the style and content of student speech in school-sponsored newspapers. The Court found that high school papers published by students in journalism classes do not qualify as "public forums"; therefore, school officials retain the right to impose reasonable restrictions on student speech in school papers (*Hazelwood* v. *Kuhlmeier,* 1988).

Courts have always framed legal decisions within a fluid social context. The particular social context of the *Hazelwood* case is the tension between two views of the purpose of education. One view holds that the primary purpose of education is to prepare students to function in society as it is. This Supreme Court accepts this view and assumes that the sole function of schools is to initiate students into the accumulated cultural traditions. This Court ignores the fact that an equally important function of schools is to prepare students to create beyond the past, to introduce novelty, to utilize freedom, to challenge existing limitations, and to offer creative solutions. The ideology that underlies the *Hazelwood* decision is dangerously wrong.

This decision provides an excellent opportunity to gain insight into the ideology of this Supreme Court, particularly the way the Court views the relationship and relative value of democracy, liberty, pluralism, individualism, and social responsibility. Although the significance of any specific Court decision is developed over time, the *Hazelwood* decision reveals an important paradigm shift. In 1969, in *Tinker* v. *Des Moines School District,* the U.S. Supreme Court put school officials on notice that they did not possess absolute authority over their students and challenged them to have a greater faith in the democratic process. In the *Hazelwood* decision, the Court made it clear that it has more faith that school officials will protect students' rights than it has in students' ability to act responsibly. The Court has placed the right of school authorities to inculcate social values over students' First Amendment rights to freedom of expression.

Supreme Court decisions depend to a large degree on the operating ideology of the justices. This Court has a clear bias toward the status quo. It has a vested interest in the past and is uncomfortable with the revolutionary function of education. It sees the unconventional as a threat. It wants schools to promote the goals of the Constitution in the abstract, but it wants them to shy away from actually teaching students the implications of the Constitution. Therefore, it denies the legitimacy of students' right to criticize the system until they have been thoroughly indoctrinated into that system. The Court promotes the premise that students in public schools are children who must accept the accumulated knowledge and values of our culture, not evaluate them. This Court believes that the teacher's primary responsibility is to facilitate acculturation by conveying those values, norms, and skills that the majority culture deems essential to individual and group survival (Yudof, 1987).

The *Hazelwood* Court assumes that there is a universally agreed upon standardized body of knowledge and an accepted set of virtues of the existing social system. Knowledge is not neutral, and there is legitimate debate about what values are in fact worthy of inculcation. As our society has become more and more diverse, minority groups increasingly need the protection of the Constitution.

This Court has failed in its role of ensuring that minority rights and points of view are protected from the oppression of the majority. It has failed to recognize the basic problem with majority control. Under the *Hazelwood* model, the majority of the people determine what values and what knowledge are of most worth. This premise results in minority viewpoints regarding politics, culture, and social organization being increasingly excluded from the curriculum. Thus the parameters of political dialogue are narrowed, and political learning is reduced to consensus values. If school boards adopt policies congruent with the *Hazelwood* decision, schools will cease to be arenas for the free exchange of critical ideas and will increasingly become institutions for the imposition of only those values and ideas that are inoffensive to a majority of the people. The *Hazelwood* Court's assumption that the primary function of schools is to inculcate cultural values will result in a curriculum that will be "democratic or majoritarian," but will be bland and insensitive to the legitimate need to give students practice at being responsible citizens. The restriction of student free speech will result in serious limitations of the free political dialogue that is necessary for the maintenance of a democratic society. A wide-ranging political dialogue is necessary for a dynamic and truly participatory democratic system. This Court has opted for stability created by limiting dialogue and narrowing the parameters of discourse. This may temporarily reduce the possibility of conflict in schools, but will also result in a dull homogeneous curriculum that does not reflect the reality of a multicultural, multiethnic community.

Good citizenship consists of more than blindly adopting the laws and values of the majority culture. Limiting dialogue limits education and will result in citizens who do not have the intellectual tools to participate in a democratic society. This Court seems to support the concept of a passive rather than active citizenship. A primary tenet of a democratic society is a free citizenry that is allowed to think and express itself freely on any subject, even to the point of criticizing the status quo. The *Hazelwood* decision is a significant step toward the erosion of the rights of students.

This decision may result in school boards adopting policies that censor legitimate student freedom of expression, resulting in a violation of the First Amendment's bar on the prescription of orthodoxy. Schools should be marketplaces of ideas where students' First Amendment rights are limited only when there is reason to believe that distribution of the material would cause significant emotional harm to a student, when substantial interference with the rights of other students would result, or when disruption to the order and decorum of the school would occur. The *Hazelwood* decision encourages school administrators to censor editorials critical of the school board or school administrators on the grounds that the students do not have the knowledge necessary to permit them to criticize adults.

In recognizing students' free speech rights, the *Tinker* Court noted that these rights were subject to limitations. The Court held that school officials could regulate student activities if student conduct would materially and substantially disrupt the work and discipline of the school. The *Hazelwood* decision has unduly infringed upon the rights enunciated in *Tinker*. It increases the likelihood that schools will exceed the intent of the *in loco parentis* doctrine and be oppressive and inhibit students' ability to learn to be responsible adults. Fear of controversy in the classroom will lead to a bland and uncontroversial school.

Allowing principals to censor material that is "inappropriate," "potentially sensitive," or "unsuitable for immature audiences" gives educators the power to censor any expression that is not officially approved. Adult journalists have limits placed on what they can write. There are prescribed punishments for copyright infringement and plagiarism, false advertising or adverting of illegal products, inflammatory literature ("fighting words" that incite to "lawless action"), obscenity, libel, invasion of privacy, fraud and trickery, threats, bribery, abuse of process, and illegal or wrongful conduct. Student journalists should have the same rights and responsibilities as any other journalists. It is up to the state and local policy makers to ensure that these freedoms are maintained. Any additional restrictions on student expression "inhibit understanding of the Bill of Rights among America's youth, and add to the general disregard for free speech guaranteed in our democracy" (Society of Professional Journalists, 1988).

The majority of students who work on school papers are bright, conscientious, and honorable. Schools that dictate behavior destroy the opportunity for these students to think critically, act responsibly, and react sensitively. State and local policy makers must be cautious in responding to the *Hazelwood* decision. School districts that adopt policies that stringently control freedom of speech not only destroy present human rights, but also threaten the existence and the proper use of those rights in the future (Hurt, 1989).

References

Hazelwood School District v. Kuhlmeier, 108 U.S. 562 (1988).

Hurt, K. (1989, October 22). Conversation between Kansas State Representative and the author.

Society of Professional Journalists. (1988). Statement adopted at the National Convention.

Tinker v. Des Moines School District, 393 U.S. 503 (1969).

Yudof, M. (1987, Winter). Three faces of academic freedom. *Loyola Law Review, 32,* 831.

EDWARD P. ST. JOHN

Who Decides Educational Policy? Or How Can the Practitioner Influence Public Choices?

Most of the literature on educational policy views the policy process as political and leaves the impression that the best, and perhaps the only, way practitioners can influence policy outcomes is through lobbying or other forms of overt political action. After more than twelve years of experience in educational planning and policy research at the state and federal levels, I have realized that practitioners can have a large influence on public policy through the actions they take, especially if those actions result in exemplary practices.

A Traditional View of the Policy Cycle

The policy cycle is generally described as a process that starts with the recognition of a problem followed by the formation of a study group, the development of policy recommendations, political decisions in the legislative and budgetary processes, implementation, and evaluation (Gramlich, 1981; Schultz, 1968; Stonich, 1977). Critics have long argued that this rational view of policy never really happens, even when elaborate and systematic public decision strategies—such as planning, programming, and budgeting systems (PPB) or zero-based budgeting (ZBB)—are implemented (Braybrooke and Lindblom, 1963; Lindblom and Cohen, 1979). These critics argue that the policy process is disjointed and incremental (Braybrooke and Lindblom, 1963) and that it can be influenced by expert analysis targeted at important policy issues (Lindblom and Cohen, 1979).

These two points of view leave us with the impression that the educational policy process is either rational and it can be shaped by objective policy research, or it is nonrational and can be shaped by policy analysts who take an advocacy position. Neither of these positions leave much room for the educational practitioner, and both assume that the political arena is the best—if not the only—place to influence the policy process.

An Alternative View of the Policy Cycle

My experiences during the past twelve years as a planner and policy researcher in education have left me with the impression that both of these traditional views of the educational policy process ignore the most important actors in the educational policy process: the educational practitioners. Innovations by educational practitioners have a major influence on the formulation of educational policy. The importance of the practitioner to the policy process can best be illustrated by discussing the roles others play in the development of educational public policy.

Politicians and their spouses often come to office with agendas for education. (The inclusion of spouses is not meant to be derogatory. The history of presidents' wives playing an active role in social policy can be traced back to Eleanor Roosevelt. During the past two presidencies, the viewpoints of the presidents' wives have had substantial influence on the development of educational policy. Nancy Reagan's interest in drug education and Barbara Bush's interest in adult literacy have had a large influence on planning activities in the U.S. Department of Education. Therefore, we should not ignore the influence of political spouses on educational policy.) At the state and local levels, education is usually the largest area of public expenditure and, therefore, it is important for political hopefuls to have views on education. At the federal level, education does not comprise as large a portion of the federal budget, but it is nonetheless still important.

However, at the top levels of the federal bureaucracy, genuine concern about education is often left to political spouses. For example, Barbara Bush's interest in adult literacy has influenced planning in adult education programs at the federal level. However, politicians seldom have the substantive knowledge of educational practices to develop meaningful policy proposals. Those who do are an exception. Instead, politicians who successfully influence educational policy usually do so by finding examples of successful practice, then developing policy proposals that might encourage these new practices to develop elsewhere. (Very often these "exemplary" practices are identified by professional policy research firms that contact educational leaders to identify successful practices. Based on preliminary studies of exemplary programs, larger studies are designed and implemented, and/or legislative and budgetary proposals are developed.)

State and federal secretaries of education also gain a lot of press and have a large apparent influence on the formulation of educational policy. For example, Secretary Bell is often credited with the development of *A Nation at Risk,* which awoke the world to the declining quality of U.S. education. (This publication was read worldwide. In the mid-1980s, when I was giving workshops on strategic planning to educational officials on the Indian subcontinent, Asia, and the Pacific, I was often asked about the book, *A Nation at Risk,* and the status of U.S. education.) He also is given credit for the state report cards–the original "wall charts"–that helped shift the public's attention to test scores as the primary means of assessing the quality of education. These actions are widely credited with initiating the educational excellence movement (Burrup, Brimley, and Garfield, 1988), but they did very little to improve the quality of education. A consensus is now emerging that a decade of top-down education reform has done little more than anger teachers and focus education on test taking; it certainly has not improved test scores (NAEP, 1990), the original focal point of the reform efforts, and it has left teachers dissatisfied (Ginsberg and Barnett, 1990).

This leaves us with the question, Who can influence meaningful educational change through the policy process? My impression is that educational practitioners can shape meaningful educational change through their own actions and that these actions can influence the policy process. In fact, bottom-up educational reform may be the most appropriate way in which meaningful educational change can eventuate and that practice leads policy, rather than the reverse. A few examples are offered here to illustrate this point of view.

Peninsula Academies

I conducted a case study of the Peninsula Academies as part of a national study of dropout prevention (Sherman et al., 1987). In the later 1970s, Sequoia Union High School District (hereafter referred to as Sequoia), which included a substantial portion of San Mateo County, California, part of the Silicon Valley, recognized it had a dropout problem. The majority of students dropping out were disadvantaged minorities and the minority population was growing as a percentage of the total population. In response to these conditions, the superintendent of Sequoia and the executive director of the Stanford Mid-Peninsula Urban Coalition developed a proposal for an innovative, occupationally oriented program that would pool resources from private industry and the schools, to benefit both. Funding for the academies was provided initially by local foundations, corporations, and local, state, and federal programs (channeled through Sequoia).

The new Peninsula Academies program, run initially by the Urban Coalition, was targeted at high-risk students who were in danger of dropping out of school due to behavioral problems. The two academies provide skills-oriented training in computers and electronics along with the necessary coursework to complete high school. The first class was recruited in September 1981, when ninety-one tenth-graders entered the program. By 1983, a full three-year program was in operation with a total of 184 high-risk students from grades ten through twelve. The program was highly successful at graduating students and placing them in meaningful positions in the local electronics and computer industries. The teachers involved in starting the academies remember it as a tumultuous but exciting period. Yet they were successful. Responsibility for the academies program was gradually shifted from the Urban Coalition to Sequoia. And the Urban Coalition became active in lobbying the State of California to fund a statewide academies program. When these efforts were successful, the Peninsula Academies received special supplemental state funding and funds were made available to start up other academy programs across the State. (Supplemental funding was needed to support academies programs because they maintained low student-teacher ratios and had relatively high equipment costs).

In the late 1980s, the Peninsula Academies gained national attention. They were included in a national study of exemplary dropout prevention programs (Sherman et al., 1987). Clearly the efforts of school teachers and community leaders in Sequoia District have not only made a difference for at-risk youth, but also have had an influence on state and federal educational policy.

Sweetwater Union High School District (St. John, 1990b)

In 1988, Sweetwater Union High School District's (hereafter referred to as Sweetwater) Adult Education Division received the U.S. Secretary of Education's Award for Outstanding Adult Education programs. Serving southern San Diego County, Sweetwater provides learning opportunities to a diverse community, from infants in parent education programs to older adults in senior work force programs. Administrators in adult education programs have received recent recognition for their contribution to the improvement of adult education programs. However, the current high level of success has not always been evident.

In the early 1980s, Sweetwater's adult education program encountered problems largely because the district was overextended; it had been expanding its adult education services during a period when state funding was capped. After the retirement of the long-term program director, a committee of principals ran the adult education program. (Sweetwater has four adult high schools.) A team approach to governing the adult education programs evolved. Principals, resource teachers, and assistant principals met routinely to plan programs. One of the principals (Jerry Rindone) was named program director when the program became financially stable. Soon after his appointment, a special projects office was established to seek funding from diverse sources.

By the later 1980s, the Sweetwater Adult Education Division had not only gotten the adult education programs operating effectively, but had also (1) taken over responsibility for the district's vocational programs, which also had encountered financial trouble, and reorganized them to improve their effectiveness and financial stability; (2) developed major new programs for at-risk students, including an innovative assessment center, with resources from JTPA; (3) created innovative computer-assisted learning programs for the GAIN program, a state welfare reform program, and for at-risk high school students; and (4) developed major new adult programs for the amnesty process. Perhaps even more important than these program expansions, the resource teachers had become actively involved in statewide efforts to develop assessment processes and curricula for adult ESL programs. In fact, one of Sweetwater's adult education teachers had written textbooks that are used nationwide.

The Sweetwater leadership team has developed a process for identifying learning needs, designing programs that meet these needs, and securing funds to create new, innovative programs. Their efforts have gained wide recognition at the state and federal levels. However, the type of cooperative action that stimulated improvement in Sweetwater's Adult Education Division is not easy to stimulate through state or federal action.

Bell Avenue School (St. John, 1990a)

Rita Wirtz became principal of Bell Avenue School in 1985. At that time, the school was considered a "dumping ground" for troubled students and ineffective teachers in the Robla School District, an elementary district that includes some of the unincorporated parts of Sacramento County, California. Bell Avenue School serves an at-risk population: Over half of the students are minorities and about 8 percent are on welfare.

During the next five years, Bell Avenue School was transformed from a place where student discipline was a major problem to a place where students used problem-solving techniques to settle disputes; from a workplace where teachers seldom interacted and did their own thing, if they did anything, to a place where teachers collaborated in curriculum improvements; from a school with low test scores to a school with the most test-score improvement of any school in the greater Sacramento area. How did these changes come about?

Early in her tenure, Rita Wirtz focused on two issues: solving the discipline problem and hiring new teachers who cared what happened to the students. She also supported teachers when they had new ideas: "Try it to see if it works" became a theme governing the change process. Teachers rapidly became innovators, finding ways to tailor instruction to the needs of their students. The teachers, with the support of the principal, also reorganized the governance of the school. They formed a new task-oriented organization with an emphasis on peer coaching and team coaching.

By 1989–90, Bell Avenue School began to receive local, state, national, and international attention. Student teachers were placed in the school for the first time in over a decade. Administrative interns were placed in the school for the first time ever. And a research team conducting an international study had developed a case study of the change process at Bell Avenue School.

So How Can Practitioners Influence Educational Policy?

These brief examples clearly illustrate that educational practitioners can influence policy research and the development of educational policies. In fact, the development of exemplary practices by educational practitioners may be the beginning point for meaningful educational policy changes, whether one holds the traditional top-down view or begins to develop an alternative view, a bottom-up view, of school reform.

If one holds the traditional, top-down view of public policy in education, then it seems apparent that exemplary practice is a good source of information for educational planning. If practitioners have ideas on educational reform, the best place to show that they work is in schools. Successful school reform can attract policy interest. The analysis of exemplary practices not only shapes the formulation of policy studies, but also the content of planning and budget proposals. Therefore, if practitioners hold the view that educational reform is a top-down process that can be shaped by public policy, then the best place to start may be to search out exemplary practices, then to publicize them—or perhaps to test reform ideas in the field, then to secure public attention.

These examples also raise another possibility: that meaningful school reform is a bottom-up process and that public officials need to find ways to foster and encourage bottom-up reforms, rather than try to change the system with stricter controls from above. Clearly the focus of the innovations described was not on the policy process; it was on the ideas of practitioners. In fact, there are no doubt many actions public officials can take to facilitate bottom-up school reform. [In the 1980s, the State of California's Department of Education seems to have recognized that school reform is a bottom-up process and to have developed a number of processes that actually encourage school-initiated reforms. Therefore, it may not be a coincidence that all of these examples are from California. However, even though the California State Department of Education has pursued a facilitation strategy, it seems to be caught in a battle for "control" of educational reform with the governor and the state board of education (Pipho, 1990).] Indeed the focus of the next wave of school reform should be on bottom-up reform strategies, in which case the government role would need to shift from "control" to "facilitation."

References

Braybrooke, D., & Lindblom, C. E. (1963). *A strategy of decision policy evaluation as a social process*. New York: The Free Press.

Burrup, P. E., Brimley, V., & Garfield, B. R. (1988). *Financing education in a climate of change* (4th ed.). Boston: Allyn and Bacon.

Ginsberg, R., & Barnett, B. (1990, March). Experiencing school reform: The view from South Carolina. *Phi Delta Kappan, 71*(7), 549–552.

Gramlich, E. M. (1981). *Benefit-cost analysis of government programs*. Englewood Cliffs, NJ: Prentice-Hall.

Lindblom, C. E., & Cohen, D. K. (1979). *Usable knowledge: Social science and social problem solving*. New Haven, CT: Yale University Press.

National Assessment of Education Progress (NAEP). (1990). *The reading risk: The imperative for educational reform*. Washington, DC: U.S. Government Printing Office.

Pipho, C. (1990, December). State departments: Change on the way. *Phi Delta Kappan, 72*(4); 262–263.

St. John, E. P. (1990a). Bell Avenue School: A case study. Prepared for instructional purposes, University of New Orleans.

St. John, E. P. (1990b). The preparation of adult educators: An examination of exemplary practices. Presented at the Mid-South Educational Research Association Annual Meeting, New Orleans.

Schultz, G. E. (1968). *The politics and economics of public spending.* Washington, DC: Brookings Institution.

Sherman, J. L., Celebuski, C. A., Fink, L. N., Levin, A. B., & St. John, E. P. (1987). *Dropping out of the school. Volume III: Program profiles.* Prepared for the U.S. Department of Education. Washington, DC: Pelavin Associates.

Stonich, P. J. (1977). *Zero-based planning and budgeting.* Homewood, IL: Dow Jones-Irwin.

PATRICIA F. FIRST
G. ROBB COOPER

Access to Education by Homeless Children

Introduction

The plight of the homeless is now recognized as a national emergency. The news media continually bring the crisis to our attention. During presidential election-night coverage, ABC's Peter Jennings reported that the problem of homelessness ranked with the deficit in people's minds as the two biggest problems facing this nation.

The numbers are staggering. Kozol (1988) has estimated that between two and three million people are without homes in the United States. It is more conservatively estimated that at least 100,000 children are homeless on any given night, among a total of approximately 750,000 homeless people (National Academy of Sciences, 1988). In their December 1987 report, the National Coalition of the Homeless reported that families with children are now the fastest growing segment of the homeless population, and that 40 percent of the homeless population consists of members of families; about 500,000 children are now homeless. Of these homeless children, 4,370 do not attend school, primarily because of residency requirements (National Coalition of the Homeless, 1987).

The focus of this contribution is the plight of the homeless children, specifically as it relates to access to schooling. That these children have been, and are, denied access to schooling because of their homeless state is well documented (National Coalition of the Homeless, 1987). The main reasons for such denial—residency requirements, transportation needs, lost records, the timelines for special education placement, and substantiated guardianship—are generally well within the legal operating parameters of the school districts involved. But the case of homeless children is a particularly poignant example of the difficult choices facing education agencies when legally defensible positions do not coincide with what many would believe to be morally responsible positions. For a homeless child, the school is a hope and a refuge for the present as well as the future. We will discuss parallels with other groups that have experienced barriers to access, impediments to access for the homeless, and the legislative response to that concern.

This work first appeared in *Education Law Reporter, 53,* 757 (July 1989).

Parallels with Other Groups

Students have a property interest in public education, where states have established such a system. That right, however, is not an absolute right to attend the school of that student's choice, unless the student has satisfied the residency requirements of the state and school district.

The groups having the closest parallel to homeless children are children of illegal aliens and migrants. The U.S. Supreme Court has addressed the right of access to education for these groups; the Court ruled that the children of illegal aliens were entitled to access to public education under the aegis of the Equal Protection Clause of the Fourteenth Amendment and that all children are subject to the laws of the state.

In *Plyler* (1982), the Supreme Court reviewed Texas legislation withholding state monies from school districts if those funds were to be used to educate students not legally admitted to the United States and authorizing school districts to deny access to children of illegal aliens. The Supreme Court found that the Equal Protection Clause applied to anyone subject to the laws of the state. Because the state had chosen to establish a system of free, compulsory education, all children were entitled to that system of public education.

The implications of *Plyler* for the homeless are clear. Every state has established a system of free public education and every homeless child in the United States is a person within the jurisdiction of some state. Therefore, every homeless child is entitled to access to a system of public education.

The question of residency is a more difficult issue to resolve. The traditional elements of residency are physical presence and an intent to remain for an indefinite period of time. The general approach used in defining residency for school purposes is to define the child's residence as that of the parent or legal guardian. In *Martinez* (1983), the U.S. Supreme Court upheld a Texas statute that allowed a school district to deny a free education to a student living apart from his or her parent or guardian if the student is in the district for the primary purpose of attending the public schools. The Court noted that although students have a right to an education, the state has the right to establish bona fide residency requirements.

The implications of *Martinez* are less clear than those of *Plyler*. The decision established that the state may impose bona fide residency requirements, but it did not specify what those requirements might be. Furthermore, many states have not codified residency requirements for school attendance purposes. Although the two-part test of common law serves the law well for many purposes, it does not clarify the situation for the homeless. All homeless persons are present somewhere, but many do not have an intent to remain for an indefinite period, so the traditional analysis cannot be used. Because of the difficulty of defining residency requirements for school attendance purposes, the McKinney Act (Homeless Assistance Act, 1987), which will be discussed later, requires every state educational agency to assure that each child of a homeless person and each homeless youth has access to free, appropriate public education; it also requires the agencies to review their residency laws to ensure that such laws do not interfere with access.

Residency Requirements as an Impediment to Access

Under the U.S. system of public school financing, local property taxes are a substantial part of the financing of the local schools. It follows that the local board of education or school committee is charged to educate children who are legal residents within the boundaries of the local school district. Because of the rising costs of education and the disparate quality and type of educational programs among districts, policies have grown in complexity through the years. The extremes to which these requirements can be taken and their dismaying impact on a child can be seen in cases involving children.

For example, in a case involving four children living with their parents in a tent in a state park within the borders of the town of Hingham, Massachusetts, the superintendent of the Hingham School Department refused to enroll the children, using the argument that they were living on state property and thus were not under local jurisdiction. The Massachusetts Commissioner of Education ruled that children from homeless families have a right to be educated in the town in which they live. Commissioner Harold Raynolds, Jr., concluded that Massachusetts state law requires local communities to be responsible for educating the children within their boundaries, "irrespective of their living situation" (Jennings, 1988).

The residency battle has been fought in other states as well. In a New Jersey town, the municipal ordinances and school district residency requirements combined to prevent homeless children's access to education. By enforcing a municipal ordinance restricting motel stays to thirty days, the town provided a basis for the school district's classification of the children as too transient to satisfy residency requirements. These policies were challenged in *Vingara* (1987).

The more common disagreements about residency occur over definitions as to what may be considered the child's true home. It is unclear whether it can be a shelter, the child's former residence in a school district until the family once again has permanent housing, or a welfare agency's placement of the family. The National Coalition of the Homeless (1987) reports that from state to state and district to district, school districts disagree on how these judgments should be made. Sometimes these disagreements effectively deny the child any education at all. In Hartford, Connecticut, for example, a child cannot attend the school nearest a shelter because a shelter is not a permanent residence, and the child may or may not be able to attend his or her former school, depending on the policies of the previous district.

In May 1988, New York became the first state to establish policy that eased the school residency problems of the homeless. This decision by the New York Board of Regents allows the parents of homeless children to choose the district in which their children will attend school. Several court decisions in New York led to this bellwether legislation. In *Richards* (1985), the court ruled that the Richards children's former school district must enroll them. In *Delgado* (1986), the court ruled that the Delgado children were residents of their shelter district and thus could not attend their former school. And in *Mason* (1987), the court ruled that bodily presence established children's residence for attendance purposes. These cases illustrate the difficulty of determining residency for attendance and the need for the state to take the initiative.

Another case that shows the difficult questions dealing with access to education by the homeless is *Orozco* (1987). Sixta Orozco is a U.S. citizen. She was born in Puerto Rico in 1980 and lived for some time in Mount Vernon, New York. She returned to Puerto Rico some time before her first-grade year and attended first grade in San Lorenzo. She and her mother returned to New York in May 1987 and, shortly after returning, applied for public assistance with the Westchester County Department of Social Services. The department accepted her case, providing emergency housing in Yonkers.

Sixta's mother attempted to enroll her in the public schools of Mount Vernon; she stated that she had friends there and intended to settle there if and when she could. The Mount Vernon schools refused to enroll Sixta, declaring that the family resided in Yonkers rather than in Mount Vernon. When her mother tried to enroll Sixta in the Yonkers public schools, the school authorities refused to enroll her on the basis that she was not a permanent resident of Yonkers. The trial court granted a preliminary injunction directing the school district of Yonkers to enroll Sixta, pending a decision on the merits.

In reaching its conclusion, the court was guided by two points of law. The first was that Sixta had a property right in free public education. The second was that she did not have an unfettered right to tuition-free education at any public school in New York but, rather, her right was limited by the residency requirement.

The court noted that no guidelines were available to help school districts to resolve this type of dispute. However, the child's property right must be protected; if the legislature would not intervene and the school districts would not resolve it, the courts must. Since the Department of Social Services was providing housing in Yonkers and would continue to control where the family lived until the family found its own housing, the court determined that Yonkers should be designated as the legal residence of the family.

Orozco settled only the case of Sixta Orozco. Since housing was being provided, the legal residence was that housing. However, the question is unsettled as to where the child is to attend school if the family is transient or divided while seeking shelter. It also illustrates the difficulty local school districts face as they try to determine the extent of their responsibility to those children without a determinable home.

Other Barriers to Educational Access

As noted previously, when children can, or must, attend school in their former school district, transportation can become an enormous problem. In a 1987 survey conducted by the National Coalition of the Homeless, 15 percent of the shelters surveyed reported that the children did not attend school because they had no transportation. In *McCain* (1986), it was established that New York City had to fund transportation back to the student's former school district until permanent residency was established. The practical problems of such a policy prevent many children from getting to school. Families must apply for the city-funded transit passes and await approval; even then, the rides are long. Children often must leave the shelters before breakfast is served if they are to arrive at school on time.

Providing appropriate records is an enormous barrier to schooling for homeless families and even more so for runaway homeless children and youth. Since the very nature of homelessness makes retaining documents such as immunization records, grades, and special evaluations so difficult, shelter workers report repeated need for advocacy on a case-by-case basis to get children to school. Sometimes the former school is uncooperative or slow in forwarding records. In special education cases, where evaluations are costly and lengthy, the lack of availability of records means long delays before appropriate services are started; and before the records finally are received, the child may have moved again.

When confronted with homelessness, a family may break up and children may stay with family, friends, or relatives. But in most states, a legal guardian or parent must register children in school. Although advocacy in individual cases has obtained waivers from these requirements, shelters in the survey by the National Coalition of the Homeless (1987) report significant numbers of children denied an education because of these requirements.

Legislative Response

In 1985, Congress mandated an exploration of the problem of homelessness. The National Academy of Sciences report, *Homelessness, Health, and Human Needs* (1988), stated that the phenomenon of homeless children "is nothing short of a national disgrace that must be treated with the urgency such a situation demands." This report further substantiated the access to education problems cited in 1987 by the National Coalition of the Homeless.

In July 1987, significant legislation to address needs of the homeless was signed into law in the form of the Stewart B. McKinney Homeless Assistance Act (1987). This law provided comprehensive federal emergency assistance for homeless persons and specifically addressed the barriers to education of homeless children. The initial appropriation for homeless persons under the McKinney Act was $1 billion, and in October 1988, Congress extended the act for another two years and appropriated another $1.3 billion.

The McKinney Act is the first systematic attempt to address the needs of the homeless. The Act addresses the concerns of emergency shelter; the provision of food, long-term housing needs, health care, training, and community services; and educational needs.

The provisions of the Act applicable to access to education are found at 42 USC Sections 11431–11435; the Act provides that:

1. Each state educational agency shall assure that each child of a homeless person and homeless youth shall have access to a free appropriate public education, which would be provided to the children of a resident of the state.
2. Each state that has a residency requirement for school attendance purposes shall review and revise such laws to assure that such children are afforded a free and appropriate public education.
3. Each state shall establish or designate an Office of Coordinator of Education of Homeless Children and Youth. This office shall gather data on homeless children in the state and develop a plan providing for their education.

4. The plan developed shall contain provisions designed to authorize the state education agency, the local education agency, the parent or guardian of the homeless child, the homeless youth, or the applicable determinations required. The plan also shall provide procedures for the resolution of disputes regarding the educational placement of these children.

5. Under the plan, the local education agency of each homeless child shall either continue the child's enrollment in the school district of origin for the remainder of the year or enroll the child in the school district where he or she is living, whichever is in the child's best interests.

6. Each homeless child shall be provided services comparable to the services provided to other students in the school being attended.

7. The educational records of each homeless child or youth shall be maintained so that they are available in a timely fashion. In addition to creating a uniform policy to guarantee access to education for homeless children, the McKinney Act also provides funds to states to develop programs to serve the special needs of homeless children.

Implementation of the McKinney Act has already spawned litigation. Homeless children in Virginia and New Jersey joined with the National Coalition of the Homeless and Shasha Bruce Youth Work, Inc., in December 1987 in filing suit in federal district court in Washington; they attempted to force the U.S. Department of Education to release, earlier than planned, $5 million in federal funds that was earmarked to help the homeless gain access to education. The groups contended that the Department of Education was not acting with all possible speed and that the delays could cost homeless children another year of schooling.

The funds are now available and are being distributed to the states as applications are received. States are at varying stages of response to the McKinney Act. Every state has received some funding, but to receive a second-year grant each state must develop by April 30, 1989, a comprehensive plan for educating homeless children. The plan must demonstrate the state's commitment to ensuring that homeless children are not denied an education.

A wide range of activity in the states is reported but only New York, with an estimated 15,000 to 20,000 homeless children, has altered its residency requirements to allow the parents of homeless children a choice in selecting a school district. New York also adopted legislation in the late 1980s to provide aid to districts that take in homeless children. The response in other selected states is discussed next.

Responses from the State

In Maine, response to the McKinney Act educational provisions is administered through the Department of Educational and Cultural Services, Office of Truancy, Dropout, and Alternative Education. The department used a planning grant from the initial McKinney funds to develop a state plan for ensuring access to education for homeless children and youth. The department awarded a contract to the Human Services Development Institute at the University of Southern Maine to collect data on homeless children and youth in Maine and to review the barriers to their access to, and participation in, schooling. The Maine state plan was submitted to the U.S. Department of Education in the spring of 1989. Maine Governor John R. McKernan appointed a cabinet-level task force to prepare legislation regarding the homeless for the Maine Legislature.

No court cases have been brought as yet in Maine regarding a homeless child's access to an education. In general, a Maine child has no barrier to attending school in a district other than the one in which he or she resides, if the superintendents of both school districts agree. Although the information has not yet been collected, these informal agreements may have been accommodating homeless children in Maine.

The Connecticut legislature passed a law in 1987 requiring the homeless child's former district to pay the sheltering district the cost of the education and transportation. In case of disputes, the sheltering district must enroll the child immediately, pending the resolution of the problem (Goldberg, 1988). Any financial dispute is not to jeopardize the child's education. In enacting this law, Connecticut became the first state to address, in a major way, the educational barriers for homeless children.

On May 20, 1988, the New York Board of Regents approved regulations that allow the parents of homeless children the right to decide where the children will attend school. The regulations that took effect in the fall of 1988 did not affect New York City, which is one school district, but they were expected to provide access relief to the estimated 2,000 homeless school children in the rest of the state. The regents also endorsed a legislative proposal that would require the state to pay receiving districts the full cost of educating the homeless. New York City was the first large city to produce a comprehensive program to address the educational needs of homeless children. But implementation problems did occur and, according to the National Coalition of the Homeless (1987), the program did not succeed in placing homeless children in school.

The state of Washington used its initial McKinney monies to set up a computer system to keep track of students' health and birth certificates. When this system is in place, homeless children will have to produce these records only once per school year.

Implementation of programs to lower barriers has been difficult because of the lack of data on homeless children and, until recently, a lack of consciousness of the problem. In a Center for Law and Education (1987) survey of state boards of education in the fifty states and the District of Columbia, only six reported a homeless school-aged population in 1987. Of these six, only two estimated how many homeless children were in their state and only New York reported state or local initiatives to deal with the problem.

Conclusion

In its extremity, the plight of the homeless may illuminate the root causes of social problems. With regard to schooling, the access barriers facing homeless children may force us to rethink our fundamental goals, our priorities, and our funding systems. It also could mark the beginning of the end of the retrenchment to basics and mark the beginning of the era when schools will become the centers of advocacy for the rights of all our children. Schools may assume the coordinating role for services to children—not to provide all of the needed services themselves but to see that services are provided and to be the link between those services and those who need them. No organization now provides such coordination, and the schools are the logical agencies to step into such a role.

References

Center for Law and Education, Inc. (1987). *Newsnotes.* Cambridge, MA: Author.

Delgado v. Freeport Public School District (1986). 131 Misc. 2d. 102, 499, N.Y.S. 2d 606 (N.Y. Sup. Ct.).

Goldberg, K. (1988, June 1). New York Board sets rules for the homeless. *Education Week,* 10–11.

Homeless Assistance Act (1987). Pub. L. No. 100–77 101 Stat. 482–538.

Jennings, L. (1988, September 28). Panel says children fastest growing portion of homeless. *Education Week,* 5.

Kozol, J. (1988). *Rachel and her children: Homeless families in America.* New York: Crown.

McCain v. Koch (1986). 117 A.D. 2d. 198, 502 N.Y. S.2d 720 [32 Ed. Law Rep. 1027].

Martinez v. Bynum. (1983). 461 U.S. 321, 103 S.Ct. 1833, 75 L. Ed. 2d 879 [10 Ed. Law Rep. 11].

Mason v. Board of Education, Freeport Union School District (1987). No. 2865/87 (N.Y. Sup. Ct. mem. op. April 22, 1987).

National Academy of Science. (1988). *Homelessness, health and human needs.* Washington, DC: Author.

National Coalition of the Homeless. (1987). *Broken lives.* Washington, DC: Author.

Orozco by Arroya v. Sobol. (1987). 674 F. Supp. 125 [43 Ed. Law Rep. 565] (S.D.N.Y.).

Plyler v. Doe. (1982). 457 U.S. 202, 102 S.Ct. 2382, 72 L. Ed. 2d 786 [4 Ed. Law Rep., 1963].

Richards v. Board of Education of Union Free School District, Number 4, (1985). No. 11490, N.Y. Department of Education.

Vingara et al. v. Borough of Wrightstown, Civil Action No. 87–7545 (S. Ct. N.J. filed September 29, 1987), Complaint at 7–8.

Federal Programs for Education and Related Activities, 1787–1988

A capsule view of the history of federal education activities is provided in the following list of selected legislation:

1787 Northwest Ordinance authorized land grants for the establishment of educational institutions.

1802 An act fixing the military peace establishment of the United States established the U.S. Military Academy. (The U.S. Naval Academy was established in 1845 by the Secretary of the Navy.)

1862 First Morrill Act authorized public lands grants to the States for the establishment and maintenance of agricultural and mechanical colleges.

1867 Department of Education act authorized the establishment of the Department of Education.*

1876 Appropriation Act, Department of the Treasury established the U.S. Coast Guard Academy.

1890 Second Morrill Act provided for money grants for support of instruction in the agricultural and mechanical colleges.

1911 State Marine School Act authorized Federal funds to be used for the benefit of any nautical school in any of 11 specified State seaport cities.

1917 Smith-Hughes Act provided for grants to States for support of vocational education.

1918 Vocational Rehabilitation Act provided for grants for rehabilitation through training of World War I veterans.

1919 An act to provide for further educational facilities authorized the sale by the Federal Government of surplus machine tools to educational institutions at 15 percent of acquisition cost.

Source: Digest of Education Statistics, National Center for Education Statistics, U.S. Department of Education, 1989.

*The Department of Education as established in 1867 was later to be known as the Office of Education until 1960, when, under P.L. 96–88, it was again designated as a "department." Therefore, for purposes of consistency, it is referred to as the "Department of Education" even in those tables covering years when it was officially the Office of Education.

1920   Smith-Bankhead Act authorized grants to States for vocational rehabilitation programs.

1935   Bankhead-Jones Act (Public Law 74–182) authorized grants to States for agricultural experiment stations.

Agricultural Adjustment Act (Public Law 74–320) authorized 30 percent of the annual customs receipts to be used to encourage the exportation and domestic consumption of agricultural commodities. Commodities purchased under this authorization began to be used in school lunch programs in 1936. The National School Lunch Act of 1946 continued and expanded this assistance.

1936   An act to further the development and maintenance of an adequate and well-balanced American Merchant Marine (Public Law 84–415) established the U.S. Merchant Marine Academy.

1937   National Cancer Institute Act established the Public Health Service fellowship program.

1941   Amendment to Lanham Act of 1940 authorized Federal aid for construction, maintenance, and operation of schools in federally impacted areas. Such assistance was continued under Public Law 815 and Public Law 874, 81st Congress, in 1950.

1943   Vocational Rehabilitation Act (Public Law 78–16) provided assistance to disabled veterans.

School Lunch Indemnity Plan (Public Law 78–129) provided funds for local lunch food purchases.

1944   Servicemen's Readjustment Act (Public Law 78–346) provided assistance for education veterans.

Surplus Property Act (Public Law 78–457) authorized transfer of surplus property to educational institutions.

1946   National School Lunch Act (Public Law 79–396) authorized assistance through grants-in-aid and other means to States to assist in providing adequate foods and facilities for the establishment, maintenance, operation, and expansion of nonprofit school lunch programs.

George-Barden Act (Public Law 80–402) expanded Federal support of vocational education.

1948   United States Information and Educational Exchange Act (Public Law 80–402) provided for the interchange of persons, knowledge, and skills between the United States and other countries.

1949   Federal Property and Administrative Services Act (Public Law 81–152) provided for donation of surplus property to educational institutions and for other public purposes.

1950   Financial assistance for local educational agencies affected by Federal activities (Public Laws 81–815 and 81–874) provided assistance for construction (Public Law 815) and operation (Public Law 874) of schools in federally affected areas.

Housing Act (Public Law 81–475) authorized loans for construction of college housing facilities.

1954   An act for the establishment of the United States Air Force Academy and other purposes (Public Law 83–325) established the U.S. Air Force Academy.

Cooperative Research Act (Public Law 83–531) authorized cooperative arrangements with universities, colleges, and State educational agencies for educational research.

National Advisory Committee on Education Act (Public Law 83–532) established a National Advisory Committee on Education to recommend needed studies of national concern in the field of education and to propose appropriate action indicated by such studies.

School Milk Program Act (Public Law 83–597) provided funds for purchase of milk for school lunch programs.

1956   Library Services Act (Public Law 84–911) provided grants to States for extension and improvement of rural public library services.

1957   Practical Nurse Training Act (Public Law 84–911) provided grants to States for practical nurse training.

1958   National Defense Education Act (Public Law 85–865) provided assistance to State and local school systems for strengthening instruction in science, mathematics, modern foreign languages, and other critical subjects; improvement of State statistical services; guidance, counseling, and testing services and training institutes; higher education student loans and fellowships; foreign language study and training provided by colleges and universities; experimentation and dissemination of information on more effective utilization of television, motion pictures, and related media for educational purposes; and vocational education for technical occupations necessary to the national defense.

Education of Mentally Retarded Children Act (Public Law 85–926) authorized Federal assistance for training teachers of the handicapped.

Captioned films for the Deaf Act (Public Law 85–905) authorized a loan service of captioned films for the deaf.

1961 Area Redevelopment Act (Public Law 87–27) included provisions for training or retraining of persons in redevelopment areas.

1962 Manpower Development and Training Act (Public Law 87–415) provided training in new and improved skills for the unemployed and underemployed.

Communications Act of 1934, Amendment, (Public Law 87–447) provided grants for the construction of educational television broadcasting facilities.

Migration and Refugee Assistance Act of 1962 (Public Law 87–510) authorized loans, advances, and grants for education and training of refugees.

1963 Health Professions Educational Assistance Act (Public Law 88–129) provided funds to expand teaching facilities and for loans to students in the health professions.

Vocational Education Act of 1963 (Public Law 88–210) increased Federal support of vocational education schools; vocational work-study programs; and research, training, and demonstrations in vocational education.

Higher Education Facilities Act of 1963 (Public Law 88–204) authorized grants and loans for classrooms, libraries, and laboratories in public community colleges and technical institutes, as well as undergraduate and graduate facilities in other institutions of higher education.

1964 Civil Rights Act of 1964 (Public Law 88–352) authorized the Commissioner of Education to arrange for support for institutions of higher education and school districts to provide inservice programs for assisting instructional staff in dealing with problems caused by desegregation.

Economic Opportunity Act of 1964 (Public Law 88–452) authorized grants for college work-study programs for students from low-income families; established a Job Corps program and authorized support for work-training programs to provide education and vocational training and work experience opportunities in welfare programs; authorized support of education and training activities and of community action programs, including Head Start, Follow Through, and Upward Bound; and authorized the establishment of Volunteers in Service to America (VISTA).

1965   Elementary and Secondary Education Act (Public Law 89–10) authorized grants for elementary and secondary school programs for children of low-income families; school library resources, textbooks, and other instructional materials for school children; supplementary educational centers and services; strengthening State education agencies; and educational research and research training.

Health Professions Educational Assistance Amendments (Public Law 89–290) authorized scholarships to aid needy students in the health professions.

Higher Education Act of 1965 (Public Law 89–329) provided grants for university community service programs, college library assistance, library training and research, strengthening developing institutions, teacher training programs, and undergraduate instructional equipment. Authorized insured student loans, established a National Teacher Corps, and provided for graduate teacher training fellowships.

Medical Library Assistance Act (Public Law 89–291) provided assistance for construction and improvement of health sciences libraries.

National Foundation on the Arts and the Humanities Act (Public Law 89–209) authorized grants and loans for projects in the creative and performing arts, and for research, training, and scholarly publications in the humanities.

National Technical Institute for the Deaf Act (Public Law 89–36) provided for the establishment, construction, equipping, and operation of a residential school for postsecondary education and technical training of the deaf.

National Vocational Student Loan Insurance Act (Public Law 89–287) encouraged State and nonprofit private institutions and organizations to establish adequate loan insurance programs to assist students to attend post-secondary business, trade, technical, and other vocational schools.

Disaster Relief Act (Public Law 89–313) provided for assistance to local education agencies to help meet exceptional costs resulting from a major disaster.

1966 International Education Act (Public Law 89–698) provided grants to institutions of higher education for the establishment, strengthening, and operation of centers for research and training in international studies and the international aspects of other fields of study.

National Sea Grant College and Program Act (Public Law 89–688) authorized the establishment and operation of sea grant colleges and programs by initiating and supporting programs of education and research in the various fields relating to the development of marine resources.

Adult Education Act (Public Law 89–750) authorized grants to States for the encouragement and expansion of educational programs for adults, including training of teachers of adults and demonstrations in adult education (previously part of Economic Opportunity Act of 1964).

Model Secondary School for the Deaf Act (Public Law 89–694) authorized the establishment and operation, by Gallaudet College, of a model secondary school for the deaf.

Elementary and Secondary Education Amendments of 1966 (Public Law 89–750) in addition to modifying existing programs, authorized grants to assist States in the initiation, expansion, and improvement of programs and projects for the education of handicapped children.

1967 Education Professions Development Act (Public Law 90–35) amended the Higher Education Act of 1965 for the purpose of improving the quality of teaching and to help meet critical shortages of adequately trained educational personnel.

Public Broadcasting Act of 1967 (Public Law 90–129) established a Corporation for Public Broadcasting to: assume major responsibility in channeling Federal funds to noncommercial radio and television stations, program production groups, and ETV networks; conduct research, demonstration, or training in matters related to noncommercial broadcasting; and award grants for construction of educational radio and television facilities.

1968 Elementary and Secondary Education Amendments of 1967 (Public Law 90–247) modified existing programs, authorized support of regional centers for education of handicapped children, model centers and services for deaf-blind children, recruitment of personnel and dissemination of information on education of the handicapped; technical assistance in education to rural areas; support of dropout prevention projects; and support of bilingual education programs.

Handicapped Children's Early Education Assistance Act (Public Law 90–538) authorized preschool and early education programs for handicapped children.

Vocational Education Amendments of 1968 (Public Law 90–576) modified existing programs and provided for a National Advisory Council on Vocational Education, collection and dissemination of information for programs administered by the Commissioner of Education.

Higher Education Amendments of 1968 (Public Law 90–575) authorized new programs to assist disadvantaged college students through special counseling and summer tutorial programs, and programs to assist colleges to combine resources of cooperative programs and to expand programs which provide clinical experiences to law students.

1970   Elementary and Secondary Education Assistance Programs, Extension (Public Law 91–230) authorized comprehensive planning and evaluation grants to State and local education agencies; provided for the establishment of a National Commission on School Finance.

National Commission on Libraries and Information Services Act (Public Law 91–345) established a National Commission on Libraries and Information Science to effectively utilize the Nation's educational resources.

Office of Education Appropriation Act (Public Law 91–380) provided emergency school assistance to desegregating local education agencies.

Environmental Education Act (Public Law 91–516) established an Office of Environmental Education to: develop curriculum and initiate and maintain environmental education programs at the elementary-secondary levels; disseminate information; provide training programs for teachers and other educational, public, community, labor, and industrial leaders and employees; provide community education programs; and distribute material dealing with environment and ecology.

Drug Abuse Education Act of 1970 (Public Law 91–527) provided for development, demonstration, and evaluation of curriculums on the problems of drug abuse.

1971   Comprehensive Health Manpower Training Act of 1971 (Public Law 92–257) amended Title VII of the Public Health Service Act, increasing and expanding provisions for health manpower training and training facilities.

Nurse Training Act of 1971 (Public Law 92–158) amended Title VIII, Nurse Training, of the Public Health Service Act, increasing and expanding provisions for nurse training facilities.

1972   Drug Abuse Office and Treatment Act of 1972 (Public Law 92–255) established a Special Action Office for Drug Abuse Prevention to provide overall planning and policy for all Federal drug-abuse prevention functions; a National Advisory Council for Drug Abuse Prevention; community assistance grants for community mental health center for treatment and rehabilitation of persons with drug-abuse problems, and, in December 1974, a National Institute on Drug Abuse.

Education Amendments of 1972 (Public Law 92–318) established the Education Division and the National Institute of Education; general aid for institutions of higher education; Federal matching grants for State student incentive grants; a National Commission on Financing Postsecondary Education; State Advisory Councils on Community Colleges; a Bureau of Occupational and Adult Education and State grants for the design, establishment, and conduct of postsecondary occupational education; and a bureau-level Office of Indian Education. Amended current Office of Education programs to increase their effectiveness and better meet special needs. Prohibited sex bias in admission to vocational, professional, and graduate schools, and public institutions of undergraduate higher education.

1973   Older Americans Comprehensive Services Amendment of 1973 (Public Law 93–29) made available to older citizens comprehensive programs of health, education, and social services.

Comprehensive Employment and Training Act of 1973 (Public Law 93–203) provided for opportunities for employment and training to unemployed and underemployed persons. Extended and expanded provisions in the Manpower Development and Training Act of 1962, Title I of the Economic Opportunity Act of 1962, Title I of the Economic Opportunity Act of 1964, and the

Emergency Employment Act of 1971 as in effect prior to June 30, 1973.

1974   Educational Amendments of 1974 (Public Law 93–380) provided for the consolidation of certain programs; established a National Center for Education Statistics.

Juvenile Justice and Delinquency Prevention Act of 1974 (Public Law 93–415) provided for technical assistance, staff training, centralized research, and resources to develop and implement programs to keep students in elementary and secondary schools; established, in the Department of Justice, a National Institute for Juvenile Justice and Delinquency Prevention.

1975   Indian Self-Determination and Education Assistance Act (Public Law 93–638) provided for increased participation of Indians in the establishment and conduct of their education programs and services.

Harry S. Truman Memorial Scholarship Act (Public Law 93–642) established the Harry S. Truman Scholarship Foundation and created a perpetual education scholarship fund for young Americans to prepare and pursue careers in public service.

Indochina Migration and Refugee Assistance Act of 1975 (Public Law 94–23) authorized funds to be used for education and training of aliens who have fled from Cambodia or Vietnam.

Education of the Handicapped Act (Public Law 94–142) provided that all handicapped children (5 to 18 years old) have available to them a free appropriate education designed to meet their unique needs.

1976   Educational Broadcasting Facilities and Telecommunications Demonstration Act of 1976 (Public Law 94–309) established a telecommunications demonstration program to promote the development of nonbroadcast telecommunications facilities and services for the transmission, distribution, and delivery of health, education, and public or social service information.

Education Amendments of 1976 (Public Law 94–482) extended and revised Federal programs for education assistance for higher education, vocational education, and a variety of other programs.

1977   Youth Employment and Demonstration Projects Act of 1977 (Public Law 95–93) established a youth employment training program that includes, among other activities, promoting education-to-work transition, literacy training and bilingual training, and attainment of certificates of high school equivalency.

1978   Career Education Incentive Act (Public Law 95–207) authorized the establishment of a career education program for elementary and secondary schools.

Tribally Controlled Community College Assistance Act (Public Law 95–471) provided Federal funds for the operation and improvement of tribally controlled community colleges for Indian students.

Education Amendments of 1978 (Public Law 95–561) established a comprehensive basic skills program aimed at improving pupil achievement (replaced the existing National Reading Improvement program); established a community schools program to provide for the use of public buildings.

Middle Income Student Assistance Act (Public Law 95–566) modified the provisions for student financial assistance programs to allow middle income as well as low income students attending college or other postsecondary institutions to qualify for Federal education assistance.

1979   Department of Education Organization Act (Public Law 96–88) established a Department of Education containing functions from the Education Division of the Department of Health, Education, and Welfare along with other selected education programs from H.E.W., the Department of Justice, Department of Labor, and the National Science Foundation.

1980   Asbestos School Hazard Protection and Control Act of 1980 (Public Law 96–270) established a program for inspection of schools for detection of hazardous asbestos materials and provided loans to assist educational agencies to contain or remove and replace such materials.

Amendments to the Higher Education Act (Public Law 96–374) provided for a new Commission on National Development in Postsecondary Education and a new Urban Grant University Program.

1981   Education Consolidation and Improvement Act of 1981 (Public Law 97–35) consolidated 42 programs into 7 programs to be funded under the elementary and secondary block grant authority.

1983   Student Loan Consolidation and Technical Amendments Act of 1983 (Public Law 98–79) established 8 percent rate for Guaranteed Student Loans and extended Family Contribution Schedule.

Challenge Grant Amendments of 1983 (Public Law 98–95) amended Title III, Higher Education Act, and added authorization of Challenge Grant program. The Challenge Grant program provides funds to eligible institutions on a matching basis as incentive to seek alternative sources of funding.

Education of Handicapped Act Amendments (Public Law 98–199) added Architectural Barrier amendment and clarified participation of Handicapped Children in private schools.

Education Consolidation and Improvement Act of 1981 Amendments (Public Law 98–211) added technical amendments for Chapter 1, and provided for parental involvement and minor changes in other programs.

1984   Rehabilitation Amendments of 1984 (Public Law 98–221) revised and extended the Rehabilitation Act of 1973. Provides for the Helen Keller National Center for Deaf-Blind.

Education for Economic Security Act (Public Law 98–377) added new science and mathematics programs for elementary, secondary, and postsecondary education. The new programs include: magnet schools, excellence in education, and equal access.

Higher Education Act of 1965 Amendments (Public Law 98–312) this act amended Title III of the Higher Education Act of 1965 by creating a new method of funding the Challenge Grant program. The act also increased the level of authorization for the Office of the Inspector General and extended the Allen J. Ellender Fellowship program through fiscal year 1989.

Carl D. Perkins Vocational Education Act (Public Law 98–524) continues Federal assistance for vocational education through fiscal year 1989. The act replaces the Vocational Education Act of 1963. It provides aid to the States to make vocational education programs accessible to all persons, including handicapped and disadvantaged, single parents and homemakers, and the incarcerated.

Human Services Reauthorization Act (Public Law 98–558) reauthorized the Head Start and Follow Through programs through fiscal year 1986. It also created a Carl D. Perkins scholarship program, a National Talented Teachers Fellowship program, a Federal Merit Scholarships program, and a Leadership in Educational Administration program.

1985   Montgomery GI Bill–Active Duty (Public Law 98–525), signed
on October 19, 1984, brought about a new GI Bill for individuals
who initially entered active military duty on or after July 1,
1985.

Montgomery GI Bill–Selected Reserve (Public Law 98–525),
signed on October 19, 1984, is an education program for members of the Selected Reserve (which includes the National
Guard) who enlist, reenlist, or extend an enlistment after June
30, 1985, for a 6-year period.

1986   Education for the Deaf Act (Public Law 99–371) places Gallaudet College and the National Technical Institute for the Deaf
on a 5-year reauthorization cycle. Establishes an 18-month
Commission to Study Deaf Education.

Handicapped Children's Protection Act (Public Law 99–372)
allows parents of handicapped children to collect attorney's fees
in cases brought under the Education of the Handicapped Act
and provides that the Education of the Handicapped Act does
not preempt other laws, such as Section 504 of the Rehabilitation Act.

Reauthorization of the Education of the Handicapped Act
Amendments (Public Law 99–457) reauthorizes for 3 years the
discretionary programs under the Education of the Handicapped Act and requires education services for all handicapped
3- to 5-year olds. Included are programs to provide demonstration projects for severely disabled individuals, research and
technology activities, early childhood education, and a new
State grant program to provide early intervention services for
handicapped children from birth through age 2.

Reauthorization of the Higher Education Act of 1965 (Public
Law 99–498) reauthorizes for 5 years the Higher Education Act
of 1965, as amended. Provides increases in maximum Pell
Grant and student loan amounts, institutes a new agency to
provide college construction funding, cuts incentives to lenders
involved in the student aid programs and extends the authorization for the Office of Educational Research and Improvement.

Reauthorization of the Rehabilitation Act (Public Law 99–506)
authorizes for 5 years programs to provide vocational rehabilitation for disabled persons. Includes increasing the State/
Federal match requirements, establishes a new State grant
program for supported employment, and sets higher education
levels.

The Drug-Free Schools and Communities Act of 1986 (Public Law 99–570), part of the Anti-Drug Abuse Act of 1986, authorizes funding for fiscal years 1987–89. Establishes programs for drug abuse education and prevention, coordinated with related community efforts and resources, through the use of Federal financial assistance.

1987   Higher Education Act Amendments of 1987 (Public Law 100–50) makes technical corrections, clarifications, or conforming amendments related to the enactment of the Higher Education Amendments of 1986.

1988   The Augustus F. Hawkins-Robert T. Stafford Elementary and Secondary School Improvement Amendments of 1988 (Public Law 100–297) reauthorizes through 1993 major elementary and secondary education programs including: Chapter 1, Chapter 2, Bilingual Education, Math-Science Education, Magnet Schools, Impact Aid, Indian Education, Adult Education, and other smaller educational programs.

White House Conference on Libraries (Public Law 100–381) authorizes a White House Conference on Library and Information Services.

Library Services and Construction Act (Public Law 100–569) extends the authorization of Title V and Title VI of the Library Services and Construction Act for 1 year.

The Handicapped Programs Technical Amendments Act of 1988 (Public Law 100–360) makes certain technical and conforming amendments to the Education of the Handicapped Act and the Rehabilitation Act of 1973.

Technology-Related Assistance for Individuals with Disabilities Act of 1988 (Public Law 100–407) provides financial assistance to States to develop and implement consumer-responsive State-wide programs for technology-related assistance for persons of all ages with disabilities.

The Omnibus Trade and Competitiveness Act of 1988 (Public Law 100–418) authorizes new and expanded education programs. Title VI of the Act, Education and Training for American Competitiveness, authorizes new programs in literacy, math-science, foreign language, vocational training, international education, technology training, and technology transfer.

The Omnibus Drug Abuse Prevention Act of 1988 (Public Law 100–690) authorizes a new teacher training program under the

Drug-Free Schools and Communities Act, an early childhood education program to be administered jointly by the Departments of Health and Human Services and Education, and a pilot program for the children of alcoholics.

Stewart B. McKinney Homeless Assistance Act (Public Law 100–628) extends for 2 additional years programs providing assistance to the homeless, including literacy training for homeless adults and education for homeless youths.

Tax Reform Technical Amendments (Public Law 100–647) authorizes an Education Savings Bond for the purpose of post-secondary educational expenses. The bill grants tax exclusion for interest earned on regular series EE savings bonds.

SECTION TWO REFERENCES

American Association of School Administrators (AASA). (1987, September 30). Bennett says studies bear out "blob" theory. *Leadership News*, 3.

American Association of School Administrators (AASA). (1983). *The Excellence Report: Using it to improve your schools.* Arlington, VA: Author.

Bakalis, M. J. (1988, Spring). The presidency and the public schools. *Loyola Leader.* Loyola University of Chicago, 1, 5, 9.

Bolman, L. G., & Deal, T. E. (1988). *Modern approaches to understanding and managing organizations.* San Francisco: Jossey-Bass.

Boyd, W. (1990, Spring). Natural goals and national politics: Beyond the bully pulpit. *Politics of Education Bulletin*, 2, 3, 10.

Bush, G. (1988, January 25). Speech to a group of teachers invited to inaugural festivities. Reported in the *Chronicle of Higher Education*, p. A23.

Campbell, R. F., Cunningham, L. L., Nystrand, R. O., & Usdan, M. D. (1985). *The organization & control of American schools* (5th ed.). Columbus, OH: Charles E. Merrill.

Cavazos, L. F. (Speaker) (1990). Senate subcommittee on labor–HHS–education appropriations. Unpublished testimony.

Chubb, J. E., & Moe, T. M. (1990). *Schools, politics and markets.* Washington, DC: Brookings Institution.

Clark, D. L., & Astuto, T. A. (1988). The implications for educational research of a changing federal educational policy. In M. J. Justiz & L. G. Bjork (eds.), *Higher education research and public policy.* New York: American Council on Education and Macmillan.

Cronin, T. E. (1989, February 1). If Bush is to be the "Education President," much work must be done at the grassroots. *The Chronicle of Higher Education*, Section 2.

Elazar, D. (1972). *American Federalism: A view from the states.* New York: Thomas Y. Crowell.

Elmore, R. (1979). *Complexity and control: What legislators and administrators can do about implementation.* Public Policy Paper No. 11, Institute of Governmental Research, University of Washington.

Elmore, R. F. (1986). Education & federalism: Doctrinal, functional and strategic views. In D. L. Kirp & D. N. Jenson (eds.), *School days, rule days: The legalization and regulation of education.* Philadelphia: Falconer Press.

Finn, C. E. (1990, May 9). Quoted in: Education department, 10 years old this month, gets mixed reviews. *The Chronicle of Higher Education*, p. A24.

"Five years after the report." (1988, April). *Education Week*, 7(30), 23.

Guthrie, J. W., & Reed, R. J. (1986). *Educational administration and policy: Effective leadership for American education.* Englewood Cliffs, NJ: Prentice Hall.

Hill, P. T. (1990). The federal role in education: A strategy for the 90's. *Phi Delta Kappan*, 71(5), 398–402.

Lippmann, W. (1914). The red herring. *A Preface to Politics.*

McDowell, C. (1990). About the education summit: Said on *Washington Week in Review.*

National Center for Education Statistics. (1989). *Digest of Education Statistics* (25th ed.). Washington, DC: U.S. Department of Education.

National Commission on Excellence in Education. (1983). *A nation at risk: The imperative for educational reform.* Washington, DC: U.S. Government Printing Office.

Reutter, E. E., Jr. (1985). *The Law of public education* (3rd ed.). Minneola, NY: Foundation Press.

Rothman, R. (1990, May 9). "Wall chart" data shows passivity, secretary warns. *Education Week,* 1, 31.

Spring, J. (1988). *Conflict of interests: The politics of American education.* New York: Longman.

Tinker v. Des Moines Independent Community School District, Supreme Court of the U.S., 1969, 393 U.S. 503.

Wimpelberg, R. K., & Ginsberg, R. (1989). The national commission approach to educational reform. In J. Hannaway & R. Crowson (eds.), *The politics of reforming school administration* (pp. 13–25). New York: Falmer Press.

Wirt, F. M., & Kirst, M. W. (1989). *Schools in conflict* (2nd ed.). Berkeley, CA: McCutchan.

State Governments and Education Policy

The State Level: Where the Action Is

"The sole advantage of power is that you can do more good."
—Baltasar Gracian (1647)

State Power

The power in educational policy making has been at the state level since at least 1980, and it is likely to remain firmly lodged there into the twenty-first century. School administrators may complain about mandates, interference, insensitivity to local concerns, and other ills, but the truth of the matter is that the states have the power. By history, tradition, and the legal framework, the education of the youth in the United States truly is the states' business. However, the school administrator in his or her policy-related roles can powerfully affect how a state's business is conducted.

The Legal Framework

Education is never specifically mentioned in the U.S. Constitution. Constitutional provisions and the means by which the federal government affects education are discussed in Section Two. The major point to remember here is that education becomes a function of the states under the Tenth Amendment.

Pierce v. *Society of Sisters* (1925), a landmark Supreme Court decision, establishes the basic constitutional framework within which the states regulate schooling (Yudof, Kirp, van Geel, and Levin, 1987). The following is a quote from *Pierce:* "No question is raised concerning the power of the State reasonably to regulate all schools, to inspect, supervise and examine them, their teachers and pupils; to require that all children of proper age attend some school, that teachers shall be of good moral character and patriotic disposition, that certain studies plainly essential to good citizenship must be taught, and that nothing be taught which is manifestly inimical to the public welfare." The state interests in requiring schooling include preparation of the individual for citizenship and economic independence, inculcating values, and preserving the security of the state (Yudof, et al., 1987).

Within the states, the state legislatures have complete legislative authority except as restricted by federal law or state constitutions. These are followed by vast numbers of statutes affecting education that are passed by the state legislatures. It is important to note that "the courts consistently say that the power of the state legislatures over the public school systems of the respective states is plenary" (Reutter, 1985, p. 7). Reutter supports this statement later in his book by pointing out that literally hundreds of citations could be given to support the point. I dwell on this point because I have found it to be a common misunderstanding among school administrators as to what are and are not the "rights" of the state, and a clear portrait of the basic structure of rights is important for meaningfully coping with policy.

The issue of compliance with legislative and administrative rules is fraught with problems. Local compliance with state standards might be voluntary, or it can result from the availability of technical assistance, informal processes of persuasion, threats of sanctions, or adverse publicity. A state agency may seek to order a school district to abide by state standards or face the actions of denial of accreditation or revocation of state grants in aid. State agencies may then face state judicial processes for the ultimate enforcement of their actions. The state courts may be called upon to determine, for instance, whether the legislature has improperly delegated its authority to the state education agency (Yudof et al., 1987).

Reutter includes some specifics regarding the power of the states: "The legislature can organize the state for the purpose of education and distribute duties and responsibilities among central agencies, intermediate agencies, and local agencies as it sees fit. Since the power over public education is legislative and plenary, it is not exhausted by exercise, and the legislature may change the educational system in any manner and as often as it deems necessary or expedient if thereby no federal or state constitutional provisions are violated" (1985, p. 9). Despite this clearly understood prevailing law, the political realities can be quite different. As many states have learned through long and bitter battles over the consolidation of small rural school districts, there are political limits to the states' power, and these powers can be "exhausted by exercise."

Centralization versus Decentralization

Arguments for Decentralization

Polsby called the issue of centralization and decentralization "one of the great, resonant themes of contemporary politics" (1979, p. 1). This is important to note because often we do not realize that this issue is one with reality and implications other than in education. Surely in education the tug-of-war between state and local agencies is a constant in the life of school administrators.

Weiler (1989) assessed the arguments for decentralization in education and, after discussing the most commonly used arguments for decentralization, offered this summary:

> The notion of decentralization as redistribution of power seems largely incompatible with the interests of the modern state in maintaining effective control and in discharging some if its key functions with regard to the system of economic production and capital accumulation. And, as has been discussed, one of the state's "key functions" is the provision of the educating system.
>
> Decentralization as a means to enhance the efficiency of educational governance by both generating additional resources and using available resources more effectively seems to have some potential in the abstract but also appears to depend on premises that, on closer inspection, are rather precarious. Thus we have seen, in the late 1980s and the 1990s more rounds in fights over school finance formulas.
>
> Finally, the notion of decentralizing the contexts and contents of learning so as to recognize the diversity and importance of different cultural environments in a society is generally considered meaningful and valid. "At the same time, however, this idea is countered by conflicting claims for a kind of learning less oriented to the specifics of cultural contexts and more to the national and international universalities of dealing with modern systems of technology and communication" (Weiler 1989, p. 37). Political considerations (conflict management in Weiler's terms) keep decentralization viable as policy making. In other words, despite the potentialities of twenty-first-century technology, political realities will probably keep the structure, at least, of decentralized educational governance in place. Nevertheless, school administrators generally seem to feel that continued centraliza-

tion of power is closing off their administrative and policy options.

There may be a need for a stronger state role than people in many states may yet wish to accept. The tradition of governance by local control is an emotional issue and will be discussed in Section Four, which covers local governance. But there are roles that only the state level of governance can perform well.

First, only the state can ensure equality and standardization of instruction and resources. And to those who say that standardization is undesirable, they must be reminded of the mobility rates in the United States in the 1990s. Families move; children move from school to school.

The state is the governance level with responsibility for the enforcement of standards. In order to link state policy and local practice more effectively, state monitoring of local programs may need to increase and be done in more depth than it has been done in the past. The state can provide the technical assistance and the information and data not available or easily accessible elsewhere, which can assist in the program work needed to meet newly enforced standards. The state also can ensure each district fiscal integrity and equitable financing.

Second, the state can exert leadership, such as curricular leadership, by providing incentives to local districts to adopt innovative programs. Such incentives need not only be financial ones. They can be promotional or practical, such as the temporary waiving of regulations that may stand in the way of innovation.

Third, the state can require local districts to be accountable for educational outcomes. The battles for equal access to education and equal treatment in U.S. schools have been fought, and to a large extent, won. The battle for equal outcomes is now being fought, as is the battle for excellence in education, but it must be excellence for all, and herein lies the importance of the states' role.

Fourth, it is the states, along with the federal government, that ensure that local communities provide for the disadvantaged and minority populations. There is evidence to show that when federal and state vigilance is relaxed, some local districts do not live up to their responsibilities to these populations. An example was the result of the lax attitude in Washington in the early 1980s toward enforcement of Title IX and Section 504 of the Rehabilitation Act. In too many districts, efforts to provide equal access to sports for girls and equal access to buildings for students with disabilities were curtailed.

The state is the level of governance best able to succeed at these tasks because societal forces have combined to make local boards and superintendents less powerful than they were in the past. From our heterogeneous society have emerged multiple existing and future goals for education. We now recognize education as a scarce good, and the distribution of scarce goods is accomplished through political means. These distribution problems are beyond the scope of a local school board and, as has been stated, it is the state's responsibility.

It is also the state's responsibility to be the protector of the public good. It is one of the historically strongest arguments for public schools that the state owes it to a child to provide some view of the world other than that of his or her parents. State policy makers can provide the broader perspective necessary to define, encourage, and protect those aspects of education that are for the good of both the individual and the larger society.

Traditionally, Americans have feared distant government. They have wanted important decisions to be made close to home. In the nineteenth and much of the twentieth centuries local control was a practical necessity. But modern communications technology has changed the practical necessity, although political realities keep in place a necessity born of conflict resolution. Both the state capital and Washington are now close to home, and the role of the local governance units, the school boards, school councils, and school committees is a changed one. The policy-related roles of the local governance structure will be explored in Section Four.

Political Concerns

Even given the realities of the legal framework for public education, we know and have read here and elsewhere that the political realities are somewhat different. As the stalling of the consolidation movement has demonstrated, there is indeed an "exhaustion" of state power in this sphere, but it is important to remember the overuse and that this exhaustion of power is a political, not a legal, reality. Public indignation may well hold in check the power of the state legislature. Since public indignation is not based on any systematic analysis of the educational point at hand, it is unlikely to be even as much based on policy analysis and the state of the research than the law making of the legislature.

Thoughtful, involved, and well-informed school administrators can serve a valuable policy-related role in mediating the extreme shifts caused by overreaction from either the public or the legislature. Called by some a public relations role, when policy matters are involved (and, by definition, long-term effects are involved), the administrators' policy-related role becomes more than public relations. The administrator becomes a point of reason, knowledge, and stability in the midst of volatile policy-making processes. In discussions of the state agency and the legislature, it is important not to forget the general principle of separation of powers among the legislature, executive, and judicial branches of government. However, the increasing complexity of society has caused some blurring in this area. As far back as 1957 in *Wall* v. *County Board of Education,* the court emphasized the fact that the mode of life has become so complex that for the legislature to enact laws in detail covering many governmental services would not only be impractical, but impossible. Thus, reasoned the court, many matters must be left to administrative agencies. Clearly then, the legislature may, and in all practicality must, delegate broad rule-making authority to the state agencies. But in many cases, state boards and chief state school officers have been pulled back by the courts for exceeding authority beyond that which was particularly delegated to them by the legislature. Where legislation is specific, state boards are not empowered to deviate from the prescriptions (Reutter, 1985). Thus, in implementing and enforcing prescriptive legislation, state boards frequently "take the heat" from irate administrators, when the boards' discretion is actually less than it is perceived to be.

There have been challenges to the ultimate control over education by the state legislature. The following excerpt from Reutter (1985) makes clear the legislature's position.

That the state legislature must be deemed to have ultimate control over education in the state in the absence of some clear constitutional provision to the contrary was held by the Supreme Court of Louisiana (*Aguillard* v. *Treen,* 440 SO.2d 704 (La. 1983). The case involved the power of the legislature to require a balanced treatment in the curriculum of "creation science" and "evolution science." The court rejected arguments that certain provisions in the Louisiana constitution allocated decisions regarding course content and methodology exclusively to the state board. The board's powers of supervision and control of public education "must yield to the legislative will as expressed by the elected representatives of the people," said the court. That the state board members also were elected did not influence the court to detach ultimate authority from the legislature. (p. 102)

Within the powers delegated by the legislature, the courts are inclined to allow state education authorities wide discretion in the promulgation and enforcement of rules. Because of the increasing complexity of the field of education and of the legal matters pertaining to it, the courts construe broadly the powers of state administrative officers so that educational aspects will be fully considered.

Political Realities

Three Styles of School Reform

"The school reform movement is peopled at one extreme by hyper-rationalists who believe that schools are infinitely manipulatable, and at the other extreme by romantic decentralizers who believe that if left alone schools will flourish" (Timar and Kirp, 1988, p. 75). The 1980s reform movement offered ample opportunity to test the power of the states and the political realities in the use of that power. Both of these aspects of reform were handled differently from state to state. Timar and Kirp identified three models of implementation that were used by the states in the 1980s reform movement. These are rational planning, market incentive, and political interaction as exemplified by Texas, California, and South Carolina.

The following terms are associated with rational planning: top-down mandates, centralized authority and decision making, standardization, and uniformity. Rational planning is also recognized by a strong mistrust of local authority and the exercise of local discretion.

In the market-incentive strategy, policy development is concentrated at the state level but implementation is encouraged through fiscal incentives and compliance is decided upon at the local level.

In the political interaction model, the state articulates broad policy goals but allows discretion and flexibility in local implementation. The purpose is to integrate state policy goals with local conditions and practices. Implementation becomes a process for problem solving instead of the imposition of a single best solution.

Important differences in the policy-development processes, as well as in the implementation strategies, can be seen in Timar and Kirp's report of their study, and the differences mean a lot to the functioning of the policy-oriented administrator. The reform process in Texas violated good policy-making principles in that no one outside of the select committee created for the purpose knew the substance of the reform bill. Few hearings were conducted as it went through the legislative process. There was such distrust on the part of this committee for the education establishment that even the "general counsel for the state department of education was unable to review the legislation until the bill had nearly cleared both houses" (Timar and Kirp,

1988, p. 77). This decidedly top-down imposition of new policy resulted in disappointment, confusion, and a fragmented reform effort.

Since the California constitution requires all state mandates to be paid for by the state, local districts in California do not have the complaint that local districts in many states have been loudly vocalizing. In many states, mandates without money has been a battle cry. Some of the skirmishes in these reform wars capture public attention and then public time and money for their settlement. As an example, the defiant motion not to comply with certain mandates by the Springfield, Illinois, Board of Education in February 1988 is reproduced as Figure 3.1, along with the prompt reply of the then State Superintendent of Education Ted Sanders (Figure 3.2). This incident did not consist only of a flurry of letters, although eventually the Springfield Board backed down. In the meantime, newspaper headlines broadcast the dispute to the entire state, hundreds of boards were said to be ready to join with Springfield, and superintendents and board members all over the state met in battle conferences. Adrenalin was running high and the fun and games of strategizing was invigorating. But what good for, and to, education do such sideshows deliver? Such intergovernmental bickering has added to the public's derision of the entire education system, and such battles between state and local education authorities were common during the 1980s.

But back to California, where money does follow the mandates

FIGURE 3.1 • *Springfield, Illinois, Board of Education (2/1/88)*

Whereas, District #186 prior to the enactment and implementation of the Illinois School Reform Act of 1985 did develop student learner objectives and did review our curricular needs on a cyclical schedule in excess of those required by the State and,

Whereas, this Board did report to our community about student achievement prior to the requirements for the district report card and,

Whereas, the specific funding provided by the State for the development of assessment plans was not provided in the current fiscal year and,

Whereas, the finances from the State of Illinois to this district are being and have been reduced, thereby resulting in reductions of services for students as has been recently reported,

Now, therefore, BE IT RESOLVED that any expenditures necessitated solely by the school reform legislation be omitted from the FY '89 budget and, further, that the Superintendent provide a report to the Board as to such reductions or savings that could be realized yet this year (FY '88) in mandated but non-funded reform activities or requirements.

FIGURE 3.2 • *Response to Springfield Board of Education*

February 19, 1988

Dr. James K. Nighswander
President
Board of Education
Springfield Public Schools
1900 West Monroe
Springfield, Illinois 62704

Dear Dr. Nighswander:

I received your letter of February 4, 1988, explaining your Board's actions regarding legal requirements, and read it with interest.

Despite your comment that the Springfield Board's action was taken with full respect for the law and for this office, I remain unconvinced of either of those assurances.

I join with the *Springfield Journal Register* in noting the obvious conflict between the special responsibility those of us in public positions have to provide models of behavior for our young people, and the Springfield Board's decision to disobey laws with which it does not agree. For it to take such action when it must realize that the effect of any penalty for its doing so will fall not upon its members, but rather upon services for children of the district, does not permit the label of respectability sometimes given to more thoughtful civil disobedience.

I find it ironic that your Board has announced its intention to willfully disobey only those laws which relate to accountability for results and full information to the public, laws which it freely admits cost a relative pittance to administer, while it has received millions of dollars from the state for other reform programs. Certainly, many will have to question both the Board's priorities and its motives in this regard.

The democratic process is available to us all for pursuing changes in laws with which we take issue. Despite that fact, the Springfield Board apparently has decided to pursue an alternative route, clearly indicating a lack of faith in and respect for the usual processes of law.

Please accept this reaction to your letter and public statements as indication of our intention to meet fully our statutory responsibility to vigorously enforce the law.

Sincerely,

Ted Sanders
State Superintendent
of Education

cc: State Board of Education
   Springfield Board of Education (copies enclosed)

and all should be easy. On the surface the California approach is appealing because of its allowance for local flexibility; however, Timar and Kirp (1988) report that although this was a politically acceptable reform strategy, the reliance upon incentives and local bargaining resulted in only marginal educational benefits.

The South Carolina example of political interaction, as described by Timar and Kirp, followed the precepts of good policy making because it involved many and diverse groups in the state and built consensus on the needed reforms. Thus, by the time reform became a reality, those affected were well prepared. They had been involved all through the process. It did help, of course, that there was state money to pay for the reforms, but money alone is not the answer as witnessed by the California example. The South Carolina case study gives an example of a state reaching a balance between state accountability and local autonomy. "South Carolina's reform strategy shows that reform can succeed if disparate, and often competing, interests can be combined to foster schools that are organizationally purposive and have the flexibility and competence to allocate and use resources congruently with their defined mission" (Timar and Kirp, 1988, p. 87). Here there was opportunity for school administrators to function in their policy-related roles.

State Monitoring Systems

Given the emphasis on excellence in the reform movement of the 1980s, state monitoring and how to do it became a subject of some debate and resentment among school administrators. Richards (1988) developed a typology of state monitoring systems after study in six states and twenty-four school districts. Richards wrote that although they may use a combination of monitoring systems, most states have a primary approach that dominates their accountability systems. Richards uses the Kiesler and Sproull (1982) definition of monitoring as a system of activities with three critical components: the regular collection of information, evaluation of that information, and resultant institutional action. This definition, if adhered to by the state agency, would have significance for the school administrator in that the often-heard complaint that information is collected and not used would be corrected. Information collected would have to be evaluated and the results acted on in order to be defined as monitoring. Thus, the information would be useful and the feedback loop would be continual and, hopefully, productive. Miscellaneous and burdensome collection of information that does not feed into the monitoring system could be argued against from a more solid base.

Richards discusses three types of state monitoring systems: compliance, diagnostic, and performance. These are exemplified by New Jersey, Minnesota, and California. Let's look more closely at these three types of monitoring. Compliance monitoring is what most administrators think of when the word is mentioned. Its goal is to ensure that schools live up to some standards and it is defined in the familiar words of laws, regulations, rules, codes, and mandates. According to Richards, it is best suited to health and safety codes. However, administrators are well aware that this kind of monitoring is inappropriately applied to scholastic purposes. The goal of diagnostic monitoring is student improvement. It is individually based and is not suitable for competitive or comparison purposes. It may appeal to the values of the educator but is not suited to schools with high rates of mobility and it does not take into account the myriad other factors outside the school that impinge upon a student's performance. The goal of Richards's last type, performance monitoring, is to promote competition between schools and school districts by focusing on school outcomes. These kinds of comparisons have been hotly resisted by teachers, administrators, and boards. Nevertheless, the technological capacity to carry such comparisons to the classroom level is here, although all state departments cannot yet afford to access it. It is hard to believe that the education establishment can hold out against the capability to provide this kind of information to parents and the public.

Experimenting with Reform

State boards of education were created to remove educational policy making from the dirty world of politics and place it firmly in the hands of objective, nonprofessional policy makers. Although this is surely a noble objective and one in keeping with democratic ideas and the importance of education, we were reminded throughout the decade of reform of the 1980s that political infighting is alive and well in educational circles and that education is a commodity to be fought over in the same political way as other scarce resources.

The 1980s saw the states experimenting with educational reform. That experimentation is necessary is said wonderfully in a quote from Supreme Court Justice Louis Brandeis, which was used at the beginning of a case study of reform in Indiana by Contreras and Medlyn (1989).

> There must be power in the states and the Nation to remold, through experimentation, our economic practices and institutions to meet changing social and economic needs. . . . Denial of the

right to experiment may be fraught with serious consequences to the Nation. It is one of the happy incidents of the federal system that a single courageous state may, if its citizens choose, serve as a laboratory; and try novel social and economic experiments without risk to the rest of the country.—Supreme Court Justice Louis Brandeis, *New State Ice Co.* v. *Liebermann,* Dissenting Opinion, 1932

The reform movement was national in nature dating from *A Nation at Risk* (1983). Education dominated governors' state-of-the-state messages between 1984 and 1988, and the similarities among states were striking in the reforms they enacted. Fuhrman (1989) noted "the leadership of general government was a common factor that crossed the states" (p. 62).

Although the movement was a national one, reform is best understood in the framework of each state's history and culture. Elazar (1972) classified the states' political culture as individualistic, where professional politicians dominate and government is limited; moralistic, where citizens believe in, and turn to, government for problem solution; and traditionalistic, where an elite aimed at preserving tradition prevails.

Fuhrman (1989) concluded that reform reflected politics as usual in the states. States that habitually resort to big legislative fixes in education continued to do so, and those packages were crafted in traditional ways, through coalition or consensus politics and strong leadership. States that normally act more incrementally maintained that approach. "The locus of policy initiative among the branches of government was also in keeping with established patterns" (p. 73). Fuhrman based her conclusions on her six-state study of Arizona, California, Florida, Georgia, Minnesota, and Pennsylvania. She expects differences to become marked over time as context and culture have time to be influential.

A traditional way of bringing about reform, consensus politics, and strong leadership was documented in Indiana by Contreras and Medlyn (1989). Consensus around reform was brought about among the various educational actors and groups in Indiana primarily through the vehicle of the Governor's Advisory Committee on Primary and Secondary Education, which was established by the General Assembly. It is interesting, however, that in many states there was marked disagreement over whether or not the reform-generated, policy-development processes allowed for the input of educators and citizens. Multiple truths emerged in some studies. For example, in a Vermont study, Johnston and Proulx (1987) point out that "contemporary epistemological theory contends that knowledge is not a single 'truth' but is rather multiple truths, each depending upon a particular perspective and an imperative to interpret the meaning of events from each perspective" (p. 196). Thus, the authors investigated local and state opinions regarding the Public School Approval Mandate in Vermont. State policy makers believed that the policy-development process that had been used permitted both citizens and educators the opportunity to participate in establishing goals and implementation procedures. Local educational actors, including school administrators, reported having no involvement in the policy making. Results were thus adaptation and pro forma of "trying to force-fit the template of governance based on rationalism." In the terms we have been discussing, it is another reported example of state policy making ignoring the steps in meaningful policy development that would involve all levels of the governance system from the beginning of the process—very different from the South Carolina example of political interaction as described by Timar and Kirp (1988).

State Characteristics

Although the states faced some common problems with reform, specific solutions varied for practical reasons such as the structuring of the school districts in the various states. These vary enormously. Thus, the vehicles for implementation also vary enormously. As can be seen in Table 3.1, the sheer numbers of school children vary greatly from state to state and district to district. The number of school districts varies all the way from the teens (Delaware and Nevada) to over a thousand (California and Texas). Hawaii is a special case as the entire state comprises one school district.

States also differ dramatically in the wealth they are able to put behind a child's education. In Table 3.2, we can see the great difference between a state such as Alaska, with $176,351 gross state product per child in 1986, and a state like Mississippi with a gross state product per child of $54,597. The gross state product (GSP) is the gross market value of the goods and services attributable to labor and property within a state. It can be used to measure the resource base available to a state from which it can raise revenue to provide services.

Uses of Comparative Data

Given the tremendous variety among the states in structure and capacity, there has been resistance to comparison of the states by measures of student outcome. The data is hard to compare as methods

TABLE 3.1 • School System Characteristics

STATE	FALL MEMBERSHIP PUBLIC SCHOOLS (1987)	SCHOOL DISTRICTS Number 1987–88	SCHOOL DISTRICTS Membership Under 1000	SCHOOL DISTRICTS Percent Membership Under 1000	NUMBER OF PUBLIC SCHOOLS 1987–88
Alabama	729,234	129	3	2.3%	1,298
Alaska	105,678	55	42	76.4%	456
Arizona	572,421	240	123 (1)	51.3%	965
Arkansas	437,036	331	223 (1)	67.4%	1,112
California	4,488,398	1,024 (2)	543 (1)	50.1%	7,123
Colorado	560,236	176	107 (1)	60.7%	1,307
Connecticut	465,465	166	55	33.1%	970
Delaware	95,659	19	2	10.5%	167
District of Columbia	86,435	1	0	0.0%	182
Florida	1,664,774	67	1	1.5%	2,379
Georgia	1,110,947	186	12	6.5%	1,724
Hawaii	165,910	1	0	0.0%	231
Idaho	212,444	115	66	57.4%	565
Illinois	1,811,446	982	602 (1)	61.3%	4,220
Indiana	962,653	303	48 (1)	15.8%	1,891
Iowa	480,826	436	332	76.1%	1,633
Kansas	421,112	304	218	71.7%	1,463
Kentucky	642,696	178	34	19.1%	1,399
Louisiana	793,093	66	0	0.0%	1,599
Maine	211,817	200	108 (1)	54.0%	749
Maryland	683,797	24	0	0.0%	1,206
Massachusetts	825,320	396	126 (1)	31.8%	1,795
Michigan	1,606,344	563	171 (1)	30.4%	3,620
Minnesota	721,481	436	286 (1)	65.6%	1,570
Mississippi	505,550	152	10	6.6%	983

Missouri	802,060	545	376	68.9%	2,087
Montana	152,207	550	513 (1)	93.3%	775
Nebraska	268,100	891	824 (1)	92.5%	1,537
Nevada	168,353	17	5	29.4%	305
New Hampshire	163,319	173	108 (1)	62.4%	435
New Jersey	1,092,962	592	306 (1)	51.7%	2,247
New Mexico	287,229	88	49	55.7%	648
New York	2,594,070	722	240 (1)	33.2%	3,971
North Carolina	1,085,976	140	4	2.9%	1,952
North Dakota	119,004	303	289 (1)	95.4%	691
Ohio	1,793,411	703	119 (1)	16.9%	3,743
Oklahoma	584,212	611	499 (1)	81.7%	1,889
Oregon	455,895	304	213 (1)	70.1%	1,214
Pennsylvania	1,668,542	501	40	8.0%	3,313
Rhode Island	134,061	40	9	22.5%	298
South Carolina	614,921	91	6	6.6%	1,103
South Dakota	126,817	194	158 (1)	81.4%	790
Tennessee	823,783	141	15 (1)	10.6%	1,578
Texas	3,236,787	1,063	617	58.0%	5,787
Utah	423,386	40	7	17.5%	725
Vermont	92,755	275	231 (1)	84.0%	333
Virginia	979,417	136	14 (1)	10.3%	1,761
Washington	775,755	296	160	54.1%	1,852
West Virginia	344,236	55	0	0.0%	1,084
Wisconsin	772,363	431	235	54.5%	2,002
Wyoming	98,455	49	23	46.9%	389
U.S. Total	40,021,518	13,267	8,127	61.3%	83,248

Source: Common Core of Data, Public Universe, 1987–88, National Center for Education Statistics, U.S. Department of Education.

Notes: Fall membership figures include Pre-kindergarten enrollment. (1) This figure may vary because some districts did not indicate the size of their enrollment. (2) Number of districts includes some county or intermediate districts that may not operate schools.

TABLE 3.2 • *States Grouped by Wealth*

	State	1986 GSP Per School-Age Child (in millions)
High Relative Wealth	District of Columbia	$316,385
	Alaska	176,351
	Connecticut	128,668
	Massachusetts	120,340
	Nevada	116,323
	New Jersey	116,190
	New York	115,337
	California	109,523
	Wyoming	109,093
	Delaware	101,791
Moderately High Relative Wealth	Virginia	101,121
	New Hampshire	99,027
	Colorado	98,793
	Hawaii	98,571
	Maryland	97,086
	Minnesota	96,216
	Florida	96,174
	Illinois	95,869
	Washington	95,083
	Kansas	93,757
Moderate Relative Wealth	Rhode Island	92,713
	Missouri	88,961
	Pennsylvania	88,505
	Texas	88,358
	Nebraska	87,818
	Vermont	86,360
	Ohio	84,868
	Michigan	84,710
	North Carolina	84,699
	Arizona	84,683
Moderately Low Relative Wealth	Wisconsin	84,160
	Oregon	83,559
	Georgia	82,668
	North Dakota	81,311
	Iowa	80,729
	Oklahoma	78,820
	Maine	78,755
	Louisiana	78,591
	Tennessee	78,362
	Indiana	78,341

Continued

TABLE 3.2 • *Continued*

	State	*1986 GSP Per School-Age Child (in millions)*
Low Relative Wealth	New Mexico	76,385
	Montana	74,620
	Kentucky	71,322
	South Dakota	71,029
	Alabama	67,082
	Arkansas	67,019
	South Carolina	65,582
	West Virginia	63,079
	Idaho	59,058
	Utah	55,703
	Mississippi	54,597
	U.S. Average	$92,854

Source: Council of Chief State School Officers (1988). *State Education Indicators.*

of data collection and definitions of measures vary from state to state. As reported by the CCSSO, "most states have comprehensive programs in place for testing student achievement. But to measure achievement, each state uses a virtually unique combination of tests and testing procedures" (1988a, p. 50).

However, the CCSSO reported in 1988 that states were adopting standard definitions and procedures for counting schools and enrollments. And standard definitions for special groups, such as dropouts, were being pilot tested in 1988. State level achievement data were expected to be available by 1991. In May of 1988, the U.S. Congress passed legislation allowing the National Assessment of Educational Programs (NAEP) to conduct a two-year pilot program to collect state-level data in mathematics in 1990 and mathematics and reading in 1992.

In order to arrive at valid, state comparative data on achievement, the states have had to arrive at consensus on what should be measured, and thus on what are the important measurable outcomes of education. For the states to arrive at such consensus was quite remarkable. As the CCSSO put it, "this is an historical development in our local-state-federal system of education" (1988, p. 50).

There are still those who object to this kind of state-comparative data gathering and others who object to "reducing" educational outcomes to those that can be measured by today's measurement devices. But good policy making depends upon good data. Until states can find out, and use in their policy making, what works in terms of statewide initiatives, future state reform efforts will be of the patchwork quilt variety of the 1980s, and school administrators will continue to be plagued by mismade state policy.

In 1989, the Office for Educational Research and Improvement of the U.S. Department of Education published an account of what the states were then doing in terms of amassing data for accountability. Figures 3.3, 3.4, 3.5, and 3.6 are from OERI (1988). These figures show the kinds of data states collect, the kinds of data on school performance, the number of states reporting performance data, and what the states are doing with their performance data.

FIGURE 3.3

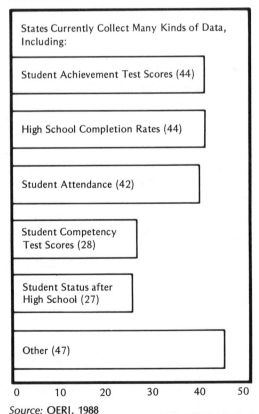

States Currently Collect Many Kinds of Data, Including:

Student Achievement Test Scores (44)

High School Completion Rates (44)

Student Attendance (42)

Student Competency Test Scores (28)

Student Status after High School (27)

Other (47)

0   10   20   30   40   50

Source: OERI, 1988

FIGURE 3.4

Data of School Performance May Include:

Indicators of Results
Graduation/dropout rates
Teacher, student attendance
Student writing samples
Achievement and competency test
    scores
Students' problem-solving skills
Participation in arts and extracur-
    ricular activities
SAT/ACT scores
National Assessment of Educational
    Progress scores
Student status after high school
Employer satisfaction
Progress toward state board goals
Course enrollments (in advanced
    placement, foreign languages, sci-
    ences, arts)

Percentage of students meeting state
university entrance requirements

Indicators about Policy
Amount and value of homework
Class size
Placement in academic tracks
Average teacher salary
Teacher qualifications
Per pupil spending
Implementation of state reforms

Indicators about Context
Community support and wealth
Student characteristics of race,
wealth, language, and parents' education

Source: OERI, 1988

FIGURE 3.5

Forty-three States Make
Performance Data Public.

*Segments show the smallest unit
assessed and the number of states
reporting data about that unit to the
public.*

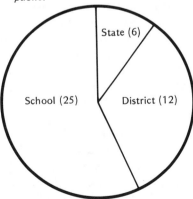

State (6)

School (25)   District (12)

Source: OERI, 1988

FIGURE 3.6

What states are doing with performance data

According to a study by CCSSO, States

Recognize one of the following		46

	Teachers	46
	Students	36
	Schools	33
	Districts	14

Require local improvement planning	14
Allocate funds for remedial programs	9
Intervene in local management	6
Provide financial incentives	5
Withhold funds	5
Waive regulations	2

Source: OERI, 1988

History of State Educational Governance

Early History

The state structures with which school administrators must deal have grown incrementally through a long history. Early in U.S. history, most states provided that common schools were to be established in each town or district, with most of the support coming from local taxes, a practice that led to the strong tradition of local control of schools. As concern for the welfare of the public schools increased, separate structures for their governance were created. At the local level, this led to separating school committees from town councils. At the state level, it led to the creation of the state education agency (Campbell and Mazzoni, 1976). The Board of Regents of the University of the State of New York was established in 1784 and was the first special structure for educational governance at the state level (Cubberly, 1927). At that time, the Regents had jurisdiction only over academies and colleges. Supervision of the public schools was added to their responsibilities in 1904.

Establishment of the State Boards

The most significant move toward establishing a state board of education for the public schools was the creation of the Massachusetts State Board of Education in 1837. The governor, the lieutenant-governor, and eight citizens appointed by the governor for eight-year staggered terms comprised the board. The board was empowered to employ a secretary as executive officer (Cubberly, 1927).

By 1900, thirty-four states had established state boards of education (Keesecker, 1950). Originally, many of these boards were composed completely, or in part, of ex officio members. However, turn-of-the-century reformers called for the separation of education and politics (Wirt and Kirst, 1989). Most states eventually removed all or most ex officio members and provided the state board seats for lay-citizen involvement in educational policy making.

Creation of the Chiefs

The creation of the office of chief state school officer in some cases preceded and in some cases occurred concurrently with the establishment of state boards of education. In 1812, New York was the first state to establish the post of chief state school officer, but the office was displaced for a time. Therefore, the post of superintendent of common schools, established by Michigan in 1829, was the first such state office created that has continued to the present time. Between 1830 and 1850, the office of chief state school officer was established in most states. Today all states have such a chief educational officer.

Twentieth-Century Growth in the State Structure

During the twentieth century there have been many changes in the state governance of education. Forty-nine of the fifty states, all but Wisconsin, have established state boards of education with jurisdiction over elementary and secondary schools. All states have chief state school officers. The number of professional personnel in state education agencies has increased enormously. As late as 1900 there were only 177 professionals in all state departments of education combined (Beach and Gibbs, 1952). From about 1900 to 1930, state departments were primarily engaged in the inspection or enforcement of standards (Beach and Gibbs, 1952). State department staffs, therefore, grew in size because the inspection of practices in local school districts required more state department personnel than did the collection of simple statistics from those districts.

About 1930, state departments of education entered a leadership phase. Campbell and Mazzoni (1976) state that although the extent to which state education agencies have provided leadership in education over the past several decades may be in question, there is no denying the fact that the agencies have taken on additional functions, greatly increasing the size of their professional staffs in the process. Most of the impetus for staff increases came from sources external to the state education agency, such as demands for school finance reform and accountability, thereby increasing the need for more information and better analyses; and federal aid to states for categorical programs, beginning with vocational education in 1917 and rapidly expanding during the 1960s with the passage of the Elementary and Secondary Education Act of 1965. Title V of that act was designed to improve state departments of education and to encourage many departments to do more than they once did in planning, research, and evaluation.

Intermediate-Level Governance

In order to implement state-level policies and facilitate the achievement of state educational goals, many states have created entities that can be called an intermediate-level of educational governance. Many would argue that these intermediate units are merely implementation arms of the state agency and not pertinent to a discussion of state-level policy development. But implementation and evaluation, which are frequently high priorities of these intermediate units, are among the steps in a complete policy-development cycle. From a policy point of view, these intermediate-level structures can be seen as instrumentalities designed for the completion of the policy-development processes. In many cases, these intermediate structures are more accessible to the school administrator for policy-impacting purposes than are the state-level offices.

Do these units make policy? The quick answer would be no, but there is a train of thought that says those who decide where the money goes are making policy decisions. Many of these intermediate units control large sums of money and distribute it, within certain parameters, of course, with wide discretion. As an example, a New York intermediate unit, which served twenty-nine districts, had a budget of $24.7 million in 1983–84 for such services as occupational education, special education, computer education, and teacher administrator training.

Thirty-nine states have some kind of intermediate unit, and their functions have grown from control alone to the providing of services (Campbell, Cunningham, Nystrand, and Usdan, 1985). In some states, such as Illinois, various kinds of intermediate units overlap. As a simplification of the very complex Illinois structure, the Superintendents of the Educational Service Regions have control and monitoring functions, while the newer Educational Service Centers provide services. But the divisions are not clear, the political rivalry is intense, and the Illinois situation at the intermediate level is confused at best. The confusion is intensified by other kinds of intermediate governance structures originating at the local level, such as cooperatives meant for a pooling of services to the member districts. These, of course, take on a political life all their own and further muddy the governance scene in many states.

States that have no intermediate level of governance are mainly those whose operating school districts are already organized on a county-wide basis. The proliferation of numerous small districts seems to lend itself to the further proliferation of confusing intermediate structures. Some intermediate units are governed by a lay board. Others are solely or chiefly in the hands of professional officers, some elected and some appointed. (The reader is referred to Campbell, Cunningham, Nystrand, and Usdan, 1985, for the history and current condition of these structures and a balanced argument as to their existence.)

State Agencies Today

Today, state agencies, certainly in the progressive states, are generally well staffed and ready to provide leadership (First, 1985b). In the early 1960s, state education agencies were perceived to be mismanaged organizations staffed by soon-to-retire school superintendents (Murphy, 1981). This folklore persists in many local districts, demonstrating a lag between perception and reality that is disruptive to the smooth operation of the intergovernmental system.

State agency capabilities today owe much to the long-term effects of the infusion of federal dollars, particularly Title V of the Elementary and Secondary Education Act. The impetus from Title V resulted in modernization, expansion, and improved professional standards. State education agencies have generally become more progressive and their managerial capacity has been markedly improved (Sherman, Kutner, and Small, 1982). This lingering federal influence is an example of our intergovernmental complexities. It is also illustrative of the difficulties inherent in delineating historical stages of influence and development.

In 1981, Chapter V of ESEA was consolidated under Chapter 2 of the Education Consolidation and Improvement Act (ECIA). There was fear that a long-range effect on state education agencies would be a reduction in their capabilities. This has not come to pass. A decade after ECIA, state agencies continue to flourish and their capabilities have been enhanced by other means such as the cooperative efforts of the chiefs through their Council of Chief State School Officers.

State education agencies today serve two major functions. One role is administrative and the other is that of policy formation. Like their histories, the policy-making roles of the state education agency are entwined with the policy-making roles of the state board of education and the chief state school officer. They are exercised through relationships with the governor and the legislature, as well as through actual formulation of policy.

Models of State Governance

Educational decisions made today at the state level fall into at least five general categories: instructional program, certification of personnel, facilities standards, financial support, and nonpublic schools. In addressing these domains, the functions of the state agency include regulatory functions; the direct operation of schools; service, leadership, and planning; research; and development.

The education agencies forced to assume these various responsibilities have evolved on individual timelines in the various states. State education agencies, state boards of education, and chief state school officers can now be grouped into eleven governance models in fifty states.

Table 3.3 shows eleven combinations of appointed and elected boards and chiefs. No particular combination has been connected to better policy making. Model 7, where the governor appoints the state board of education and the board appoints the chief state school officer, and Model 8, where the board is appointed by the governor and the chief is elected in a partisan election, are the most common models used in the states.

The State Boards

As indicated in Table 3.3, the structural arrangements of the state boards vary. In 1988 board members in thirty-three states were appointed by the governor; in twelve states they were elected by the

TABLE 3.3 • *State Governance Models*

MODEL	DESCRIPTION
1	Board elected in partisan election Chief appointed by the board
2	Board elected in non-partisan election Chief appointed in partisan election
3	Board elected in partisan election Chief elected in partisan election
4	Board elected by joint session of the state legislature Chief appointed by the board
5	Board elected by state legislative delegation (plus 1 governor's appointee) Chief elected in partisan election
6	Board elected by local district boards Chief elected in partisan election
7	Board appointed by the governor Chief appointed by the board
8	Board appointed by the governor Chief elected in partisan election
9	Board appointed by the governor Chief appointed by the governor
10	Ex officio board Chief elected in partisan election
11	No state board Chief elected in partisan election

*Models 1, 3, 7, and 8 could be further divided into state boards which have one to three ex officio members and those that have none.

people (in seven states on a partisan ballot), and in four states they acquired office in other ways, elected by the legislature, local districts, or a mixture of state leaders (CCSSO, 1988). The number of board members varies from six to twenty-one and terms of office range from four to eleven years. All state boards of education are responsible for the general supervision of elementary and secondary education and most are additionally charged with the responsibility for vocational education and rehabilitation. A few are responsible for higher education, such as the powerful Board of Regents in New York. The policy leadership functions of state boards of education include strategic planning and goal setting, the creation and operation of policy review cycles, and assessment and reporting on educational quality (NASBE).

The Tasks of a State Board

State boards exist to make education policy. Encompassed within this broad charge are the tasks, jobs, and projects that keep the mechanisms of a state board running. The National Association of State Boards of Education (NASBE) suggests an action plan for state boards in which concentration on the following tasks is encouraged:

1. Creating effective state board members
2. Seeking able leaders
3. Ensuring efficient use of board items
4. Working with state education departments
5. Enlisting constituency group support
6. Developing legislative strategies
7. Communicating with governors
8. Working with local school boards

NASBE further recommends that state boards of education develop a series of three- to five-year policy review cycles covering the seven major state education policy domains: school program accreditation and requirements, school personnel training and certification, student testing and assessment, school governance and organization, curriculum materials development and selection, school finance, and school building and facilities. Each domain should be targeted for review at least eighteen months before the review process begins. The process should consist of a frank, comprehensive public review of current policies and careful consideration of proposed improvements.

A Policy-Making Process

Illinois is an example of a state where the state board of education, shortly after its creation, established a formal policy-making process (Figures 3.7 and 3.8). It has been modified in ensuing years and although in practice it may not be followed in its "pure" form, it is a good example of an attempt at thorough and systematic policy making. It is clearly a formal process leading to policy decisions and it demands that all aspects of education under the state board's authority are systematically addressed. It involves the study of alternative courses of action relative to a particular educational problem and it leads to the eventual adoption of educational policy statements by the Illinois State Board of Education. Note that Figure 3.8 is a further charting of what happens during Step 8 of Figure 3.7.

In Figure 3.8 we see all the actions and activities of the state board itself. The activities of the state agency may be more visible to the administrator in the field, but in terms of policy development, what

FIGURE 3.7 • *SBE Policy Development Process*

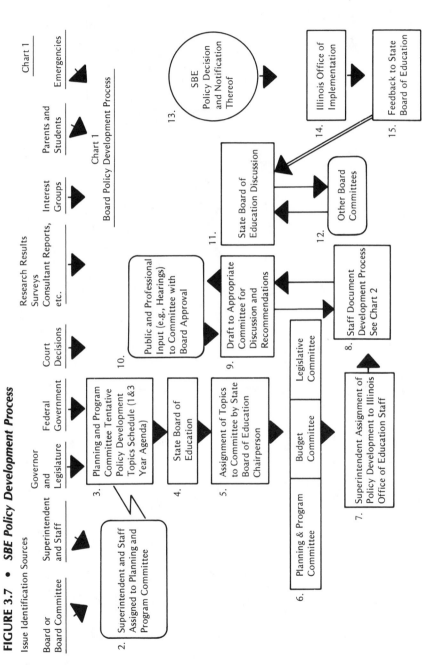

Source: Illinois State Board of Education, "The State Board of Education Policies and Procedures Handbook." Springfield: Illinois Office of Education, Policy Development Process Section, n.d.

FIGURE 3.8 • *Illinois Office of Education Procedures for Policy Development*

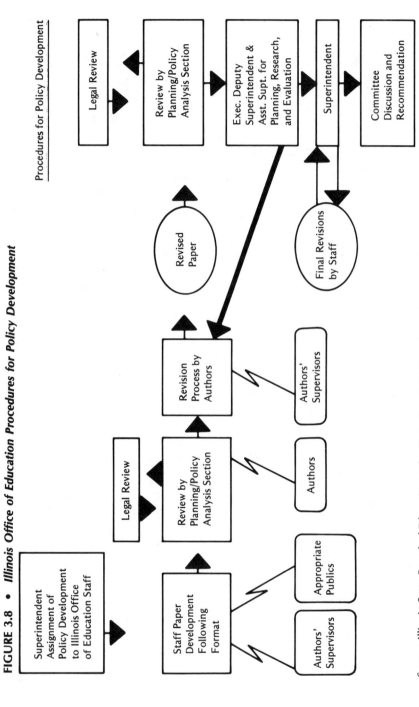

Source: Illinois State Board of Education, "The State Board of Education Policies and Procedures Handbook." Springfield: Illinois Office of Education, Policy Development Process Section, n.d.

the state agency does is only one step in the board's complex policy-development process. A brief explanation of the steps in this process follows (First, 1979).

Step 1: Issue Identification Sources. A key function of the Board Planning and Program Committee was to identify the likely policy issues for board consideration for both a one- and three-year period, thus shaping the content of future board discussion and deliberation. In developing its topic agenda, the committee looked at current and projected issues and needs, as identified by the various school interest groups, both state and national; various studies and surveys done by the state agency, by government agencies, and by university people; recent or possible court decisions; the federal government; rules and regulations existing or under consideration; the governor, the legislature, and their staffs; and the interests and concerns of the board, the board's committees, and the superintendent and the staff of the state agency.

Step 2: Superintendent and Staff Assigned to Planning and Program Committee. The superintendent and the agency staff assigned to the Planning and Program Committee had opportunity for significant input into the committee's tentative schedule of policy-development topics. The time and talents of agency fiscal, program planning, research, and other specialists were heavily used in the development of policy-analysis papers.

Step 3: Planning and Program Committee Tentative Policy Development Topics Schedule. The Planning and Program Committee had the function of identifying and evaluating current and projected policy issues and needs and setting up tentative one- and three-year policy-development agendas. Among the functions of this committee was the development of the agendas—tentative schedules of issues for policy document development and presentation. Some topics were scheduled more than two years in advance of discussion by the state board. Other topics were scheduled so that discussion by the board was to occur half a year or less after the topic was placed on the tentative agendas by the Planning and Program Committee. In emergency situations, some topics received state board discussions and a decision very soon after the topic emerged as an issue needing board action. However, emergency policy decisions should be few if there has been a sound, systematic planning process in developing policy issue agendas. Of course, unexpected issues do arise. All through the 1980s, state boards of education across the country found themselves forced into a responsive, as opposed to a planning, mode as reform reports and legislatures demanded attention.

Step 4: State Board of Education Review. The one- and three-year agendas, the schedules of issues prepared by the Planning and Program Committee, were presented to the full board for its approval subject to discussion and modification. At a regularly scheduled board meeting, the full board votes on approval.

Step 5: Assignment of Topics to Committee by State Board of Education Chairperson. Upon approval of the one- and three-year agendas, the chairperson of the board assigned the various issues to a board committee. Study of an issue by a committee constitutes a strategy-delineation process.

Step 6: Planning and Program Committee, Budget Committee, Legislative Committee. Some topics were assigned to the Budget and Legislative Committees, particularly those topics on the one-year agenda that related to the annual board budget or the board's legislative package. However, the policy-development aspects of these topics could be referred by the Budget and Legislative Committees to the Planning and Program Committee, although such referral did not preclude continuing involvement by these committees in the policy-development aspects of the topic. Board bylaws are the documents that would provide information as to where in the board structure responsibility rests for monitoring the policy-development processes. In this case, such responsibility rested with the Planning and Program Committee.

Step 7: Superintendent Assignment of Policy Development to IOE Staff. The superintendent assigned to members of the agency staff the various topics on the policy-development issues agenda. Background work then began in order to provide the committees in Step 6 with the information necessary to delineate possible strategies.

Step 8: Staff Document Development Process. The internal agency procedures for policy development are outlined in Figure 3.7. As indicated in the figure, the primary responsibility for document development was in the hands of agency staff members assigned by the state superintendent. Such responsibility included literature research, exploration of similar existing programs and policies, consideration of staffing and budget, and legislative needs. Document development involved many sections of the agency as well as internal compromises and negotiations before a document was returned to the board.

Step 9: Draft to Appropriate Committee for Discussion and Recommendations. Upon completion of the internal agency policy-development procedure, the superintendent presented the document to the appropriate board committee for its discussion, deliberation, and recommendations for further action.

Step 10: Public and Professional Input. The committee, with board approval, sometimes held public hearings or otherwise sought public input on the policy topic.

Step 11: State Board of Education Discussion. When the committee handling the topic was satisfied that the topic had had adequate staff work and public input, it presented the paper, with its recommendations, to the board for discussion, deliberation, and decision.

Step 12: Other Board Committees. The board sometimes decided that the topic, because of its budgetary, policy, legislative, or higher education implications, merited review by another committee prior to making its decision.

Step 13: Board Policy Decision and Notification. The board made its policy decision on the topic and appropriately notified the education community and the public. Such notification was done in various ways. Examples are news releases, conferences, and letters from the state superintendent to superintendents of local districts. The policy decision decided upon through this process was a strategy chosen from a pool of possible delineated strategies. Implementation of the strategy chosen was then the responsibility of the state agency.

Step 14: State Agency Implementation. Once a policy decision had been made, that is, the particular strategy was selected from the alternatives, the staff of the state agency had the responsibility for implementing that decision in an appropriate manner, through use of guidelines, technical assistance, hiring and training staff, program development, and development of legislative proposals.

Step 15: Feedback to State Board of Education. The remainder of the process consisted of monitoring, evaluating, and reporting back to the state board.

The preceding description of state board policy development in one state is presented in some detail so that administrators can see the multitude of steps and people involved in such a process. Either formally or informally, a similar process is taking place in every state. If administrators, individually or through their consortia and associations, discover the mechanics of the process and the names of the players, they are more likely to be able to influence educational policy development at the state level.

State Board Policy Development in the 1990s

It used to be said that modern state boards served to insulate education from the dirty world of politics, but the reform decade of the 1980s once again made it obvious that education is just one more resource to be allocated, and that the provision of education is undeniably political. The state boards were intended to ensure lay citizen involvement in educational policy making. "Lay" was intended to mean nonpolitical, but let's look again at how most state board members obtain their seats. Gubernatorial appointment can hardly be called nonpolitical. Neither can membership by partisan election (seven states). Combine this political activity with the equally political mechanisms for obtaining chief state school officers (sixteen elected, ten in partisan elections, seven appointed by the governor, and twenty-seven appointed by the state board) and the myth of nonpolitical lay control of educational policy making at the state level is exposed. Guthrie and Reed comment, "However effective such arrangements have been in providing the public with the illusion that education and politics are separate, it has made for cumbersome governmental arrangements" (1986, p. 36).

Granting the intertwining of the policy-making roles of state boards, chiefs, and state agencies, acknowledging the power of the governors and the legislatures, and granting the complexity of state-level policy making, it does not appear that state boards are major contributors to the governance system. For one year, July 1988 to July 1989, First and Quaglia (in press) read the agendas, minutes, and information packets from state boards of education in four states: Connecticut, Illinois, Maine, and Washington. After reading one year's worth of materials prepared from state boards of education, little evidence was found that meaningful policy making was taking place. Even after allowing leeway for variations and constraints from state to state, it was disappointing to read page after page of what might be called educational trivia.

Among the four boards, there were differences in the completeness and professionalism of the minutes and packets. There were some references to policy-development process, but little evidence of results of these processes. In two of the states, there were reports of goals and objectives for the year, strategic plans as it were, but even these did not rise to the level of far-reaching, creative, or disciplined policy making.

In one of the states, which sets goals for the year, some of the goals concerned educational issues but these were listed along with goals for hosting a convention for the National Association of State Boards of Education (NASBE). Virtually all the goals actually listed by the state school boards were immeasurable and read as mere political jargon. There were many references to NASBE and its meetings, who was to attend, who was to be nominated for this office or that honor, but no evidence that the excellent materials from NASBE on the policy-making capabilities of state boards were being consulted. There was evidence in the minutes of the existence of board committees but their reports most often consisted of lists of which members attended what event and where it had been held.

State board members receive many, many reports (for example, on at-risk students, adult education, and early childhood curricula). While they seem to be flooded with information, the minutes, which are after all the official records of their proceedings, provided little evidence that this flood of information resurfaces in thoughtful policy making. Task forces are created, blue-ribbon committees are recommended, reports are received and transmitted to other communities, and more task forces are created to further study the problem. When one follows the tortuous trails to some conclusions, the matter almost always is referred to state legislatures. This research suggested that state boards may constitute a redundant layer of government. Such matters could probably have gone to these duly elected representatives of the people in the first place, for the underlying research will be done yet again by legislative staffs or consultants brought in for that specific issue.

All four boards were dealing with pretty much the same administrative and regulatory business, giving evidence for Sam Harris's 1973 remark that "the tendency of state boards of education to become too involved in administration and less attentive to, and hence less competent and comprehensive in important legislative and policy-making responsibilities is a problem in many states." When these boards vote, most of the action falls into these categories:

1. Procedural items, such as approval of their minutes, acceptance of financial reports, travel plans, their own rules (making and suspending them), statements of their own activities, board elections, and NASBE activities.
2. Public relations items, such as awards, commendations, thank yous, and correspondence of a ceremonial nature.
3. Personnel functions, such as appointments, transfers, and resignations.

4. Approval of plans, grant applications, regs and more regs (their creation and amendment).
5. Motions for the CSSO to proceed, transmit, investigate, discuss, report back, and so on.
6. Formalization of certification actions.
7. Approval or just acceptance of priorities and plans from various programs in the state department. Varying among the states, these corresponded to specific requirements of state legislation.
8. Adoption of legislative proposals and budget proposals from the chief.
9. And very occasionally, the adoption of something called a policy that is intended to give direction to the schools of the state. The best examples of these are policies evolving around the certification of teachers and administrators.

The reality is that state boards of education today operate under real constraints that prevent their taking active roles in state policy making. Following are some of these constraints:

- Boards have essentially no accepted route to the state's resources.
- While policy determination is explicit, most boards have no legislative powers. State legislatures enact education policies, as the 1980s proved.
- Board members at the state level typically have little influence with either the governor or the legislature as sources of information, advice, and policy. The chief state school officer is more often the person to whom other actors on the educational policy-making scene turn for information.

Are state boards, in fact, making policy for state education systems? Many observers say no. The state board has been characterized as a weak policy actor, primarily because of its inability to hire or remove the chief state school officer, who has major constitutional oversight of state education. However, that inability may be largely due to political realities rather than constitutional or statutory authority. Legally, it is the boards, not the chief state school officers, that have most of the authority for the governance of elementary and secondary education in the states. Only in California is there any marked deviation from the prevailing legal pattern whereby the chief is largely dependent on state board authorization for the power to govern the schools. However, the state board is also often poorly staffed or organized to operate effectively and often lacks political lines to the legislature and the governor. "They seem to wander about in the wilderness while the battle is being fought on a plain somewhere else" (Wirt and Kirst, 1989, p. 287).

Experts question whether state boards of education or the chief state school officers exert more influence in policy-making arenas. Most often it is the chief state school officers and their staffs who formulate board meeting agendas and supply nearly all the information related to agenda items. Judging from the perusal of the agendas from these four states, the chiefs are keeping their boards very busy, but one must question the value or the policy implications of the "busyness." Contributing to the power of the chief is that many board members appear to make little effort to have input on the agenda or to react critically to the material that is presented to them (Campbell and Mazzoni, 1976). What Friedrich (1941) has called the "rule of antici-pated reactions" still operates in state board of education-chief state school officer relationships. What the chief state school officer does in preparing the agenda or developing information is based to some degree on his or her anticipation of what board members want or need. Summerfield (1971) describes the same phenomena as "cuing."

Campbell and Mazzoni did a case study investigation of three issue areas in which state boards of education make policy decisions: certification, school desegregation, and education program improve-ment. In studying the respective policy roles of the boards and chief officers, they found that the basic policy-making functions of initiation, formulation, and support mobilization were largely exercised by the chief state school officers and their staffs. State board of education members sat on policy-oriented committees or task forces and gave formal approval to the major decisions (Campbell and Mazzoni, 1976). Campbell and Mazzoni found it hard to identify many clearcut exam-ples of state boards actively involved in the performance of policy-making functions other than formal legitimation.

It may be helpful, while considering state boards of education, to remember that any group's policy influence is contingent on access to resources that can be drawn upon to command, persuade, or bargain in the course of a decision process. Additionally, it is instructive to re-member again in this context that it is in the legislature that power really lies, no matter how extensive the policy-making authority of a state board may appear.

Influence with the legislature is the critical factor in whether or not state boards of education really set policy. Other factors are the opinions, assertiveness, and knowledge of governors; the power of the interest groups; and the legacies of the 1980s reform movement.

In the late 1960s Sroufe (1971) inferred that "state boards of education, rhetoric to the contrary, have little capability as actors in the education policy system of the state." Campbell and Mazzoni (1976) later reached the same conclusion about education policy making in the ten states they studied. The policy-making role of the ten boards of education were marginal in the legislative arena, and the boards were overshadowed by the chief state school officers in the agency arena. All of the studies mentioned give evidence to contradict the traditionally held perspectives that education policy making is apolitical and operates in a state of considerable autonomy through the efforts of state boards. All the more recent evidence suggests that state boards of education lack policy influence (Wirt and Kirst, 1989).

There is no evidence that at the state level it is the state boards of education either exerting power or "doing more good." As Baltasar Gracian (1647) would phrase it, "Cumbersome, and expensive to operate, state boards may be dinosaurs in the educational policy system." The public is paying a high price for this "illusion," if in fact members of the public take note or care (First and Quaglia, in press). School administrators do take note and do care and thus need to decide whether and how to influence the structure as well as the process.

The Chief State School Officers

In twenty-seven states, the chief state school officer is selected by the state board of education and serves as its executive officer. In the remaining states, the relationship of the chief officer to the state board of education is less well defined and there is more possibility of role confusion (Campbell, Cunningham, Nystrand, and Usdan, 1985). Sixteen chiefs are elected, ten in partisan ballot, and seven are appointed by the governor (CCSSO 1988). As of 1988, in addition to the chief state school officer, New Mexico, Oklahoma, South Dakota, and Virginia also have an appointed secretary of education in the governor's cabinet.

The chief is, of course, the chief executive officer of the state education agency (SEA), a large and complex bureacracy in many states. Who these agencies serve and how well they provide these services are topics of major importance for school administrators.

SEAs and Their "Clients"

Holt (1987) questions the effectiveness of the services SEAs provide to their "major clients, the local school districts." SEAs are frequently criticized in this manner, that is, with the assumption being that the client, or major client, of the state agency is the local district.

However, given the governmental structure, the "real" client of the SEA may be the state legislature. The client is not the local district which is itself also a creation of the legislature. And, if one regards the major client of the SEA to be the legislature, then evaluations of the SEA may look quite different. Of course, there would be variations from state to state and certainly we recognize that the legislature is also often displeased with the SEA in every state, but the SEA in operation considers what the legislature thinks and wants.

To further complicate the matter, the federal government is the primary client of many sections of the SEA. Given the complex intergovernmental system, sections of the SEA are really mini federal bureaus, created to implement and monitor the federal education programs. Funding comes from the federal government, loyalty is to the federal bureau, and indeed the federal level is the client. From this point of view, SEAs are likely to score quite well in an evaluation of their functioning.

Hanson (1980) devised a classification of SEA tasks (management, service, and leadership) based on a study of six states. In the management category are the regulatory functions, the essential jobs prescribed by the state constitution, statute, state board of education rules, federal regulation, and department policy. Some of the specific tasks in this category would include distributing funds, certifying personnel, prescribing curriculum, accrediting schools, operating special programs, evaluating and monitoring performance, and enforcement activities.

In the service category are activities that offer technical assistance. (Notice that there is a lot of overlap here, that is, while in a district doing something regulatory some service can be performed too.) It is important to note here that we are leading into the problem of how to provide this technical assistance without overlap of functions because such overlap can undermine trust and responsiveness. Thus we are leading into the creation of the intermediate level of state educational governance, which may include the county systems, educational service regions, and educational service centers.

Hanson (1980) considered the technical assistance factor the core of the SEA function, but this can be disputed. As was discussed in the section about changing structures, state boards seem to spend what substantive time they do have on regulatory functions. Thus, regulatory functions become a priority for the state agency. In this light, we could probably say that the SEAs should be applauded for managing any technical assistance at all instead of criticizing them so vehemently. What, in the best interests of education and children, they ought to be doing is another question entirely and if technical assistance is the answer to that question, some of the other burdens of the SEAs may need to be shifted.

Within his technical assistance category, Hanson includes planning curriculum development and implementation, evaluation devices and strategies, pupil personnel, and fiscal and administrative concerns.

In the leadership category, Hanson includes new directions and structural and organizational change to bring about new directions. Here again a point can be made that the critics have been too hard on SEAs. An example may be consolidation attempts in Illinois. For many years, bolstered by study after study, Illinois chiefs, agency, and the board attempted consolidation, but there are still nearly a thousand local school districts in Illinois, protected by rhetoric and emotion and legislative threat, despite careful planning and analysis by the state board and the state agency.

SEAs can and do provide real contributions through their planning and research functions, including the policy-analysis function, which other governmental layers within a state cannot do as well. This includes translating educational initiatives and the newest information from research, government, and other states' practical information for school districts in a particular state.

Some of the constraints on the smooth operation of the SEAs are listed here. Fiscal constraints include fluctuating resources from the states, and since the bloc grants, less money is retained by the SEAs because the bloc grants flow almost directly from Washington to local school districts (Holt, 1987). SEAs relied upon federal funding generated from the Elementary and Secondary Education Act (ESEA) of 1965. When the individual title programs, particularly Title IVc and Title V, were incorporated into the bloc grants (ECIA of 1981), the states had difficulty funding some staff positions and activities.

Coordination constraints occur particularly with other state agencies, especially the other human service agencies. (This was the reason for the ex officio members on many state boards of education at the beginning of the century.) Some solutions to coordination problems include umbrella committees with supposedly coordinating functions, task forces for specific tasks, and so on, but this is a constant problem as the services get bogged down in turf wars. (But remember, it happens at every level; at the federal level remember the Drug Czar versus the Attorney General over the strategy in the drug war during 1989.)

In fact, it is almost ludicrous to speak of local school districts as the clients of the SEAs when the most far reaching interventions of both state and local government have been those that corrected long-standing wrongs perpetuated by the local districts: discriminatory actions against minority groups and the poor. In the case of homeless children and their access to schooling, the pattern of LEAs refusing to act in a socially responsible manner until forced to do so by federal and state action continued into the 1990s. "To think that distributive measures could be accomplished without legal rules and pressures, on the basis of exhortation and 'trust' of local educators alone, surely is utopian. But it is also a mistake to dismiss complaints about regulation as unfounded or unimportant" (Kagan, 1986, p. 65).

The states derive their power directly from the people. That power is exercised in the legislature. Agencies such as SEAs are implementation and evaluation arms of the state, created to carry out the wishes of the people as they are expressed through the legislature. Thus, their client is the people through the legislature. The client is not the local school district; the local school district is merely the implementation mechanism of the state. This sounds simplistic and, of course, life is so much more complicated than this, but if we strip away some of the governmental complexities and look at the skeleton of the system, we can get some perspective on the competing arguments regarding the "interference" of the state in local school district affairs. The real operating room for school administrators in state policy making may then be more easily perceived.

Other Actors on the State Educational Scene

The Governors

During the 1980s the growth in the importance of governors in educational policy making can hardly be overestimated. There is no question that a number of governors seized the policy leadership role in education and set new legislative directions in their states.

Adler and Lane (1988) viewed the governor as the most important state policy maker for education and examined the three principal roles of the governor: chief state executive, chief budget officer, and chief opinion leader. The following are examples of gubernatorial powers in each role. As chief executive, the governor may appoint state board members and sign or veto education legislation. As chief budget officer, he or she can exert tremendous power over the budget by setting the tone and priorities, lobbying the legislature, and approving or disapproving annual appropriations for all of education. And, finally, the governor is chief opinion leader, the voice of the people of the state, and as such is able to attract considerable media attention.

In his case study of three Minnesota governors, Mazzoni (1989) summarized factors that impinged upon gubernatorial leadership: the press of other issues, such as economic issues; the availability of state revenues, that is, surpluses made innovation more possible; and the legislative subsystem, the legislators who specialized in education issues.

Mazzoni ended his summary of the case studies by suggesting a number of generalizations about the educational leadership of governors. A governor's leadership is difficult to sustain. Governors perform on a national as well as a statewide stage. Governors now rely on sources of information and opinion other than the traditional education establishment. (Becoming a source of information and opinion for educationally interested governors could be an important goal for administrators operating in their policy-related roles.) A fourth point made by Mazzoni is that "governors have enormous, albeit not exclusive, capacity to shape the state policy agenda for K-12 reform" (p. 89). Finally, in education as in other arenas, the governor must be willing to take risks to be successful.

We saw the governors performing on the national education stage in the fall of 1989 when President Bush called his Education Summit and met with the governors in Charlottesville, Virginia. That summit and the resultant National Education Goals, which were released in February 1990, are discussed in Section Two.

The State Legislature

All through the 1980s, state legislatures packaged combinations of educational reform initiatives. Reactions to this activity were mixed. In some states reform was welcomed, but in others it was resented and resisted. When the legislature is active in an area, it uses three basic legislative control mechanisms: resource allocation, rule making, and ideology articulation. These control mechanisms interact with structural arrangements, decision-making processes, and work orientations to determine the impact of any legislative policy within a school district (Mitchell and Iannaccone, 1980). During the 1980s we saw much (some say too much) legislative rule making applied to education.

The state legislatures have not often been so active in educational affairs. The legislature is the general government, and usually education is more or less left in the hands of the special educational governance structures.

General versus Special Government. The roles of the state-level policy makers are still evolving. Administrative control of education has cycled from direct control by the general government, that is, the legislature of a state, to control released by the legislature to an established special government, that is, a state education agency; and through the 1980s to an era where control was retrieved by the general government, although the structures of special government were left in place and the players remained on the scene in varying stages of influence.

This flurry of action in the state legislatures in the 1980s can be explained as a return to control of educational policy making by the general government. (For a discussion of general versus special government in educational policy making, see Campbell, Cunningham, Nystrand, and Usdan, 1985). In brief, the legislature is the general government and over time, in order to carry on the myriad functions of state government, the various legislatures have created entities to attend to specific functions. The state board of education and the chief state school officer are examples of special government entities that are empowered to handle the education arena. The point is that general government can pull back power from the created special government when the need or whim arises; in the direct involvement in educational policy by the various state legislatures in the 1980s we saw such a pull back. To capture the attention of special government, it was called by some the "window of opportunity," but most school administrators observed the phenomenon with far less enthusiasm, as the attention resulted in more mandates than money.

After the highly publicized and complex reform era of the 1980s the furor over educational issues in state legislatures naturally waned. Education had captured the attention of the state legislators far longer than most would have predicted, as it was, and other issues demanded the bulk of legislators' attention. As the decade closed, concern for the environment was on everyone's mind, the Supreme Court had thrown the abortion controversy back to the states, and civil rights was again a hot item on the public agenda due to Supreme Court decisions during the spring and summer of 1989. It looked as if the success or failure of the reform movement, its implementation and evaluation, were back in the hands of special governments, squarely on the shoulders of the state education agencies. And then, in the fall of 1989, President Bush called the Education Summit and the spotlight shone again on educational reform.

Other State Agencies

It is important to remember that state agencies other than the specifically designated education agencies have some control over various aspects of the education system. In most states, these would include some variation on the following list:

1. Auditor of Public Accounts–apportions state school funds
2. Department of Children and Family Services–oversees child abuse legislation
3. Attorney General–may give legal opinions on educational questions
4. State Teachers' Certification Board–administers the teacher certification function
5. Department of Labor–exercises some control over the employment of minors
6. Board of Trustees of the Retirement Fund–administers the teachers' retirement program
7. Scholarship Commission–awards scholarships to high school graduates
8. School Building Commission–allocates state funds to "needy" school districts for school building purposes.

Because of the proliferation of agencies with often overlapping functions, there has been great emphasis for many years on fostering coordination among agencies serving the same populations. However, little success has been reported with this seemingly desirable technique. "The activity of coordination is itself fraught with peril. Amid all the attempts and all the species of coordinating mechanisms, this message is clear. Many devices are tried, but few human service programs designed to do so ever result in more coordination" (Weiss, 1981, p. 24).

Education Stakeholders

A broad array of educational interest groups affect the policy-making process at the state level. Their numbers grow as educational specialties grow. There are administrators' organizations, teachers' organizations, organizations for the leadership of various special population groups, organizations of subject matter and curricular specialists, and subgroups of all the above. Which ones are truly influential and when is a powerful question.

In a six-state study, Marshall, Mitchell, and Wirt (1990) clustered state policy players into Insiders, Near Circle, Far Circle, Sometime Players, and Other Forgotten Players. It may come as a shock to school administrators to hear that the school board association and the state administrator group are in the cluster called Sometimes Players. We tend to think of our own associations as quite powerful, or at least we cling to a hope that they are. Legislators were found in the Inside Circle. The chief state school officer, teacher organizations, the governor and the governor's staff, and the legislative staff were found in the Near Circle. State boards of education were in the Far Circle and the school board and state administrator associations were classified as Sometimes Players. There were Other Forgotten Players such as the courts, educational research organizations, and producers of education materials. Here is another arena in which the administrator acting in his or her policy-related role can try to make a difference by restoring the respect, influence, and activity level of administrator organizations in the state policy-making processes.

Since the rise of the teacher unions, the grouping of kinds of administrators into professional associations separate from teachers and from each other, the education "community" has been fragmented in policy making and in the support or nonsupport of various legislative initiatives. This has been seen by legislators as justification for legislative initiatives since even the educators apparently cannot agree on what is good for education. In some states, the state agency has acted in a leadership role in leading the various interest groups to common action on some reform measures. An example was in Illinois in 1985 when leadership from the state department led to a massive reform package supported by the major groups. This kind of leadership is a natural for the state agencies. In the ideal policy-making arena, the agency would have the broad and interest-free state perspective that the other groups lacked. But to wish for the ideal is naive. Today's school administrator must be an effective operator within the policy-making world that really exists.

A wide variety of political, economic, and social forces were responsible for shifting the initiative in education policy formation away from local and federal actors to state-level policy systems during the 1980s (Mitchell and Encarnation, 1984). These forces included the need for more money for education, the demand for accountability, growing teacher power and the deliberate decrease in the federal role which was debated during the Nixon and Carter years and swiftly implemented during the Reagan years. As the 1990s opened, the problems of the state reform packages that had been passed with little or no analysis were becoming evident.

Governors were still directly involved in educational policy making and legislators were still seeking quick solutions to problems in schooling. As the 1990s opened, school finance forumlas were once again being challenged and choice was on the legislative agenda in a surprising number of states. Amidst the dangers of more inappropriate measures being passed into law, there was a leadership vacuum that state education agencies in the progressive states were ready to fill.

Those with strong departments of planning, research, and evaluation were staffed with professionals whose expertise and leadership are critically needed to guide further educational reform.

Nevertheless, school administrators cannot forget that through constitutional and statutory language, court interpretations and long practice make it clear that the legislature of each state is the most powerful educational policy maker, the "big school board."

Contributions

In the first contribution, Louis Miron illustrates administrator leadership in affecting school-level policy decisions with analysis of a challenge to the Louisiana school finance formula. The case demonstrates the importance of coalition building and national networking in order to meaningfully impact state policy making.

In the next piece Gordon Donaldson also discusses the building of a coalition—a coalition of administrators' associations, preparation programs, the state board and state educator agency—which seeks to improve the principalship in Maine. It is an example of administrators leading in policy initiatives to improve their own profession and impact schools and children's lives in a positive way. With the publication of its "Open Letter," this coalition began to influence state policy processes.

In the next contribution, we learn the story of a controversial state policy initiative from the state administrator who was responsible for the implementation. Sally Bulkley Pancrazio explains the roles of the policy-making participants and the reaction of school practitioners to the introduction of the Illinois Report Card. Note that when this controversial measure was first suggested by the governor, there was "little public response." It illustrates the need for administrators to respond quickly if they wish to influence state policy making.

Russ Quaglia explains in the next selection how a state reform policy was quickly developed in the aftermath of *A Nation at Risk*. A significant change in the Maine Administrator Certification law took place quickly, without sufficient reference to the accumulated literature on the subject or the evaluation of pilot sites.

Caroline Cody presents an analysis of textbook policy, how it is made, and how influential the textbook industry has become in making and influencing policy choices in the schools.

Finally, James Meza takes us through the state policy-making process by illustrating how an important reform measure in Louisiana was handled by the policy-related actors influential in the process.

LOUIS F. MIRON

Impact of School Leadership on State Policy

School administrators often assume what Henry Levin calls a role of "policy compliance." That is, they often take a structural position on leadership, one that attributes the school leader with the legal authority to implement educational policy or to enforce policy decisions set forth by the state.

Such a structural view of school leadership becomes problematic when schools need internal professional support for change or parental and community support to fulfill school goals and objectives. Particularly troubling is the fiscal condition characteristic of financially strapped urban school districts, a situation in which urban school administrators often find themselves. Here, a broader definition of school leader must prevail if the school site administrator is to be successful in finding the financial and human resources to effectively implement either state policy decisions (e.g., curriculum mandates) or school-level educational policy.

School Leadership in Action

The potential to influence state-level educational policy may be illustrated by the case in Louisiana in which a coalition of legal experts, school-site administrators, and the local school board and its administrative staff have mounted a challenge to the state finance formula (the Minimum Foundation Formula) which, according to consultants recently hired by the State Board of Elementary and Secondary Education, has historically discriminated against large urban school districts that lack the tax base to support the at-risk populations they serve.

The Data

This coalition in New Orleans followed the lead of successful court challenges in the states of Kentucky, Texas, and Montana by first assembling the massive amounts of data and information to support the legal claim that the state of Louisiana (namely, the Legislature, the State Department of Education, and the state's governing board) had not lived up to their constitutional responsibilities to deliver a minimally adequate level of public elementary and secondary education. The group (which had only marginally relied on the "legal authority" figures in the school district) could point to any educational measure (achievement levels, dropout figures, teacher pay) and categorically conclude, as did the courts in those other states, that Louisiana as a state fared very poorly when compared to the rest of the nation. Moreover, the levels of inequality of educational outcomes in large urban school districts were such that the life chances of blacks and other minorities in cities such as New Orleans, Baton Rouge, and Shreveport were slim.

The Strategy

This coalition of education activists/leaders realized that it would need to extend the concept of the school community to include members of neighborhoods and community organizations if it were to be successful in securing the prerequisite public support to mount a successful legal challenge in state supreme court. It set out immediately, therefore, to enlist the support of both local and national civic and public interest organizations. First, locally it requested that the superintendent's office schedule briefings with major and minor community-based organizations, especially those representative of the low-income minority students enrolled in the school district. These locally based community organizations included the Urban League, NAACP, Parents Community Alliance, United Teachers of New Orleans (the teachers' union), and others. Nationally, the group sought the advice and counsel of the American Civil Liberties Union, the Lawyers' Committee for Civil Rights, and some established law firms in Washington, D. C. and New York City.

It was the informal policy of the working group in New Orleans that no national organization, whether working pro bono or for a contractual fee, would dictate to the local group the tactics it should take. This attitude was shared by the representatives of the national organizations who made several voluntary trips at their own expense to gauge the depth of public interest and the quality of the case that was being assembled in New Orleans. Thus, a mutual feeling of respect between "leader" and "follower" cemented a unity of purpose so essential to change.

Policy Impact

Working in concert with the Orleans Parish School District, the coalition was successful in obtaining the support of area legislators to change the Minimum Foundation Formula to reflect the needs of urban school districts in Louisiana. The threat of litigation (which has resulted in substantial change in the funding formulas in the states of Kentucky, Montana, and New Jersey) caused the State Department of Education and the state governing board over elementary and secondary education to propose changes in the formula that were to be presented to the legislature in the April 1991 legislative session.

Perhaps most significant, in addition to the prospects of altering education policy in Louisiana through a change in finance strategies, is the heightened public awareness of the dire needs of "property poor" urban school districts with their unique role in educating large numbers of at-risk students. Prior to the work of this coalition (whose work was supported by many school-site administrators, teachers, and parents), little attention was paid by policy makers and the news media to the plight of large urban school districts in the state.

Regardless of which, if any, of the proposed changes in the funding formula the legislature ultimately approves, the informational value of articulating the current inequities in the formula has been substantial.

Summary

When school administrators adopt a concept of leadership that extends beyond the legal authority figures in the school, the potential to achieve substantial change in educational policy is significant. Indeed, principals, assistant principals, and others with a formal legal role in the administration of the school should have no fear of allowing teachers, parents, community members, and, yes, even students, a leadership role. To embrace such a model of leadership at the school level will likely unify the school and its surrounding community in achieving its purpose and goals. This contribution has illustrated the processes school leaders may follow in seeking to change educational policy at the state level. Although there are several models upon which to draw, the central tenet remains clear: The school administrator should embrace a concept of leadership that gives a pivotal role to "followers" as well as to formal leaders. Leadership style is also important when the goal is to have school-level administrators make an impact on state education policy. A style fundamentally receptive to change within the confines of the internal school community is much more likely to influence the community outside the school, thus making it possible to garner community and public support for new state education policy.

GORDON A. DONALDSON, JR.

Evolution of "An Open Letter"

In the fall of 1989, Maine educators and policy makers were surprised by the statewide circulation of an "An Open Letter Concerning the Revitalization of School Leadership in Maine." Unsolicited statements of consensus among school administrator groups are rare events in Maine. Few public initiatives have emerged from such groups, let alone focused on their collective future needs and purposes. Moreover, the composition, publication, and circulation of the letter were accomplished collaboratively; consensus was not only articulated in the letter but demonstrated in the work of issuing it and following it with other initiatives.

How did an ad hoc group of administrator leaders form and by what chemistry was it moved to action? The convergence of often disparate groups—elementary and secondary principals, vocational school directors, university personnel, and state department of education and board of education representatives—around concerns for the school principal was the product of several developments in Maine. Since 1979, when Maine had been the second state in the nation to begin a professional development academy specifically for principals, awareness of the need to rethink principals' performance and training had grown. The Maine Principals' Academy was jointly sponsored by the state's elementary and secondary principals' associations, the Maine Department of Educational and Cultural Services, and the University of Maine System. The presence of the academy during the 1980s focused concern in each of these parent bodies for innovative training systems, professional development practices, and support mechanisms.

Within this climate, it was the accidental availability of funds that led eventually to "An Open Letter." Two members of the Principals' academy board of directors obtained a grant to run an intensive seminar on interpersonal skill development for principals as a follow-up academy experience. When they were unable to attract enough participants, they found themselves in the unusual predicament of having funding for a program that they could not float.

After consulting numerous leaders, they decided to use the grant to foster open thinking about the condition of the principalship in Maine and its prospects for improvement in the ensuing five to ten years. The money, that is, was to be used simply to assemble individuals who had a stake in building leadership in Maine's schools and whose institutional bases might play a part in carrying new thinking forward into new practices. Importantly, the state department of education grant administrator supported the notion of paying to bring people together, to stimulate their thinking, and to give them time to develop consensus around a common vision.

Since the spring of 1989, the group continued to meet and to work in two arenas: reinforcing changes in the programs and practices of constituent institutions and stepping up political pressure on elected bodies to recognize the need for greater support and innovation for school leadership positions. The group is still an ad hoc group—it has no permanent location or budget, but it now has adopted a name: the Forum for the Emerging Maine Principal. The forum's Purposes and Procedures include coordination of existing professional development for principals, expansion of professional development opportunities for principals, review of principal preparation programs at the University of Maine and the University of Southern Maine, the communication and integration of appropriate elements of the emerging principal model in on-going activities of principal groups, and the exploration of partnerships with other organizations, private and public, that have relevant training expertise for middle managers. In Figures 3.9 and 3.10, An Open Letter Concerning the Revitalization of School Leadership in Maine and the Purposes and Procedures of the Forum for the Emerging Maine Principal are displayed.

The group gathered three times in a retreat format at Tenants Harbor, Maine. Most of its members were, by design, school principals. With the assistance of a facilitator hired for the purpose, the group explored individual and institutional interests in assisting school leader development. Differences among institutional interests and among individuals were apparent, but of greater impact were the similarities, and particularly the wide agreement that the reform era had forced principals and vocational directors into increasingly untenable roles. Through extensive discussion, shared readings, and survey data about Maine principals' views of their jobs, the group was able to move beyond the current ills of school leaders to create a common profile of the "emerging Maine principal" and to explore ways to support principals in transition to this emerging model.

The Open Letter was only one product of the group's work. At its third and final "funded" meeting, participants drew up a long-term strategy for raising awareness of school leaders' needs both as professionals and as people. Further, the constituent institutions vowed to take action: The professional associations would alter their professional development strategies; the University would review its master's degree program and reformulate courses; and the state department would pursue legislative initiatives to support greater professional development activity for principals and vocational directors.

FIGURE 3.9 • *An Open Letter Concerning the Revitalization of School Leadership in Maine*

The school you attended as a child is gone. In its place is a complex social service agency whose purpose is not only to educate children, but also to nurture their physical, emotional, and social growth. The Education Reform Act of 1984, the need to educate young people to compete in a rapidly changing global economy, and the diminished role of the extended family, church, and community in the lives of children are but a few factors which have greatly altered the mission of the school.

The school principal you remember is gone. Today's principals do far more than discipline students and ring the bells; they need knowledge and skills in areas their predecessors never had to think much about. In addition to the "traditional" duties of managing and leading school programs, building, staff, students, and budgets, today's principal must serve as:

- an Articulate Advocate for Education
- an Instructional Leader
- A School Law Expert
- A Change Agent
- a Facilitator
- a Collaborator
- a Planner
- a Negotiator
- an Enabler
- a Visionary

In order to meet these challenges, principals must develop and maintain balance in their personal and professional lives.

Maine's schools of the 90's will successfully meet the challenge of higher community expectations only if they are led by strong principals. The effective schools research points to the building principal as the person most crucial to the school's success. When asked what one thing could be done to improve schools today, former Assistant Secretary of Education Chester E. Finn, Jr., said he would "hire the best principal I could find and give that person ample authority and heavy responsibility." Clearly, meaningful improvement in Maine schools cannot and will not happen without the full involvement and commitment of the building principal.

But in Maine, policy makers have focused no attention on the changing needs of school principals in this age of reform. 252 of today's principals (44%) will be retiring or leaving the profession by the year 1992. According to the Administrator Supply and Demand Report prepared by DECS in 1988, school systems around the state, especially in rural communities, report few applicants for advertised vacancies. Many of the principals who do remain will need their professional development refocused if they are to successfully lead Maine schools into the future.

Your role in preparing principals for the 90's is crucial. A consortium of concerned educators and citizens urges your action and support for a refocus of principals' professional development for the coming decade. The Governor, the Commissioner, DECS, the Maine Association of Vocational Administrators, the Maine Elementary Principals Association, the Maine School Boards Association, the Maine School Superintendents Association, the Maine Secondary School Principals' Association, the State Legislature, and the University of Maine System must heed the alarm. Only by re-tooling the pre-service and the in-service training of principals will Maine schools—and the youngsters they serve—successfully meet the challenges of the coming decade.■

FIGURE 3.10 • *Forum for the Emerging Maine Principal*
Purpose and Procedures

The Forum is a confederation of associations, institutions, and individuals committed to expanding and improving the professional development of Maine school principals, assistant principals, and vocational education directors.

The Forum combines the energies, ideas, and capabilities of its members to plan and coordinate professional development activities for Maine school site leaders. The Forum thus permits members to deliver services that are both complementary to one another and, through joint planning, purposefully to relate services to common models of the changing Maine principalship or directorship.

Membership in May, 1989 was drawn from the following organizations: Maine Elementary Principals Association, Maine Secondary School Principals Association, Maine Principal's Academy, Maine Association of Vocational Education Administrators, Maine Department of Educational and Cultural Services, University of Maine, University of Southern Maine, Maine Leadership Consortium, Maine State Board of Education. Other members whose purposes comply with the purposes of the Forum are always welcome.

A majority of Forum member representatives are practicing Maine principals, assistant principals, or vocational education directors. Meetings are called when needed by circulating an invitation to all representatives and obtaining attendance of a majority of member representatives. A Forum Meeting may designate committees to perform functions between Meetings. Accounts of its activities are circulated to member representatives following meetings.

SALLY BULKLEY PANCRAZIO

State Policy Initiative:
The Case of the Illinois School
Report Card

Content

Public clamor concerning the quality of student performance and achievement led state policy makers to extend their sphere of influence during the 1980s. As a result, the state's role in regulating and monitoring its public schools was clearly strengthened.

Accountability emerged as a predominant theme across state legislatures as education leaders asked for more state financial resources in response to legislated reform. State legislators, in turn, asked school administrators to provide information to the public on how well the schools were performing. In order to obtain support for the necessary increases in state funding, legislators, taxpayers, and business and industry spokespersons asked as a condition of support that educators become more accountable for meeting their expectations for schooling, primarily student learning.

While accountability has several different meanings, the primary connotation given to accountability began to mean that fair return has been given to the public for the value given. One way in which fair return can be measured is by providing the public with information about the service it receives.

Several assumptions underlie the importance of making information available to the public about the performance of public services in general: The public has the right to know how institutions using public money are performing; having such information contributes to the public making more informed decisions; and through public disclosure, tax-supported services will be motivated to improve their services.

For school personnel, this means that the public expects to receive information about how well students do on achievement measures. Accountability may mean providing other information about other outcomes, but measures of student learning must be included. It is believed that if the public has information about how the schools are doing, the public will engage in behavior that ultimately leads to improving the education system.

The Illinois Response to School Accountability

On February 25, 1985, then Governor James R. Thompson (Republican), in an unprecedented state-of-the-state address on education, introduced the school report card concept for Illinois schools as part of his proposed Illinois Better School program. His proposal identified a set of data he wanted to see on report cards from school districts, including student test scores, graduation rates, and dropout data. There was little public response to his proposal.

During this same period, the Illinois Commission for the Improvement of Elementary and Secondary Schools, a group of twelve legislators from the Illinois House and Senate and eight lay members formed by a Senate resolution, proposed a series of reform proposals. The proposals emerged from the results of a comprehensive study of educational mandates conducted by the Illinois State Board of Education, under the supervision of Nelson F. Ashline, Executive Deputy Superintendent and the testimony from public hearings that the commission conducted around the state. While the commission's report made no reference to school report cards, its more than 100 recommendations became the nucleus for the package of education legislation considered by the Illinois General Assembly in spring 1986. Other education groups, such as the teachers' unions, introduced legislative proposals containing their versions of educational reform.

In the waning days of the legislative session scheduled to end July 1, 1985, Governor Thompson called on the leaders of the House and Senate, the newly appointed Illinois State Superintendent, Ted Sanders (now Deputy Secretary, U. S. Department of Education), and others to engage in a summit to reach consensus on a proposed Education Reform Act. At the point of agreement by all summit partners, the Senate Republicans threatened to withdraw support on the nearly 170 provisions comprising the act unless information about schooling was released at select periods of time. To do otherwise would have resulted in all information being required for all grades.

The law also required information on indicators that suggested the extent to which resources, human and fiscal, were being expended on schools for a given period of time. These included pupil-teacher ratio, pupil-administrator ratio, operating expenditure per pupil, per capita tuition charge, district expenditure by fund in graphic display, average administrator salary, and average teacher salary. For the most part, these indicators were reported at the district level rather than at the school level.

Indicators characterizing the achievement or performance of students included composite and subtest means for college-bound students (for Illinois students, this requirement essentially meant ACT scores for the graduating students in a particular year), and percentage of students placing in the top and bottom quarters of nationally normed achievement tests. The reason for this last data element was that Illinois schools use a variety of tests to assess achievement (some out of print, some with norms a dozen or so years old) and this method provided the only appropriate way to display and compare the data across schools and across tests. State staff interpreted the requirement to refer to tests at only grades three, six, eight, and eleven as those points were identified for future state testing in another piece of legislation.

Other information that helped identify the school was added: the name of the school and school district, statistics regarding the composition of the school, and information regarding the teachers in the district (years of experience and degree status), for example.

Most of the required data were already collected by and available in the state agency, leaving approximately 25 percent of the required statistical indicators to be collected as new information. School officials were given the opportunity to verify their school data before the cards were released. Because of the review process and the scrutiny by the public of the information, the state staff believe that the accuracy of the state data bases has been improved markedly.

Procedures Taken to Implement the School Report Card Requirement

A broad-based advisory group of representatives of various special interest groups was established by the state superintendent to advise the staff on the definitions of the indicators, other information to be reported on the cards, procedures for collecting and reporting the information, and guidance for managing the public and media upon release of the first cards.

Groups represented on the Report Card Advisory Council were: School Boards Association, State Chamber of Commerce, Association of School Administrators, Farm Bureau, Principals Association, Association of School Public Relations, the state affiliates of the AFT and NEA, Taxpayers' Federation, Chicago Public Schools, Parent/Teacher Association, Designs for Change (an advocacy group based in Chicago), and researchers with special expertise in school finance and educational equity. State staff coordinated the meetings of the advisory council.

There was rarely consensus among the various constituencies on the advisory council. Arguments regarding the potential use or harm from the school report cards, or additional information, or the use to which such information would be put generally resulted in the emergence of two camps: the education establishment (which included the PTA) and the community groups (which included businesses, taxpayers, and advocacy groups). The community camp argued for more information. The education camp argued for less. The former argued for strict compliance with the law and the addition of sanctions for any school official found manipulating or changing the information on the printed card. The education camp argued that the law would hurt schools and should be changed. Its position was if the law couldn't be changed, then the impact should be minimized as much as possible by complying with a strict and narrow interpretation of the law.

Working out the technical definitions and the statistical formulas was the responsibility of the state staff. For the most part, the operational definitions of the data elements were the same or similar to ones already being used in the agency. Definitions such as "graduation rate" and "percent of college preparatory students" had particular technical and political ramifications and were changed several times, depending on the reaction of one group, then another.

The Media

The Illinois law required that the school district release its school report cards to a newspaper of "general circulation." The state staff defined this as a daily newspaper serving the geographic area in which the school was located in order to enhance the probability of the information being circulated over a wide area in a timely fashion (as opposed to being distributed in a monthly newspaper).

State staff, including public relations staff, held regional meetings with representatives of Illinois newspapers, television, and radio to prepare them for the release of the information. The major concern was that the media would use test scores only, generalize beyond the information provided, or would not put the information in context. Therefore, emphasis was given to the importance of looking at the composition of the school, the resources being provided to it, and the performance of the students. The limitations of the data and the definitions were also emphasized in these meetings.

The press coverage on Illinois was unprecedented in its volume the first year the cards were released. Never before had so much information been available to the public on Illinois schools. Many school superintendents used the opportunity to showcase good programs or identify needs in their districts. Some superintendents denigrated the requirement to have to make the information public or blamed state staff for making errors and taking too long to print the cards.

Newspapers were the primary users of the information. A state agency survey of Illinois district superintendents following the first year of the release, with a response rate of 92 percent, showed that 93 percent of the respondents said that their newspapers had reported their school report card information, followed by radio (24 percent), and television (6 percent). Apparently, the advance work with the media was successful. A surprising 80 percent of the superintendents said the media reported accurate information for their schools and 75 percent said the reporting was fair.

Counselors and school administrators objected to the media listing ranks of high schools by ACT scores, however, even when contextual information was provided. While the media tended to place the test results next to the proportion of students who came from low-income families or along with an indicator of district wealth, many school officials thought such ranking procedures to be unfair to the public relation's image of their school or district.

Opposition by the Education Establishment to the School Report Cards

The education establishment was united in its opposition to the requirements to disseminate a school report card. The Education Reform Act had 169 separate provisions including a statement that established the primary purposes of schooling; identified the primary role of the principal (instructional leadership); required studies for school consolidation; mandated state assessment in reading, mathematics, and language arts; provided the option for full-day kindergarten; and established a new state program for educational services to children aged three and four found to be at risk of educational failure. The three provisions that generated the most controversy were consolidation, required criminal checks for teachers, and the school report card. (The requirement for consolidation studies was dropped about a year later under extreme political pressure to the general assembly by community members.)

Organizations opposing the requirement for school districts to disseminate information about each of their schools included all the major educational lobbying groups (with the exception of special education lobbyists, a highly vocal group in Illinois): Association for School Administrators, Association for School Boards, the two major teachers' unions, a lobbying group for affluent school districts in the northern part of the state called ED-RED, and a lobbying group for large, unit school districts, LUDA.

A new state representative from northern Illinois was urged by lobbying groups to introduce legislation to change the requirement to a card with district data instead of school data. The Illinois House Elementary and Secondary Education Committee heard the bill in June 1986. The governor did a "fly-around" to various parts of the state and publicly expressed his opposition to "watering down" the accountability requirement.

The only education group testifying in support of the school report cards (and opposing any change to the original language of the bill) was the State Board of Education. Groups similarly testifying included the Farm Bureau, State Chamber of Commerce, the Taxpayers' Association. The Chicago-based advocacy group, Designs for Change, wired its opposition to the proposed change in requirement. (State staff had called representatives of these groups prior to the hearing to inform them of the proposed changes and urged them to testify if they wished the legislature to consider their views. They did.)

The Arguments

Anti-School Report Cards

The arguments of the bill's sponsor to change the cards from school reports to district reports focused on the "negative effects associated with pitting one school against another." Curiously, he emphasized the point that since about half of Illinois' school districts were one-school districts (a true statement, even though the Chicago school system has nearly 600 schools), the district, not the school, should be required to report on its performance.

Arguments from the education groups supporting changes in the report card focused on several themes:

- We are already releasing this information in our annual reports. A mandate is not necessary.
- Schools are so different that they can't be compared with each other. It's like comparing "apples to oranges." Publicizing this information will destroy our schools.
- There are problems more important in education than accountability, like funding.

- People in the schools will cheat and manipulate the data to make the schools look good. The data won't mean anything.
- Test scores don't measure every important component. The effects of parenting, self-esteem, and motivation won't get included.
- Parents won't understand the school report card. All they care about is how their child is doing, not the school.
- Parents will want to select their child's school on the basis of the school's test scores or other noneducation reasons.
- Some of our best teachers are in the worst schools and the cards won't show their efforts.
- Our kids are dumber than the kids in the suburban schools. Our schools are going to look bad because the kids aren't as smart.
- Our kids are poorer than the kids in the suburban schools. Our schools are going to look bad because their families aren't as wealthy.
- Families in the suburban schools expect their kids to do well in school. Expectations aren't so high in my community. It isn't the school's fault, yet we'll be blamed.
- We tell our parents that all of our schools are good. Now, with the school report cards, the people will think we lied to them.

Probably the most frequently heard argument against school report cards was that the data permitted comparisons, indeed, encouraged comparisons, from school to school. (Prior to this time, only the Chicago Board of Education regularly released the results of its testing program by school.) Conventional wisdom held that certain suburban schools in northern Illinois (e.g., New Trier High School in Wilmette or Deerfield High School in Deerfield) were the state's "best high schools" on academic grounds but there were no uniform or standard data on which to make such a claim. The notion of "best high schools" on athletic grounds, of course, had some empirical basis if one accepted the results of athletics tournaments and win-loss-tie records as measures of performance.

The issue of comparisons had other dimensions. Many district superintendents said that they wanted their schools to be compared only with themselves, that is, the school report cards should contain data only about their schools over several periods of time. Since the Reform Act called for state assessments in reading, mathematics, and language arts in grades three, six, eight, and ten (later changed to eleven), it was difficult to reconcile the cross sectional nature of the requirement with the longitudinal methodology requested by local officials. Conflicts and political tensions about the purposes of state testing and how the results should be reported remain today.

Pro-School Report Cards

Citizen groups, taxpayers, and community activist and business groups—those who tend to take an oversight or monitoring role for schools and educational costs—argued for more information about how schools and school children were doing. The central themes in their arguments were:

- Given the amount of public tax dollars spent by the schools, the public has the right to know how its schools are doing.
- It is necessary to have information at the school level since the most likely site for improvement in the educational system is at the school level. Reporting information by district washes out any differences across schools. Broad comparison groups such as districts do not take into account the vast differences among schools.
- School personnel blame school children or their parents (or their race, ethnicity, lack of wealth, lack of education) when children do not do well in school but take credit when children do well in school. While children learn in places other than schools, the primary mission of schools is learning.
- For too many school officials, school improvement means changing the kids instead of changing the conditions of schooling. More and better information is needed to monitor the conditions of schooling that support learning.
- Although school districts release information about how the district is doing—its test scores, Merit Scholars, athletics, Advance Placement rates, and so on—uniform and comparable data, showing state results disaggregated by size of school, wealth of school, or by region are necessary to make meaningful and fair comparisons.
- Most parents were educated in Illinois schools. To say they will not understand education statistics is another condemnation of the schools. Besides, people can certainly understand baseball and football (e.g., the Cubs and the Bears) statistics and, with time, they can interpret school statistics.
- Making comparisons among things, services, and expenditures requires informed judgments. This is a component of critical thinking. Our schools are too important to society to make decisions on guesstimates, opinions, or whimsy. We need hard data on schools.
- If the educators do not want to be accountable for public monies based on what kids know, let them argue for better measures of school performance. To accept their plea that we should just give them money and leave them alone is naive and irresponsible.

- If the airlines can report the rate at which they lose luggage or delay flights, hospitals can report their mortality rate, or police departments report their crime rates, it seems very appropriate that schools report information on how well or how poorly students are learning.
- The first step in solving a problem is knowing that we have a problem. Specific information about our schools, the context in which schooling takes place, and the resources we use to support the learning environment helps us to know where our problems are and which ones we need to work on.
- The schools are the only public service institutions that compel people to attend them, require people to pay for them even when they are not using the services directly, and then refuse to tell people what they are doing and how well they are doing it.
- It is not enough to say we scored a 10 on something. In order to get any meaning out of the score of 10, we have to know what scale we are using, what the usual score is, what the conditions are under which we conducted the measurement, and the limitations of that measure.
- When superintendents say that we should expect low performance from students whose families are poor, we should judge their comments for what they are: a cop out. We need to ask these superintendents how they are supporting early childhood education, full-day kindergarten, special tutorial and counseling programs, and alternative high school programs for at-risk kids. As educators, they are suppose to know what schools can do to help all kids, not just privileged kids. Information on schools is vital to knowing how all our children are doing.

The preceding arguments were among those given in support of or in opposition to changing the requirement of a report card from a school card to a district card. One outspoken legislator, Representative Mary Lou Cowlishaw, the minority leader and a former teacher and journalist, said to the bill's sponsor as she shook her finger at him, "The public has the right to know how the schools are doing. Indeed, the General Assembly has the right to know."

With one exception, the House Elementary and Secondary Education Committee voted to retain the original language in the law requiring that districts issue school report cards. No further changes were made in the original language of the law until July 1988 when the General Assembly added the requirement for schools to report the number of students who were chronic truants. State Superintendent Ted Sanders did not encourage further changes in the law during the period of significant opposition to the concept of public reporting. There was a need, he said, to show strong support for accountability, particularly at a time when the schools were asking for additional funding.

Aftermath

In retrospect, the Illinois education system did not crumble as a result of the schools publicizing information. After resisting the requirement so vociferously prior to the first release of the cards, many school administrators now express a blasé, bored attitude with the whole process. It is considered a nonevent. The new state superintendent, Robert Leininger, in office since August 1989, has called for an external evaluation of the school report card. He says it is "filled with educator-ese" and is not understandable. His comments signal a readiness on the part of the state agency to open the doors for possible changes.

It is clear that the school report cards did not hurt the schools. How they helped remains to be seen. While no one strategy can make our schools better, educators who argue for valid and systematic measures of schooling and work to better inform the public on the results of those measures are more likely to find responsive legislators, taxpayers, and members of the public than those who do not. Then, educators can better earn the public's trust.

RUSSELL J. QUAGLIA

The Development of Educational Administrator Certification Law in Maine

The Maine Legislature passed, in 1985, a certification reform act that turned over control of the profession to administrators in the field. Legislative Document 1228, An Act to Provide for State Certification of School Administrators, toughened standards and decentralized the review process by granting recertification authority to regional consortia of school districts. These consortia are governed by administrators representative of the groups affected by the act.

Historically, Maine's certification requirements for administrators were weak, especially for principals. Two courses in administration were required for certification. According to State Board of Education Chair Carol Wishcamper, "there was concern that traditional certification standards for administrators were loose and initial access to the administrative ranks would be quickly and easily met; and, there was little correlation between attendance in a required course and the development of skills and competencies needed by administrators to perform their jobs."

Renewal requirements were even more loosely defined. Administrators had to complete six credit hours of university coursework or equivalent alternate activities. There was limited quality control regarding what constituted acceptable coursework and although alternative activities received some scrutiny, both activities and courses were self-determined. Improving specific skills was left to the discretion of the participating administrator. There was general consensus that the traditional approach to certifying administrators was perhaps efficient, but certainly not effective.

Thus, in Maine, administrative certification reform became part of the reform turmoil that swept the nation after the publication of *A Nation at Risk*, the report of the National Commission on Excellence in Education (1983). As the commision portrayed our nation's educational system as a system in crisis and called for reform, it included in the areas identified as capable of change the quality of educational leadership. The commission's implementing recommendations identified principals and superintendents as crucial leaders in developing community and school support for the proposed reforms. The commission cited "lack of leadership" as one cause of the "current declining trend" in education and made a clear distinction between "leadership" skills and "managerial" skills. During the remainder of the 1980s, dozens of major and minor educational reform reports continued discussion of the themes so dramatically begun in *A Nation at Risk.*

Maine followed the national lead by creating a Commision on the Status of Education in Maine. The report of the commission was presented to Governor Joseph Brennan in 1984. The report addressed most areas of possible reform, and specifically addressed the issue of educational administrators. Administrators were viewed as being responsible for the quality of education and accountable for managing resources to that end.

Further echoing the federal report, the state's report pointedly distinguished between responsibility for education quality and responsibility for mere caretaking functions. Although leadership is not mentioned explicitly in the Maine Commission's report, the need for leadership quality is clear in its conclusion that "school administrators are the front-line managers to whom we entrust our educational investment . . . and they must be more than overseers of school rules." This belief came to be reflected in new certification standards intended to upgrade administrator performance, which were adopted by the Maine legislature in 1985.

Maine's new administrator certification law identified twelve knowledge areas as standards for administrator certification. A unique feature of the twelve areas was that they were generic to all administrator certificates (e.g., principal, superintendent, vocational director). The list includes the following:

1. community relations
2. school finance and budget
3. supervision and evaluation of personnel
4. federal and state civil rights and education law
5. organizational theory and planning
6. educational leadership
7. educational philosophy and theory
8. effective instruction
9. curriculum development
10. staff development
11. knowledge of the learner and the learning process
12. teaching the exceptional student in the regular classroom

With the enactment of the 1985 Administrator Certification Law, new induction and professional development expectations were also established. Practicing administrators are now required to conduct a formal needs assessment of their knowledge in relation to the twelve knowledge areas and to develop a comprehensive action plan to be completed under the guidance of a support system every five years. Additionally, the support system process requires that individuals seeking certification renewal have mentoring relationships through a support team. There is an implication (but no requirement) that mentors will be "journeymen" administrators with strong professional backgrounds. Their purpose is to assist the certification candidate along a pathway of professional development by cooperatively assessing the candidate's strengths and weaknesses, identifying strategies to address areas that need improvement, and generally supporting the candidate throughout the renewal period.

Because this new approach challenged the traditional routes to administrator certification, the statutory language was intentionally broad and provided for the creation of pilot projects. Following adoption of the new law, three pilot sites were established to explore various approaches to certification and recertification under the new law. Between July 1985 and September 1987, three multidistrict sites tested the new law. Evaluations were conducted of the experiences at two of these pilot sites, the 1–95 Consortium and the Kennebec Valley Consortium (Donaldson and Seager, 1988).

> The authors evaluated the pilot sites and concluded that the pilots demonstrated flaws in both the conceptualization of the legislation on which the pilots were based and in the pilot processes themselves. Maine's administrator competencies were not framed to match the integrated nature of a school administrator's tasks, initial assessment of participants' competencies was inadequate, and the learning plans which emerged from the process did not appear to demonstrate that the legislatively defined knowledge areas would be learned. The authors also found that despite these problems and the significant commitments of time and energy required, participants reported an enthusiasm and a sense that significant learning had taken place. (Donaldson and Seager, 1988, p. 1)

The State Board of Education began rule making in the fall of 1987 and rules were adopted in March 1988. Considerable political activity was observed between 1985 and adoption of the rules. It appears that this activity superseded a careful use of the evaluation of the pilot sites in the rule-making process. However, it should be noted that this is not at all unusual in state-level policy making (First, 1987). Unfortunately, it is the rule rather than the exception.

As implementation of the new law proceeded, it became clear that formative evaluative research was needed in order to provide Maine policy makers with information necessary for any needed modifications in the rules and regulations or the act itself. Two strands of research converged to provide a "snapshot" of the impact of the Maine certification law in 1990 (First and Quaglia, in press). The first strand consisted of an impact evaluation of the legislation conducted in the manner of naturalistic inquiry and reported as multiple case studies of the consortia that had formed to implement the new law. The second strand consisted of survey research designed to determine:

1. Which of the identified areas certified elementary and secondary principals perceive as impacting their effectiveness in their administrative role
2. Which component(s) of the recertification process (i.e., needs assessment, action plan, mentoring) have the greatest impact on administrative effectiveness as they relate to the identified areas.

The results of both strands were available to policy makers for reconsideration of the Maine Administrator Certification Law beginning in 1990.

References

Donaldson, G. A., & Seager, A. J. (1988). Field-based competency assessment and development: Lessons from Maine's administrator certification pilot project. Paper presented at the annual meeting of the American Educational Research Association, Washington, DC.

First, P. (1987). Evaluation research in state level decision making. An interview with Sally Pancrazio. In J. Nowakowski, (Ed.), *The client perspective of education.* San Francisco: Jossey-Bass.

First, P., & Quaglia, R. (in press). Educational administrator certification law in Maine: Its development, its impact and its relationship to principal effectiveness.

National Commission on Excellence in Education. (1983). *A Nation at Risk.* Washington, DC: U. S. Department of Education.

CAROLINE B. CODY

Policy Making about Textbooks in the 1990s

No doubt, to many educators, textbooks seem an insignificant feature of the education enterprise and not one around which important policy issues arise. It is with textbooks, however, that American values, big market forces, and the dispersed powers of the education enterprise converge. In the past, Americans' beliefs that textbook purchases provided opportunities for the misuse of public funds and that what children read in school is what they will grow up believing have led to policy controversy. Policies intended to make the process of textbook selection free from graft and conflict of interest and subject to the influence by the majority culture yet sensitive to the impact of special interest groups from a broad spectrum of the American populace have resulted (Cody, 1990). It is not surprising, therefore, that many policy makers and most of the public will think of these areas of controversy when they think of textbooks—if they think of them at all. During the last decade, however, textbooks and the policies surrounding them have become the subject of new interest for several reasons, reasons very central to policy makers' efforts to improve schools.

First, in the late 1970s and 1980s, it become clear to many policy makers that the public's expectation for improved reading achievement was the new political reality. That reality created an interest in the findings of research which indicated that some reading achievement problems resided not with the reader, but with the material to be read. Scholars analyzed the factors about text that impact on readability and textbooks' ability to bring about learning: the instructional design, the style of writing, the use of illustration, the content, and so on (Cole and Sticht, 1981; Anderson, Osborn, and Tierney, 1984). Using these factors to study and evaluate textbooks, researchers found many books lacking, and a movement to improve the quality of textbooks used in classrooms took hold among farsighted policy makers (Cody, 1986).

Efforts to improve the books available for purchase must confront a complex market system and the loosely linked system by which books are selected. Publishers respond to market demands transmitted in large part by the selection process (Squire and Morgan, 1990). But since educators find it difficult to be cynical about the beautiful books presented and since the areas in which the new research-based standards are important are difficult to evaluate, we often send the wrong messages to publishers. Time and expertise are often missing from the selection process; selectors often use proxies such as renowned authorship, recent copyright date, attractive presentation, easy-to-use manuals, and the like as indicators of quality. There are no shortcuts for choosing quality books, and when the best books presented are not chosen, we lessen the chance that books will improve. Publishers assure us that they will provide what the market demands; policy makers are challenged, therefore, to construct selection processes that will result in books that justify readers' efforts.

The second reason that policy makers must take another look at textbook policy has to do with efforts to tighten the linkage between what is taught and what is tested. This tenet of the effective schools movement leads many policy makers to look at the textbook as a mechanism important to the reform movement. The idea that the textbook is the de facto curriculum and the teacher's manual the major pedagogy gives encouragement to efforts to change books in order to change teaching.

Tightening the linkage has taken two forms. First, many school districts have created curriculum specifications for textbooks that are designed to ensure that books presented by publishers for consideration will cover the curriculum of the district. Increasingly, computer programs have permitted publishers to create correlation studies to demonstrate to selection committees on what pages specific curriculum objectives are covered. Such computer studies look important and bring much comfort to selectors, but instructional design is more complicated than such studies would indicate. No study can evaluate the quality of content on a topic or its appropriateness for teaching and learning.

Influential states that have used curriculum specifications to influence what is included in books have met with some success— sometimes improving the quality of books available to all districts; such efforts, however, are appropriate for only the most influential purchasers and their influence is not always positive. Correlation studies required by many jurisdictions throughout the country, however, have created new pressures on the editors of textbooks that often result in books designed to include everything and please everyone. No longer is it likely that a working educator or a professor can invest a lifetime of experience in writing a textbook; it is more likely that editors will develop an outline based on the curriculum specifications of important constituencies and hire a professional writer who can write with such a formula in mind. Since the books will be marketed throughout the country, there is pressure also to homogenize the books so they will meet as many guidelines as possible and satisfy teachers on the selection committees. High standards for content, quality of writing, and instructional design are difficult to maintain under such a formula (Tyson-Bernstein, 1988).

Using the textbook to tighten the linkages in decision making has also had its impact on teaching and teachers. The use of the textbook to bring about standardization of teaching takes several forms. Many school districts have advocated centralized decision making about what books will be used throughout the district. Such decisions are seen to have several advantages: negotiating with a single publisher increases the likelihood that an advantageous purchasing package can be worked out to include free materials and training programs; a single book used throughout the system permits students to move from school to school without "loosing their place"; and using a single book facilitates distribution of textbooks in times when school populations fluctuate. A single book also makes the instructional supervisor's job easier. Instructional leadership can concentrate not on the complexities of teaching, but on monitoring the efficient use of the materials. Some districts have gone so far down the standardization route as to prescribe what chapter a teacher should be on during any week during the year. Teachers, on the whole, have not complained. Some, feeling at risk, have welcomed clear directives about what and how they should teach.

The use of the textbook as the program of instruction has often meant that a criterion for the selection of the book often has been the ability of the weakest teacher to use the book and follow the manual. The teachers' manuals that accompany textbooks have differed from decade to decade (Woodward, 1986). In some periods of educational history, the manual has been a resource guide for teaching and has contained discussions of professional issues and research; in other periods, manuals have avoided challenging new ideas or even ideas at all and have been characterized by scripted questions for teachers to read for which acceptable answers are given. In recent decades, schools have experimented with the textbook-delivered "teacher proof" programs, and manuals have attempted to make teaching effortless and thoughtless. Current textbooks come in packages that include not only manuals, but materials and teaching aids that in better times teachers would have used their professional knowledge and creativity to prepare. Publishers have invested a great deal in the development of such programs, perhaps at the expense of the books themselves. To use such programs, the teacher becomes a technician, needing only to follow the directions; critic Michael Apple (1986) has described this trend as "deskilling" the teacher. It is tempting to believe that a district could adopt a textbook that would do all this—ensure the curriculum is taught, improve instruction, and so on. In the next decade, policy makers will have to address the issues, pro and con, of using textbook policy to standardize curriculum, teachers, and teaching.

A third movement is at work in the United States in the 1990s, and it speaks to a countermovement and teacher empowerment. Frustration with the lack of success with previous reform movements has brought many policy makers to a point wherein teacher professionalism and increased decision making at the school level seem promising as a reform strategy. They seek to bring to life professional prerogatives and to involve teachers in the reform of the schools in which they teach. In all jurisdictions, legislation and policy require that teachers dominate the textbook-selection process. In states that have a centralized process by which they create a list of approved books for purchase with state funds, teachers have the votes on the state committees as they do at the local level. In states that have no state level process, teachers also dominate the process, either as members of selection committees or as individuals when all-teacher vote is the selection process (California State Department of Education, 1984; Education Research Service, 1976).

A recent study of teacher decision making in the various states released by the Carnegie Foundation for the Advancement of Teaching found that of all the decisions made in schools, teachers feel the most involved in textbook selection. In the Gallup poll published in the June 1989 *Kappan,* when asked how much and in what areas teachers should have control in the educational process, sampled teachers responded that they should have control of "selecting textbooks to be used in class" at the level of 4.2 on a 5.0 scale. When asked "How much control teachers in your school actually have" on the selection process, teachers indicated 3.1. Clearly, in the minds of many teachers, selection of textbooks is an area of clear professional prerogative; they feel involved at present and would seem to want to be more involved. It is also clear that teachers are selecting the books now in use—the books so often found lacking.

The three movements—to improve the quality of books, to use textbooks to ensure that the curriculum is delivered, and to involve teachers in increased professional decision making—provide an interesting conundrum. Textbooks need to be improved. It is the belief of many scholars that requiring textbooks to deliver the curriculum—its content and its pedagogy—is having a detrimental effect on the quality of textbooks. It is a loosely linked system; the people who develop the specifications are not the people who select the books. Teachers select the textbooks and feel it is an important professional prerogative. It is also believed that increased professionalization of teachers and their involvement in choosing textbooks are not congruent with efforts to control teaching by the use of books, and it is clear that present less-than-adequate books that are designed to be selected by teacher committees do not merit the faith of administrators who cannot resist the efficiencies of standardization and centralization.

The new decade provides a challenge for policy makers. Policy makers in large jurisdictions must create mechanisms for designing specifications for school books that focus not on the shortcuts, but on the quality features of books. Policy makers in all jurisdictions must challenge publishers and convince them that textbooks must continue to improve to meet the highest standards research can provide us. Policy makers must design processes that can result in the selection of the best books, thereby encouraging publishers to market excellent books; policy makers must send the message to teacher selectors that they must not be distracted by the glitz of textbook programs, but must look long and hard for excellent content and instructional design that address the best pedagogy available. In addition and even more basic, it is this author's opinion that textbook policy is one area where policy makers should resist the temptation to use textbooks to centralize and standardize; decisions about how to use textbooks are best made by teachers—perhaps even at the school level. Centralization, as irresistible as its efficiencies may seem, has high risks and a negative impact on the quality of books available and on the quality of teachers and teaching. No doubt, policy makers have some important decisions to make as they think strategically about textbooks and school improvement in the 1990s.

References

Anderson, R., Osborn, J., & Tierney, R. (Eds.) (1984). *Learning to read in American schools.* Hillsdale, NJ: Erlbaum.

Apple, M. (1986). *Teachers and texts: A political economy of class and gender relations in education.* New York: Routledge and Kegan Paul.

California State Department of Education. (1984). *Survey of textbook evaluation and adoption processes in adoption states and in sample districts in nonadoption states.* Sacramento: California State Department of Education.

Cody, C. (1990). The politics of textbook publishing, adoptions, and use. Textbooks and schooling in the United States: Eighty-ninth yearbook of the National Society for the Study of Education, Chicago: University of Chicago Press.

Cody, C. (1986). *A policymaker's guide to textbook selection.* Alexandria, VA: National Association of State Boards of Education.

Cole, J., & Sticht, T. (Eds.). (1981). *The textbook in American society.* Washington, DC: Library of Congress.

Education Research Service, Inc. (1976). *Procedures for textbook and instructional materials selection.* Arlington, VA: Educational Research Services, Inc.

Squire, J., & Morgan, R. (1990). The elementary and high school textbook market today. *Textbooks and schooling in the United States: Eighty-ninth yearbook of the National Society for the Study of Education,* Chicago: University of Chicago Press.

Tyson-Bernstein, H. (1988). *A conspiracy of good intentions: America's textbook fiasco.* Washington, DC: Council for Basic Education.

Woodward, A. (1986, Spring). Over-programmed materials: Taking the teacher out of teaching, *American Educator,* 26–31.

JAMES MEZA, JR.

How Local School Administrators Can Influence State-Level Policy

The U.S. Constitution does not mention education in a specific way as the business of the federal government, and the Tenth Amendment to the Constitution states that those powers not delegated to the federal government rightly belong to the states. Thus, education becomes a prerogative of the state or the people themselves. States have enacted through constitutional provision and legislative acts school policy governing the financing of education, control of education, and the organization of state and local school boards. Therefore, governmental bodies such as the executive branch-office of the governor, state legislatures, and state boards of education become the vehicles through which education policy is formulated, enacted, monitored, and in some cases administered. This process is currently referred to as top-down policy making.

This top-down approach to education policy making has caused local school administrators to become critical of most aspects of policy formulation. Local school administrators want to express their voice and participate in the development of the policy that forms the basis of their school operation. The problem, however, is that most school administrators feel powerless and uncertain about their role in influencing state-level policy.

The purpose here is to describe the processes of state-level policy formulation and to explore practical methods and strategies for local school administrators that will enable them to play a policy-related role. This contribution will frequently refer to the "Children's First Act," which was an omnibus education bill designed by the governor of Louisiana, enacted into law by the state legislature and implemented into policy by the state board of education.

Policy Formulation

Education policy formulation is an aspect of public policy formulation that requires a framework that ensures an opportunity for the general public to influence its development and final form. Policy decisions made by governors, state legislatures, and state boards of education are subject to the scrutiny and influence of the general public. Their role in policy formulation is as follows.

Office of the Governor

The 1980s have been characterized by governors taking a proactive leadership role in establishing policy and programs to reform public education. Frequently, governors are elected because their educational platforms are supported by the majority of the public. Therefore, the legislature usually supports the governor's education package. The governor also has an extraordinary amount of power in influencing and controlling the state budget, thus the chances of funding his or her program or policy are very probable. Finally, the governor can establish policy through the use of executive orders and can alter the direction of policy development through his or her veto power.

In his 1987 election campaign, Louisiana Governor Buddy Roemer placed education as the most important issue of his campaign. The prioritizing of education and his education reform initiatives were strongly supported by the voters of this state. As a result of this public support, he passed his education reform bill during the first legislature session.

The Children's First Act did not pass, however, without some controversy. The bill mandated the replacement of lifetime teaching certificates with five-year certificates renewable upon evaluation. Many teacher groups and some legislators were opposed to this aspect of the bill. The governor, however, using his budgetary power of influence, coupled the teacher evaluation plan with increases in annual pay and extended step increases to raise the average teacher's salary 30 percent over five years. Through his budgetary power, he was able to successfully negotiate with opposing legislators and teacher groups.

State Legislatures

State legislatures create policy through the establishment of laws. In the developmental process of law, bills are referred to House and Senate committees where issues of bills are discussed. These committees simplify the process of deciding which bills have merit and which are unacceptable. The fate of approximately one-half of proposed legislation is determined at this point. The House and Senate rarely differ with a recommendation rendered by a committee, although the potential does exist to override. Also, the legislature can influence policy making through the budget and oversight process. Although a bill has been passed by the House and Senate, funds must be appropriated to implement the policy. The legislature can control the implementation of policy by not appropriating or only partially funding education programs or policy. Finally, the legislature has oversight over the final adoption and implementation of education policy. This has particular impact for policy established by state boards, since their policy-making authority must be in accordance with the law. Thus, through its oversight power, the legislature can delay or prevent the implementation of policy.

The Children's First Act was referred to the House Education Committee. The bill was presented by the governor and his staff. Special interest groups such as business and industry, parent associations, school boards, school administrators, and teachers' associations also testified during the committee hearings. After listening to testimony, both for and against the bill, the education committee reported the bill favorably and forwarded it to the full House for consideration. The House discussed the bill, voted favorably, and referred it to the Senate. The Senate passed the bill and forwarded it to the governor, who signed the bill into law.

This legislative process for the omnibus education bill was not complete, however, because funds needed to be appropriated to implement the Children's First Act. The governor's reform bill was part of the appropriation bill. The appropriation bill was discussed by finance committees of the House and Senate. Testimony was heard during the finance committee hearings. The appropriation bill was discussed by the full House and Senate and forwarded to the governor for his signature. At this time, the Children's First Act was approved for implementation.

State Boards

State boards of education are responsible for providing the lay governance of education and separating education policy making from partisan politics. The state board is expected to establish policy that focuses the needs of public education and serves the interests of the public and children of the state.

As nonpartisan education policy makers, state boards solicit input from public groups and individual citizens before final decisions are made. Statewide public hearings are usually held for controversial issues and matters of significant educational interest. The state board, like the legislature, refers issues to committee and that committee makes a recommendation to the full board. All policy that is adopted by the state board must be publicly advertised for a specific period of time to provide the public an opportunity to comment on the matter. Although the state board is considered by many to be the chief education policy maker in the state, frequently it establishes policy based on state statute or as required by law.

Once the Children's First Act became law, the state board of education had the responsibility to develop policy that would assist local school districts in the implementation of the reform initiatives. The state board and its administrative arm, the state department of education, utilized public hearings, organized technical and advisory committees, and encouraged public input throughout the development process. Frequently, the same special interest groups that testified during the legislative process were now testifying in the policy-development process. The advisory committees provided local school districts an opportunity for input as the committees consisted of teachers, principals, supervisors, and local school district superintendents.

After the policy was approved by the state board of education, the legislative oversight committee reviewed the policy issues and its development. There was no objection and the policies for the Children's First Act were finalized.

Methods of Influencing Policy

Although state-level policy is formed in a top-down approach, the process of development is designed to enable local school administrators to play an active role in policy formulation. Following are some suggestions that will assist local school administrators in influencing education policy.

Planning

Since state-level policy is developed over a period of time ranging from weeks to months, and since time is a scarce resource for school administrators, effective planning is essential if school administrators are to be actively involved in policy development. School administrators must prioritize time to meet with state legislators and educational leaders, serve on state and regional level committees, play an active role in professional associations, and closely monitor the policy-development process on a continued basis.

Planning Associations

Even the most effective planning may not release the time that is needed to impact education policy. Therefore, school administrators should select a spokesperson to represent their interests. This can be achieved through the use of professional organizations such as the local principals' association, superintendent's association, or school board associations.

Consensus Building

Because educational issues are contextual, policy that is good for one school or school district may not be good for another. It is important, therefore, that consensus building and priority of issues be established in professional organizations. Without this unified approach, the issue appears to be self-serving and not in the best interest of the children we serve. Consensus is necessary to influence policy development. School administrators should also look to establish consensus with other professional education associations and special interest groups.

Continuous Communication

Finally, local school administrators should maintain continuous communication with area legislators and key education leaders at the state level. State-level policy makers need to know the feelings of constituent groups in the early stages of policy development, not only after the final adoption. Building support with policy makers sustains the necessary interaction with those who make the final decisions.

SECTION THREE REFERENCES

Adler, M. W., & Lane, F. S. (1988). Governors and public policy leadership. In S. Gove & T. Beyle (Eds.), *Governors and higher education* (pp. 1–16). Denver, CO: Education Commission of the States.

Aguillard v. Treen, 440 SO 2nd 704 (La. 1983).

Beach, F. F., & Gibbs, A. H. (1952). Personnel of state departments of education. Washington, DC: U.S. Government Printing Office.

Campbell, R. F., Cunningham, L. L., Nystrand, R. O., & Usdan, M. D. (1985). *The organization and control of American schools* (5th ed.). Columbus: Charles E. Merrill.

Campbell, R. F., & Mazzoni, T. L. (1976). *State policy making for the public schools: A comparative analysis of policy making for the public schools in twelve states and a treatment of state governance models.* Berkeley, CA: McCutchan.

Contreras, A. R., & Medlyn, W. (1989, April). *Case study of educational reform in Indiana.* Paper presented at the American Educational Research Association, San Francisco, CA.

Council of Chief State School Offices (CCSSO). (1988). Directory of state education agencies, 1988–1989. Washington, DC: Author.

Cubberly, E. P. (1927). *State school administration.* Boston: Houghton Mifflin.

Elazar, D. (1972). *American federalism: A view from the states.* New York: Crowell.

First, P. F. (1979). *A study of a state board of education policy development process.* Doctoral dissertation, Illinois State University.

First, P. F. (1985a). An historical examination of state education agencies. *Thresholds in Education, XI*(2), 1–5.

First, P. F. (1985b). The evolving role of the state education agencies. *Planning and Changing, 16*(3), 167–176.

First, P. F., & Quaglia, R. (in press). State boards of education: Fact or fiction.

Friedrich, C. J. (1941). *Constitutional government and democracy.* Boston: Little, Brown.

Furhman, S. H. (1989). State politics and education reform. In Hannaway, J., & Crowson, R. (Eds.), *The politics of reforming school administration* (pp. 61–75). New York: Falmer Press.

Gracian, B. (1647). *The art of worldly wisdom,* 286, tr. Joseph Jacobs.

Guthrie, J. W., & Reed, R. J. (1986). *Educational administration and policy: Effective leadership for American education.* Englewood Cliffs, NJ: Prentice Hall.

Hansen, K. H. (1980). *State education agency staff development: A function of agency role and mission.* Portland, OR: Northwest Regional Education Lab. (ERIC Document Reproduction Service No. ED 225 254).

Harris, S. P. (1973). *State department of education, state boards of education and chief state school officers.* Bethesda, MD: ERIC Document Reproduction Service, ED 072 566.

Holt, S. L. (1987). State education agency services: Limitations and prerequisites for change. *Planning and changing, 18*(3), 170–177.

Johnston, A. P., & Proulx, R. J. (1987). State education policy: Old rules, new agendas. *Planning and Changing, 18*(4), 195–201.

Kagan, R. A. (1986). Regulating business, regulating schools: The problem of regulatory unreasonableness. In Kirp. D. L. & Jensen, D. N., *School days, rule days: The legalization and regulation of education* (pp. 64–90). Philadelphia: Falmer Press.

Keesecker, W. W. (1950). *State boards of education and chief state school officers.* Bulletin no. 12, Federal Security Agency. Washington, DC: U.S. Government Printing Office.

Kiesler, S., & Sproull, L. (1982). Managerial responses to changing environments: Perspectives on problem sensing from social cognition. *Administrative Science Quarterly, 27,* 548–570.

Marshall, C., Mitchell, D., & Wirt, F. (1990). *Culture and education policy in the American states.* Bristol, PA: Falmer Press.

Mazzoni, T. L. (1989). Governors as policy leaders for education: A Minnesota comparison. *Educational Policy, 3*(1), 79–90.

Mitchell, D. E., & Encarnation, D. J. (1984). Alternative state policy mechanisms for influencing school performance. *Educational Researcher, 13*(4), 4–11.

Mitchell, D. E., & Iannaccone, L. (1980). *The impact of California's legislative policy on public school performance.* Berkeley, CA: Institute of Government Studies.

Murphy, J. T. (1981). *Differential treatment of the states, a good idea or wishful thinking?* Papers prepared for the School Finance Project. Washington, DC: U.S. Department of Education.

National Association of State Boards of Education (NASBE). (Undated). *The challenge of leadership: State boards of education in an era of reform.* Alexandria, VA: Author.

Office of Educational Research and Improvement (OERI). (1988). *Measuring up: Questions and answers about state roles in educational accountability.* Washington, DC: U.S. Department of Education.

Pierce v. Society of Sisters, 268 U.S. 510, 45 S.Ct. 510, 69 L.Ed. 1070 (1925).

Polsby, N. (1979). Preface. In Sharpe, L. J. (Ed.), *Decentralist trends in western democracies.* London: Sage.

Reutter, E., Jr. (1988). *The law of public education* (3rd ed.). Mineola, NY: Foundation Press.

Richards, C. E. (1988). A typology of educational monitoring systems. *Educational Evaluation and Policy Analysis, 10*(2), 106–116.

Sherman, J. D., Kutner, M. A., & Small, K. J. (Eds.). (1982). *New dimensions of the federal-state partnership in education.* Washington, DC: Institute for Educational Leadership.

Sroufe, G. R. (1971, April). State school board members and the state education policy system. *Planning and Changing, 2,* 23.

Summerfield, H. L. (1971, August). Cuing and the open system of educational politics. *Education and Urban Society, 3,* 425–49.

Timar, T. B., & Kirp. D. L. (1988). State efforts to reform schools: Treading between a regulatory swamp and an English garden. *Educational Evaluation and Policy Analysis, 10*(2), 75–88.

Wall v. County Board of Education, 249 Iowa 209, 86 N.W.2d 231 (1957).

Weiler, H. N. (1989). Education and power: The politics of educational decentralization in comparative perspective. *Educational Policy, 3*(1), 31–43.

Weiss, J. A. (1981, Winter/Spring). Substance vs. symbol in administrative reform: The case of human services coordination. *Policy Analysis, 7,* 21–45.

Wirt, F. M., & Kirst, M. W. (1989). *Schools in conflict* (2nd ed.). Berkeley, CA: McCutchan.

Yudof, M. G., Kirp, D. L., van Geel, & Levin, B. (1987). *Educational policy and the law.* Berkeley, CA: McCutchan.

Local Government and Education Policy

School Boards: The Great Responsibility

> The most numbing phrase in the American vocabulary must be 'local government' followed by 'federal government,' and then, perhaps, by 'electoral politics.' Even 'Sears catalogue' carries livelier possibilities, in everyday usage, than those terms that refer to our collective enterprise as citizens.—Barbara Ehrenreich, *The Worst Years of Our Lives,* (1990)

School administrators have their most immediate access to policy-making processes at the local school board level. It is at this level that the school administrator typically acts in his or her policy-making role. Yet, given the pressures, responsibilities, and restraints defined for the local school board by the federal and state levels of educational governance, there is the question of how many significant policy decisions are left to the discretion of the local school board. There is also the question of how representative of demographically changing communities these boards really are. Yet, that local school boards represent their communities and are close to the scene of education for a particular group of children remains popular justification for their place in the educational governance system.

But, not many people vote in school board elections, which also raises the question of how representative of their communities local school boards really are. Like other types of local government, school boards are pretty much taken for granted, even ignored. But people do think it is important that we have local school boards even though the same people confess to not knowing very much about what school boards really do (Institute for Educational Leadership, 1986). They are, and are seen by citizens as, symbols of our democratic processes, as providers of future opportunity and the good life for our children.

Since the reforms of the 1980s, local school boards have been under tremendous pressure to justify, restructure, and define their role. The early rounds of reform ignored local school boards and the institutionalizing power of their policy-making processes (Nowakowski and First, 1989). Later rounds of reform called for new structures and functions for local school boards as in Chicago where the power was shifted to school-site councils or "miniboards." And the controversial choice reforms opened Pandora's box to ask whether school boards were really needed anymore. In 1936 Franklin D. Roosevelt said that "wise and prudent men–intelligent conservatives–have long known that in a changing world worthy institutions can be conserved only by adjusting them to the changing time." In the 1990s, pressures are converging upon U.S. school boards that are forcing them to adjust to changing times.

But, in the midst of all the reform and controversy, school board members continue to give of their time for the public good, and their neighbors still think it is important to have someone close to home overseeing the children's education. And wise school administrators know it is still important to build strong relationships with the board as a whole and with individual school board members even when times and functions are changing.

At the local level it is this board of lay citizens, commonly called the local school board, that is the policy-making entity. Given the already delineated powers, duties, and responsibilities of the federal and state levels of educational governance, the question of what is left of a policy-making nature for a local board to do must be seriously addressed. It is a fair question; in fact, it is one of the most important structural issues in educational governance in the 1990s. As Shanker (1989) put it, "it is a question worthy of national debate. It is time for these 'worthy institutions' to adjust to changing times" (p. 29).

Over 15,000 local school boards meet regularly to provide policy-level guidance for education in the United States. The school board story as told by the National School Boards Association (1987) is impressive. School board members have educational responsibility for nearly 40 million students, fiscal responsibilities for more than $160 billion each year, and responsibility as the employer of nearly 4 million individuals. Almost 4 percent of the entire U.S. gross national product goes to expenditures for elementary and secondary education.

In just one state, Illinois, close to 1,000 school boards comprised of some 7,000 elected citizens meet for twelve to twenty-six three-hour-plus school board meetings annually. To say this is an enormous expenditure of citizen time and public money is certainly an understatement. What do these people do? A major portion of these people's time appears to be devoted to the business of running a school–the funding, upkeep, and contractual agreements that provide the structure that permits education.

The list in Figure 4.1 serves to remind us of the matters school

FIGURE 4.1 • *Procedural and Routine Motions Passed by Sample School Districts in 1986–1987*

Procedural

Approval of minutes
Recognition of visitors
Move to executive session
Adjournment

Report Approval

Superintendent report
Board president report
PTA report
Standing committee reports
  curriculum
  finance
  substance abuse
  legislative
Coop agreements reports
  special ed
  voc ed
Special information reports
Annual report

Personnel

General personnel matters
  hires
  retirements
  releases
  leaves
Recruitment
  minority recruitment
Salary schedule
Teacher appreciation week
Teacher awards
Insurance and compensation
  programs
Staff development
  salary credit workshops

Students

Student accident insurance
Suspensions
Expulsions
Special programs
  young authors
  youth soccer
  crossing guards
Adoption of aptitude test

Finance/Business Management

Bills approval
Payroll
Claims
Donations and gifts
Working cash fund
Annual budget
Budget calendar
Public hearing budget
Transfer of funds
Tax levy
Public hearing/tax levy
Bond resolution
Building fund data
Auditor selection
Audit report
Bids
  photographer
  office supplies
  transportation
  towel services
  gym floor
Insurance
  liability
  property
  auto insurance
Purchases
  equipment
  property
Investments
Loss and damage reports
Contracts
  school leasing agreement
  school attorney
  heating and air conditioning
  natural gas
  transportation
  community use of facilities
  food service management
  custodial and maintenance pro-
    gram
Grants
  technical assistance
  approval to request
  approval of reports regarding
Fees
  textbook rental
  pool rental rates
  school rates
  tuition rates

Continued

FIGURE 4.1 • Continued

District Policy	Finance/Business Management (cont.)
Policy readings	Lunch program
AIDS policy	lunch policy
Approval of policies	lunch fees
Adoption of board policies	lunch supervision program
Adoption of board goals	Life safety code
Adoption of school calendar	change orders
Adoption of mission statement	safety committee recommenda-
Adoption of textbook-selection	tions
policy	Litigation
	vendors
Professional Linkage	
Professional memberships	**Evaluation**
IASB	Community surveys
NASB	Special education self-study
PTA	
Conference delegates selected	
Conference reports accepted	

Source: From "School Board Minutes: Records of Reform" by J. Nowakowski and P. F. First, 1989, *Educational Evaluation and Policy Analysis, 11*(4). Copyright 1989 by the American Educational Research Association. Reprinted by permission of the publisher.

board members must attend to. It can also be seen as a list of all the areas in which the school administrator can provide leadership to the board and help it operate on a policy-oriented level. The diverse topics the list represents will not come as a surprise to anyone who has either served on a school board or attended school board meetings for any period of time (Nowakowski and First, 1989).

Among thoughtful people there are wide-ranging differences of opinion regarding the efficacy and importance of the local school board. That school boards waste their time on trivial matters has become a stereotype. Anne C. Lewis, in lamenting the lack of exciting public debate about education, states bluntly, "School boards tend to concern themselves with trivia" (1988, p. 324). Denis Doyle, communicating directly with boards via the *American School Board Journal,* says that "no corporation could run for a week with the kind of niggling oversight school boards habitually practice" (cited in Reecer, 1989, p. 34). Reecer's panel of school board watchers suggested to boards that they do more looking outward, more representing of education to the community, and more linking with the growing segments of the population not directly connected to the public schools.

But others still see the local school board as an important, if neglected, link in the governance of education. As Nellie C. Weil,

TABLE 4.1 • *Public School Districts and Enrollment, by Size of District: 1986–87 and 1987–88*

Enrollment Size of District	1986–87			1987–88		
	Number of districts	*Percent of districts*	*Percent of students*	*Number of districts*	*Percent of districts*	*Percent of students*
Total	15,713	100.0	100.0	15,577	100.0	100.0
25,000 or more	173	1.1	27.9	171	1.1	27.3
10,000 to 24,999	447	2.8	17.1	464	3.0	17.4
5,000 to 9,999	915	5.8	16.5	937	6.0	16.5
2,500 to 4,999	1,823	11.6	16.4	1,912	12.3	16.8
1,000 to 2,499	3,504	22.3	14.7	3,561	22.9	14.7
600 to 999	1,754	11.2	3.5	1,796	11.5	3.6
300 to 599	2,257	14.4	2.5	2,290	14.7	2.5
1 to 299	4,071	25.9	1.3	4,041	25.9	1.3
Size not reported[1]	769	4.9	–	405	2.6	–

Source: U.S. Department of Education, National Center for Education Statistics. Common Core of Data survey. (This table was prepared April 1989.)

Note: Because of rounding, details may not add to totals.

[1] Includes school districts reporting enrollment of 0.

– Data not reported.

President of the National School Boards Association, pointed out in 1986, "Improvement in the instructional program, to be truly effective, needs the support of the people in the local communities. Those people look to their local school boards for leadership in this task. Therefore, state efforts to improve education must involve school boards as an integral part of the process" (Institute for Educational Leadership, 1986, p. iii).

Belief in local control and the importance of keeping power "close to the people," at the "grass roots," is a deeply held American value. We are unique in the developed world in allowing over 15,000 groups of private citizens to make hiring, firing, and curricula decisions about the education of the country's youth. That a child's education can differ from community to community confounds visitors from other countries. Yet we take it for granted, and there are many who maintain the importance of keeping the governance of the vital function of education physically close to the people. The districts that school boards govern vary tremendously in size, type, and the quality of the education they offer. (See Table 4.1.) "Their diversity illustrates the tenaciousness with which Americans hold to these remnants of socialism and grass-roots expression of public will" (Campbell, Cunningham, Nystrand, and Usdan, 1985, p. 78).

The Legal Framework for Local Boards

The Powers of School Boards

The powers of school boards seem broad to the public and to the administrators who work with the boards. In fact, when there are challenges courts do tend to uphold school boards (Reutter, 1985). In an overwhelming number of instances of legal challenge to new educational practices, the decisions of school boards have been upheld by the courts. Nevertheless, it is important to remember that local school boards are creatures of the legislature, created by the legislature as instrumentalities to carry out a decidedly state function: the provision of public education. School board members are state, not local, officers and this fact does not change whether they are appointed or elected. Even where school board members are appointed by a mayor, they are still state, not municipal, officers and it is worth reemphasizing that the education function is a state responsibility. This legal fact does not change even though certain aspects of the education function may be delegated to local authorities. Local school board members are selected as the legislature chooses, they hold office by virtue of legislative enactment, and their powers may be extended or limited at the discretion of the legislature (Reutter, 1985).

Because of this awkward placing in the governance system, school boards have sensitive relations to cultivate with many other layers of government. In any geographic location there exist both a school government and a general local government and perhaps many of both kinds overlapping each other's territory. Relations are easily strained and disputes are frequently before the courts. School boards can do what the legislature in their state has authorized them to do. These are called the express powers of the board. But legislatures cannot be expected to foresee every eventuality and, therefore, school boards also have implied powers, that is, the powers necessary to accomplish the tasks of the express powers. It is in this large, gray area of implied powers that there is room for much disagreement and thus much litigation.

Boards cannot delegate away their powers. But they can establish policy and procedure by which their powers are exercised by the superintendent. The degree to which this can be done and the areas in which it may be done vary under different state laws, and each educational administrator needs to consult the appropriate laws for his or her state and when in doubt seek legal counsel. When the board has established procedural parameters for the carrying out of board powers by the superintendent, these policies and procedures need regular reviewing as part of a regular board policy-development cycle.

Constituencies of the School Board

In exercising their powers, school boards must respond to a wide range of constituents with a wide range of viewpoints. What Peterson (1976) calls the core constituents include parents, students, teachers, taxpayers, minorities, and the federal and state governments. In Peterson's study, these constituent groups were identified with issues with which they were concerned: Parents were concerned with community control, advisory input, and decentralization; students with rights of governance, expression, dress, and behavior; teachers with teacher power (we would now call it empowerment and restructuring); taxpayers with having the state pay a larger share of the costs of schooling; minorities with desegregation/integration; and federal and state representatives with guidelines, mandates, and court orders. These constituents pressure a school board for attention to their issues through the intervening variables of the community structure and the interaction of the demands of all the groups. Visualizing all of these groups as continually making demands about their special issues, we can see that the pressures on a school board are enormous as it wields both its expressed and implied powers.

Two Views of the Local School Board

That the American public finds school boards important has already been mentioned (Institute for Educational Leadership, 1986). The National School Boards Association captures this view in these words: "The school board is the unit of government best suited to the needs of public schools, because school boards not only represent the public but also translate the public's desires into policies, plans, and goals. . . . The school board is perhaps the very best example of representative and participatory government, its members derived from the community, serving at the public's pleasure, and making decisions based on community needs, values, and expectations (NSBA, 1987, p. 1).

The reform movement of the 1980s, however, caused some reflection on this traditional and still widely held view of local school boards. Given the massive changes that impacted the U.S. educational system during the 1980s, school boards could not remain immune to scrutiny. In the 1990s, two views of the desirability of local boards have begun to emerge. The first is that local school boards are still necessary arms of government, are the voice of the people in the community, and are best placed in the educational governance structure to ensure what is best for the community's children. Succinctly stated, the second viewpoint is that local school boards are archaic inhibitors of educational progress.

Following are some of the reasons local school boards are considered by some to be performing necessary functions for the governance of schools:

1. School boards are a legal necessity. They are required by law and they provide a legal entity that can conduct the business of the school district. Without that legal entity, school districts would be unable to enter into contractual relationships or perform other functions that require the presence of a legal entity.
2. They are a societal necessity. Given the system of funding for public school districts, it is imperative that a board responsive to public concerns have the ultimate responsibility for providing direction to the professionals it engages to provide educational services.

3. The nature of public education requires an independent governing body. Without an independent governing body that is responsive to its constituents, there is ever present concern that the form and function of public education would be decided solely by professional educators. While professional educators exercise a justifiable pride in their profession, the nature of public education requires that the public have a strong voice in how education is administered, delivered, and evaluated. The existence of school boards ensures accountability on the part of the professional educators to those they serve.
4. The education of our children is too important to be left to the professional educational community. Parental concerns and ideas are entitled to an audience before a group that is legally responsible to them and able to provide direction to those individuals who deliver educational services to their children.

Some of the reasons local school boards are sometimes considered superfluous or worse follow:

1. Constitutionally, the basic responsibility for providing education belongs to the states. Local boards are created entities that can be seen as out of control and, in state after state, in virtual competition with state governance structures for power and influence. Challenges, often petty, to the power of the legislature, the state board, and/or the chief state school officer eat up precious court time and public money. The power of the state has been continuously upheld, but local boards never want to give up the struggle, surely a sign of their organizational immaturity.
2. Local school boards have shown themselves too often to be an impediment to reform efforts. By simple inaction they can diminish or halt the effects of reform, and in many cases, inaction is not all they do to sabotage reform efforts. As an example, there are cases of local boards refusing to provide programs for those with disabilities over almost two decades after the landmark legislation in this area. As another example, attempts to consolidate school districts, even when based on long study and sound research, are almost always hotly contested by local boards for reasons that can only be called reactionary compared to the potential educational benefits for the children involved.
3. Societal complexity, rates of change, and population mobility make ludicrous a situation where a child's education can differ markedly from that of a child a mile away. And technology has made obsolete the need for actors physically close to the scene.

4. Restructuring within local districts cannot stop at the board level. These artificial governance boundaries can prevent innovative combinations of programs and choices. The logical conclusion of the establishment of real choice in public schooling could be the elimination of this level of governance.

The Public and the Local Board

An interesting study of school boards was done by the Institute for Educational Leadership in 1986. IEL found that the nation's basic commitment to the concept of local governance of education has not changed, but the public seems unaware of what the school board in its own local community actually does. The discrepancy between the words of support for local boards and the lack of knowledge about a particular local board was rather startling. IEL concluded that school boards are facing serious challenges to their future given the findings of low voter turnout for school board elections, increasing controversy in decision-making processes, a growing reluctance among civic leaders to serve on school boards, and the almost total exclusion of school boards from state and national education reform efforts. Among the study's major findings were the following:

1. Boards tend to be solidly middle and upper-middle class in composition, with women and minorities underrepresented except in large, urban districts.
2. There is strong public support for maintaining the basic institutional role and structure of the school board, but little public understanding of school boards' actual roles and functions.
3. Boards are frequently perceived to spend too much time on administrative responsibilities and "trivial" matters and not enough time on educational issues.
4. Boards are perceived as reactive rather than deliberative and as representative of special interests rather than of the entire community.
5. Boards have only sporadic interaction with general government and tend to be isolated from mainstream community political structures.
6. Board members are seriously concerned about state-level intrusiveness, but have not yet developed a strong response that would make them full partners in educational improvement.
7. The public has high expectations for board member performance and holds school board members to a greater evidence of ability and commitment than other office holders.

8. Board members continue to grapple with tensions over necessarily gray areas between the board's responsibility for policy
   making and the superintendent's responsibility for administration.
9. School boards recognize the need for their own development, but
   the resources and systems to provide this are inadequate.
10. Few boards conduct evaluations of their performance, and very
    few involve the "outside" in such evaluations. (IEL, 1986)

Boards at Work

Nowakowski and First (1989) noted with concern the bypassing of local
school boards in the reform movement of the 1980s. Their research
supports the view that local school boards are important players in the
reform game if reform is to be lasting and meaningful. By simple
inaction, these boards can prevent or delay the institutionalization of
reform. Thus, while we still have this level of educational governance,
it is not wise to bypass it during serious school reform efforts. This
research also supports the view that local school boards have invested
considerable time and expense on reform efforts only to have external
constraints such as diminished state funding undermine their progress
and success.

The nation's slightly more than 15,000 local school boards were
neglected players in the decade of educational reform. Mountainous
packages of state mandates bore witness to the fact that the basic
responsibility for providing public education is a state function and
that the state legislature has the ultimate power and authority over
local school boards to make policy decisions regarding the schools. As
an example, let us look at Illinois.

Eighties-style reform came to Illinois in 1985 via a massive state
reform package covering 169 topics. Although once again it was "clear
that the legislature of each state is the 'big school board' " (Campbell et
al., 1985, p. 60), it was noted that the importance of local boards of
education in implementing these educational reforms could not be
overlooked. The Illinois boards were diminishing or halting the effects
of reform by simple inaction, either planned or by happenstance, as
other items, important or trivial, occupied them.

But the school board is, after all, the policy-making body in the
local school district and should be addressing the items of most importance in the local district. It is the policy-related leadership of the
school administrator that is needed to keep the local board operating
on a policy level and addressing the items of greatest concern. In fact,
the argument can be made that both administrators and boards are

acting neglectfully or worse if they do not address and implement the gigantic strides in knowledge about teaching and learning that are available today to help children. If education-reform-related activity is not among the items occupying the agendas of local boards, concern for the institutionalization of these reform initiatives should be very real.

The purpose of the study by Nowakowski and First (1989) was to evaluate the degree to which the 1985 Illinois Reform Act was being implemented at the local school district level as measured by the number of reform-related board motions, discussions, and reports documented in local school board minutes the year preceding passage of the reform act and the two years following its passage. Since "it is only through the minutes that a board actually speaks" (Hudgins and Vacca, 1985, p. 68), school board minutes were chosen as a measure of local reform-related activity. The study provided evidence of the amount and nature of local policy making directly responding to legislated reform. It indicated that school boards were responding to some areas of the reform bill more than to others and that some school boards were responding to reform provisions more than others.

There was evidence in the school board minutes studied that these school boards undertook some substantial projects in response to reform, but the constraints in the political environment surrounding these boards prevented a sustained reform effect. Some of the boards studied documented concern in their minutes over abandoning newly developing programs and reform activities when expected state financial support did not materialize. These boards saw the withdrawal of support for reform as consequential and they did not lightly modify their own response to reform.

This research did not support the stereotypes of local school boards wasting time on trivia. Minutes of meeting after meeting in this research showed a record of concerned citizens struggling mightily with a massive influx of state mandates on top of agendas filled with largely substantive, though non-reform-related activity. In the context of political strains and fiscal constraints, boards must choose where to be responsive to all the demands upon them. The regular routines and obligations of a board do not disappear in the years a state chooses to pass new mandates. Kimbrough and Nunnery addressed the widely different patterns of responsiveness of school boards. "They [local school boards] must decide whether they are to be responsive to their constituents, other leaders on the board, professional leaders, national demands, or state policies" (1976, p. 356).

As displayed in Figure 4.2, the percentage of attention that the boards in this study gave to reform could be termed disappointing. Nevertheless, it is important to note that many of the responses to

FIGURE 4.2 • *Percentage of Reform-Related Motions versus Nonreform Motions: 1986–1987*

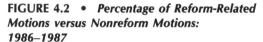
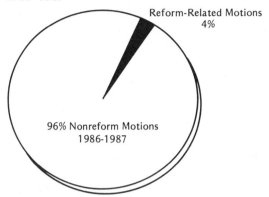

Reform-Related Motions
4%

96% Nonreform Motions
1986-1987

Source: From "School Board Minutes: Records of Reform" by J. Nowakowski and P. F. First, 1989, *Educational Evaluation and Policy Analysis, 11*(4). Copyright 1989 by the American Educational Research Association. Reprinted by permission of the publisher.

reform were significant and potentially could have enduring effects. Among these were included new personnel evaluation procedures, articulated learning objectives, all-day kindergarten programs, new programs for at-risk preschoolers, discipline policies, and reconfigured districts. Although the bulk of activity remained in nonreform areas, much of it was important, such as the passing of a referendum. Time devoted to such an activity is hardly evidence of the trivia in the stereotype, given school funding systems. However, it is important to note that in the later 1980s and early 1990s we have seen state educational finance systems come under careful scrutiny. If funding for education changes away from local property taxes to more and more state responsibility, the justification for the existence of local school boards will further erode.

Three kinds of constraints were identified in Illinois as preventing school boards from devoting more attention to reform (internal, external, and historical). The strongest constraint was an external one: the need for fiscal support beyond the local district level to implement and sustain reform activities and programs. This was substantiated by a 1986 study for the Illinois State Board of Education in which all Illinois school districts were surveyed regarding what they identified as constraints to a proposed second wave of reform. In that study, districts overwhelmingly identified financial concerns as the most powerful constraint over six other constraints: labor agreements, state mandates, public concerns, teacher attitudes, time constraints, and district size (First and Nowakowski, 1986).

It is important to note here that in these studies Illinois school boards were identifying a very real fiscal constraint to proceeding with reform, not simply a perceived obstacle. The Illinois Reform Act of 1985 came, bringing its 169 new mandates, during a decade when Illinois was establishing a dismal record for funding education. Between 1978 and 1988, Illinois dropped from sixth from the top among the fifty states in expenditure per ADA to the twentieth position. This drop of fourteen ranks sounds significant enough, but "when adjustments are made for relative purchasing-power of the dollar, Illinois is burdened with the worst reputation in the nation, having fallen 24 ranks" (Hickrod et al., 1989).

If local school boards and their concerns continue to be overlooked in educational reform movements, then we must ask the very basic policy question of why have them at all; then we stray beyond reform to the realm of reformation as explained by Soltis (1988). We will no longer be accepting the "basic form and purpose of the institution in question" (p. 24). The policy-making responsibilities of the local school board make the inclusion of their functions in meaningful and lasting reform imperative. Attention to their potential roles in board policy making should be a priority for school administrators at all ranks in the school district system. The involvement of all administrators in board policy making is a policy-related leadership function of the school district superintendent. It is also the responsibility of the superintendent to insist that the board become knowledgeable about the best and latest in educational practice and address its time to policy making for its implementation.

The Members of the Local School Board

While school populations are growing increasingly diverse and political parties show signs of representing a broader mix of the ethnic and minority groups that make up U.S. society, communities continue to elect (nearly all board members are elected rather than appointed) to their local school boards a preponderance of middle-aged, college-educated, well-off, white males.

In January 1989, the *American School Board Journal* described the typical U.S. school board member as a white male, forty-one to fifty years old; a married college graduate with one or two children in school; in a professional rather than a managerial job, making $40 to

50 thousand a year; and owning his own home in a suburban or rural setting. He is elected to a school board with seven or eight other board members much like him and he serves one to four years in a school district serving 1,000 to 5,000 students. In our increasingly multicultural society, in a nation that will be comprised of minorities rather than containing minorities by the year 2000, this is a typical school board member with policy-making powers for the education of the children of the twenty-first century. Even the most ardent supporter of local school boards must pause with concern.

Only 4 percent of popularly elected school officials in the United States in 1987 were black or Hispanic, according to data compiled by the U.S. Bureau of the Census. Based on a review of elected officeholders in that year, the bureau reports that 85 percent of the 86,772 school board members, superintendents, and other elected officials in school districts nationwide were white. Two percent were black and another 2 percent were Hispanic. Sixty percent of the officials were men. Data on sex or race, or both, were not available for approximately 10 percent of the officials.

The Bureau of the Census also reports that 87 percent of elected board members that year were chosen on an at-large basis, while 13 percent were elected from subdistricts. A total of 2,574 school board members were appointed, the bureau found. Whether their membership was appointed, elected, or a combination of the two, boards had an average of six members. The data include officials in the 14,721 independent school districts nationwide, but not in the 1,492 dependent districts that are considered part of another government entity (U.S. Bureau of the Census, 1987). Table 4.2 contains percentage of elected school officials by race and sex in 1987.

TABLE 4.2 • *Elected School Officials by Race and Sex*

	Total	*%*	*Male*	*%*	*Female*	*%*
Total U.S.	86,772	100	57,174	100	20,648	100
White	74,003	85	54,380	95	19,673	95
Black	1,825	2	1,276	2	549	3
Hispanic	1,415	2	1,101	2	314	2
Native American	488	1	347	1	141	1
Asian	91	0.15	70	0.5	21	0.5
Not reported	8,950	10	N/A		N/A	

Source: U.S. Bureau of the Census, 1987

Note: Details may not total 100% because data on race or sex was not reported, or due to rounding.

The Role of the Local School Board

The role of the school board is generally considered to include policy making, advocacy for students, staffing and employee relations, fiscal matters, accountability to the community, and planning of the future. All categories can be covered by the one phrase, policy making. A local school board exists to make policy, and everything that happens in a local school district flows from that policy, whether it is made well or poorly. Board policy making can be visualized from a systems approach as displayed in Figure 4.3.

Inputs or pressures force the processing of policies which leads to the outcomes or policies, procedures, and plans that form the backbone of a school district. Policies made are part of the process. The results of those policies in terms of their effect on children's lives and opportunities are the true measure of the effectiveness of a local board of education (First and Nowakowski, in press).

FIGURE 4.3 • *Systems View of Local School Board Policy Making*

Inputs	Processes	Outcomes
Commission reports	Local school board	Budget
Community/parent concerns	deliberations	Calendar
Court cases (fed/state)	Local school board	Class size
Demographics	learning	Curriculum
Economy	Local school board	Discipline
Elections	policy making	Graduation
Federal initiatives and	recorded in meeting	requirements
policies	minutes	Improved learning
Foundations		Improved lives
Media		Salaries
Postsecondary requirements		Staff development
Results of research and		Staffing
development		Tax rate
Special interest groups		Teacher evaluation
State mandates/policies		Textbooks used
Students		Working conditions
Superintendent/		
administrators		
Tax base		
Teacher organizations		
Teachers		

A policy is a broad guideline that describes what course of action the board approves in a given situation. A policy has long-term effects and wide influence, and when properly implemented and evaluated can stand as testimony to the board's leadership and guidance.

Boards make policy to foster stability and continuity in the district, to provide the crucial climate for better learning and life chances, and to build the framework within which school administrators can lead good schools. It is a crucial part of a school administrator's policy-related role to help the board achieve this level of policy making and governmental leadership. Policies inform everyone of board goals and clarify the board-superintendent relationship, thus saving time and effort for the superintendent for leadership to and with the schools. Policies also save time and effort for the board. They are a public decision point and a signal that deliberation of an issue has stopped for a time. The board moves on to other policy matters while the administrators continue the policy cycle with implementation and evaluation phases.

Policies eliminate school district confusion in all areas and at all levels of school district management. Policies that are developed in an atmosphere of study and consensus provide the basis for further good management decisions by the school board, and the repetition of discussion and argument over similar district problems and solutions is eliminated when written policies provide consistency to school board decisions.

The school board delegates to the administration the authority to implement and evaluate policies and to handle problems that may arise. The superintendent serves as the school board's chief school official and under board policy establishes procedures for action within the school district. Each time a decision is to be made, the superintendent does not have to go to the board, but may address a problem based on established policy.

Policies inform everyone about the school board's philosophy, intents, and goals. Board policies are discussed and adopted in open meetings, and the content and impact of a policy needs to be communicated to those most directly affected immediately following a meeting. Policy statements and policy manuals should be easily available to any member of the community at every school site. Written policies foster stability and continuity for the district when board members and school district personnel change. Personnel change is not as traumatic when written policy provides direction and guidance to newcomers and assures students, parents, and the community that the district's vision and purposes will be carried on (McCormick and First, 1991).

Legality of Board Policy

Policies are legal documents enacted by a school board that has the legal authority to determine district goals and management. The courts ask that board discretion—policies—be written statements. And so, although we know that informational/organizational processes may, and often do, result in ad hoc policy, it is the written policy on which the board and the administrators must stand if a challenge develops. Also, the process of developing and revising a policy statement becomes an educational tool in itself for both board and administration. As the board adopts policy, its members become more knowledgeable about school district management.

From a legal perspective, the presence of absence of board policy is particularly important in matters that affect the educational or employment interests of students or staff members. This is because these matters are most vulnerable to potential litigation against the school board or its members. In cases where a policy is open to legal challenge, the standard used by a court of law to determine its enforceability is much the same standard that is used to judge legislation at other levels of government. This standard has been cogently outlined by Reutter (1985):

1. The rule should be publicized. School authorities must take reasonable steps to bring the rule to the attention of students, staff members, or others who are affected by it.
2. The rule must have a legitimate purpose relating to the effective functioning of the school system.
3. The rule must have a rational relationship to the achievement of that purpose.
4. The meaning of the rule must be reasonably clear. It must not be so vague as to be almost completely subject to the interpretation of the school authority invoking it.
5. The rule must be sufficiently narrow in scope so as not to encompass constitutionally protected activities along with those that may constitutionally be proscribed.
6. If the rule infringes on a fundamental constitutional right, a compelling interest of the local school board in the enforcement of the rule must be shown.

A policy that does not meet this standard will be deemed to be unenforceable in a court of law. Additionally, courts will review the consistency with which such policies are applied by the school district and will look askance at actions that give an appearance of partiality or capriciousness.

Why Boards Do Not Make Policy

Written policies are the means by which school districts operate most effectively and efficiently. Why then do so many school boards neglect this important duty? The National School Boards Association discovered the following reasons in a nationwide survey: lack of time or staff, lack of administrative leadership, negative board attitudes about written policy, lack of policy-making "know-how," frequent turn-over of board members and superintendents, the high cost of consulting assistance, and lack of available resource information. Administrative leadership in the policy-development realm is needed to overcome all of these obstacles to board policy making.

Boards need to consider and reconsider the policies that provide leadership to all aspects of school district operations as part of an ongoing policy formulation and review cycle. There are times other than its own preset calendar and cycle that a board needs to attend to certain policy areas. These are following a legislative session, after a Supreme Court decision, when a policy is causing problem, and in response to societal problems.

In this last area, local boards can assume a leadership posture without waiting for compelling directives from state or federal agencies. For example, local school districts could have examined their own policies in order to be more welcoming to growing numbers of homeless children in the late 1980s without waiting for forced compliance to the provisions of the McKinney Homeless Assistance Act.

In taking such a leadership stance, boards need to consider the various levels of priority among policies, procedures, and law and decide which level needs to be changed or influenced in order to address the problem. These levels are case law, statutes, state board of education rules and regulations, agreement with teacher group, board of education (local) policies, superintendent regulations, principal's rules, and teacher's classroom rules.

A school board should always practice preventative law. One way to do so is to have the board attorney question each policy or procedure to reveal potential legal problems after the board has decided the educationally sound direction it wishes to take.

The Policy-Development Cycle

A board needs to know that, in some carefully planned fashion, it is addressing in a policy-related way all of the domains of an education system. Every three years on a published rotation, every domain of the board should be reviewed. Advice on policies all districts should have and the policy areas all boards must address is readily available to administrators and the board from the National School Boards Association and its affiliate state school board associations. Good publications that can be of help to the school administrator are also available. Examples are NSBA's *Becoming a Better Board Member: A Guide to Effective School Board Service* (1982) and *American School Boards: The Positive Power* (1987). There are similar sources of guidance available from national and state administrator organizations.

One of the most positive ways that the school administrator can exercise leadership with the board in its policy development is by assisting the board in establishing a workable policy-development cycle. In Figure 4.4 a policy-development cycle is presented. As can be

FIGURE 4.4 • *A Policy-Development Cycle*

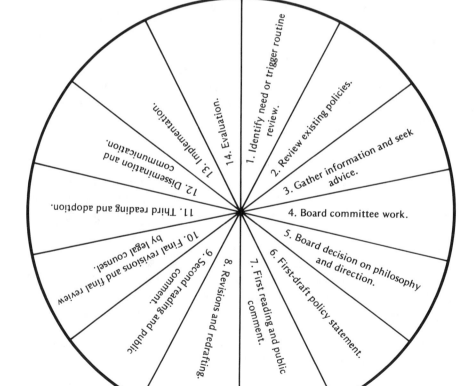

seen from the configuration of Figure 4.4, policy development is continuous and overlapping. Various policies, problems, and domains will be in various steps of the cycle simultaneously. Fourteen steps are presented in this policy-development cycle. Each step may have a variety of tasks which will vary depending upon the particular policy area being addressed. A discussion of each of these fourteen steps follows.

Step 1. In Step 1 the need for attention to policy may happen in a variety of ways. A district policy domain such as reading curriculum may be due for review on the regular policy-development calendar. The Supreme Court may have decided another student's rights case, triggering a need for the board to review its discipline policies. The district superintendent or a building principal may identify a policy that has caused numerous implementation problems, thus signalling the need for a policy review. The state board may enact a new mandate or the state legislature may revise a statute. The U.S. Department of Education may announce significant findings of accumulated research on middle school science curriculum. Or a school site, particularly in districts that have embraced site-based management, may bring to the board's attention policies needing reconsideration so that the site may proceed with its creative direction. In some way and from some person or group (see Figure 4.3), a need or a problem comes to the attention of the board of education.

Step 2. In Step 2 the superintendent and staff review existing policies to determine which ones need attention, given the particular problem that has been raised. In big urban districts, a big staff exists to provide such services. In small rural districts, the superintendent may be the only person available to provide this kind of staff work for the board. But in both cases the elements of a good policy-development process remain the same.

Step 3. Information needed for consideration of the problem is gathered. Reviews of the latest research and literature are needed. Advice must be sought from as many sources as possible: teachers and other staff with particular expertise in the area; staff committees (both standing or ad hoc for this particular problem); the district citizen advisory committee; or a special commission established for this purpose. If a grave or momentous policy decision is under consideration, consultants may be needed and legal advice should be obtained. Regarding the legal advice, it certainly is important that the board "stay out of trouble," but it is equally important that the board first make educationally sound decisions, hopefully even ground-breaking and creative decisions, and then find a legally sound method of implementation. For an issue that is expected to be quite controversial, the appointment of a special citizen commission is a good idea. Such a group can hold public hearings and consider opposing ideas that may otherwise delay the process in later steps in the policy-development cycle.

Step 4.   Once information has been gathered, it is time for a committee of the board (whichever standing committee of the board has leadership responsibilities in the policy domain) to study, deliberate, and determine the basic issues involved. The board committee then fashions recommendations for the board as a whole regarding the board's policy direction in this matter, consistent with the board's educational philosophy.

Step 5.   The board receives the board committee report and agrees on the philosophy, direction, and intent or sends the issue back to committee. At some point, the board as a whole needs to agree on philosophy, direction, and intent in this policy matter as it related to the broader educational philosophy, direction, and intent of the board. Only then can the cycle meaningfully and smoothly continue.

Step 6.   Staff now actually writes the first draft of the policy statement. Note that the statement itself, even a first draft, is left to Step 6, after fundamental agreement on "what the board is about" has occurred. The superintendent and/or staff writer now knows what the words on the paper are supposed to reflect. If time and effort have been expended for thoroughness in Steps 1 through 5, the rest of the cycle can proceed more quickly. And obviously the amount of time and effort will vary greatly depending upon the problem (or opportunity) under consideration.

Step 7.   Before the first reading and subsequent deliberations at a board meeting, the public and those most affected by the proposed policy must have adequate notice that the policy is being considered. Some states have specific laws regarding adequacy of such notice. Time for public comment on the proposed policy takes place at the board meeting where the board first reads and deliberates upon the proposed policy statement.

Step 8.   Revisions and rewriting take place in response to the board's deliberations.

Step 9. There is a second reading of the proposed policy at the next board meeting, and time is provided again for public comment and further board deliberation. It is important that a policy keep moving through the cycle and that proposed policies not just "disappear" from board consideration.

Step 10. This is the time for final revision and for a careful review by legal counsel.

Step 11. At the time of the third reading at a board meeting, the board acts on the policy.

Step 12. There is immediate communication of the policy to those immediately affected and the public at large.

Step 13. The policy is implemented under the direction of the school district superintendent. Plans for evaluation should be built into the implementation plan.

Step 14. The evaluation, both formative and summative, leads to revisions, updating, and improvement and eventually to the "beginning" again of the policy-development cycle.

In the steps of the policy-development cycle, we can see the school administrator in his or her policy-related roles: policy maker, policy implementor, consumer of policy research, and policy analyzer and evaluator. By exerting leadership in establishing and implementing a policy-development cycle, the administrator can avoid the undesirable policy-related role of victim of policy mismade. At the local governance level, we can see opportunity for educators in all parts of the school district to positively influence educational policy making and of the local administrator's response to policy set at other levels of the educational governance system.

Contributions

In the first contribution, Thomas Glass discusses the importance of the school district policy manual and steps for its development when no manual exists or when policy development has been so neglected that a total revision of the manual is necessary. The sections of the manual suggested here could also be used as a classification of policy domains to be scheduled for the regular policy-development review.

Contributions dealing with specific policy areas then follow. In discussing literacy, Rosemary Salesi points out how expectations change over time and how changes in instructional policy must follow. In the area of reading, the innovative changes come from the classroom. It is a reminder to boards and superintendents not to overlook the policy-development expertise in their own staffs. Challenges to administrators regarding policy development and implementation are then delineated.

In the next contribution, Lawrence Rossow provides policy-related advice to principals regarding search and seizure. In this example, policy has been set, beginning with the Supreme Court. The policy-related problem for the principal then becomes proper implementation within existing law.

Charles McCormick stresses the importance of the policy-related roles of the school business official. There is discussion in the contribution of the policy-related functions of the school business official in policy areas not directly impacting the business function, as well as of those that directly impact the school business official's role. The district's business official is the contact throughout the policy-development process for expertise on the legal, insurance, building, and other external information that policy development in any area requires, in addition to the crucial budget information.

Joan Curcio discusses the conversion of policy into practice using the example of restructuring. For a school board to embrace restructuring in its fullest sense requires a districtwide commitment to fundamental change. The policy implications of such a philosophical shift are enormous as this contribution makes clear. It is an opportunity for the most skillful leadership on the part of committed administrators.

Using the voices of principals, Ira Bogotch gives us examples of the burden principals must assume from policy made at other levels of the governance system. In his discussion of the "managerial virtues of necessity and choice," we see the deliberation and the stress as principals strive to further their educational and personal beliefs within the policy constraints placed upon them.

And lastly, we return to that complex policy question being debated at all levels of the educational policy-development system: parental choice of school. John Maddaus explores more of the policy-related complexities of this new direction for public education. As he points out, the movement toward choice is such a fundamental policy change that it opens for everyone involved the basic question of what the fundamental purposes of schooling ought to be. It is an issue that can serve as example for the discussion throughout this book of the need for policy-related leadership by educational administrators at all levels of the educational governance system. Persistent and inspired educational leadership really can lead to better education and better lives for all our children.

THOMAS E. GLASS

The District Policy Manual

The development of policies is one of the most important responsibilities of school boards. The development of procedures to implement policies adopted by the board is the responsibility of the district administration and is no less important.

What is a school district policy? In general, it is a broad or specific statement of purpose. Some policies are very broad in scope and some are more limited in nature. For example, a policy on educational opportunity is a broad type that states the board's intent of providing educational programs to meet the needs of all students in the district. A more specific intent is addressed in a personnel policy that states that employees must not possess a conflict of interest with district business operations.

Often, there is a great deal of confusion as to what is policy and what is procedure. Generally, procedures are the steps the district administration will take to implement a board policy. Sometimes these procedures, as in the case of a reduction-in-force policy, need to be quite detailed and guarantee due process.

In this age of litigation, school districts periodically find themselves in court defending their policies and procedures. Generally, it is the procedures used in the implementation of policies that run afoul of the law.

To be sure, many procedures need to be adopted by official board action along with the policy. Also, districts need to understand that just because an item is included in a state statute does not mean that a district policy should not be written at the local level. Procedures specifically fitted to the local scene need to be developed and, in many areas such as personnel, the courts expect employees to be familiar with district policies, not necessarily state statutes. This also follows for items in the negotiated agreement.

How Should a School District Organize to Develop District Policies?

Step 1. In most districts there is already an existent policy manual. The new manual may be a revision, or the district may decide to start from scratch and develop a totally new manual. This decision

An earlier version of this work appeared in *Thresholds in Education, 12*(2), May 1986.

should be based on a needs assessment made by a committee of administrators, board members, staff, and, probably, consultants. Many states have organizations that furnish a policy-development service to districts. The committee should look into what types of technical assistance are available from these groups. More specifically, the committee should look carefully at the district's policy needs, which often will be determined by district size, experience, and programs.

Step 2. The following are the usual sections of a school district policy manual. The committee might wish to establish a priority list as to what section should be developed first.

Sections

Board of Education	Community Relations	Noninstructional Operations
Instruction	Administration	Special Education
Students	Financial	School Facilities
Personnel	Management	Miscellaneous

Step 3. Once the schedule of work is determined, the committee should then assess the types of resources needed to develop each section. Timelines also need to be established in order to make sure the project will be completed at some point. Also, in the case of a major revision, board members will have to carefully read and consider each policy before its formal adoption at a board meeting. This takes much coordination.

Step 4. An administrator should be appointed by the board to work with the committee on what probably will be a year long task. Many districts release an administrator for a school year to work on the project. The committee will likely have other responsibilities, and a facilitator between the committee and outside resource persons is essential.

Step 5. Policies need to be developed on a schedule and, most importantly, be previewed before all concerned parties in the school district. Better yet, as many staff members as possible should be involved in development of the policies so they will feel ownership and involvement.

Step 6. Procedures need to be developed along with the policies because many times the board will want to know specifically how a policy, such as reduction in force or dismissal, will be implemented. Additionally, a legal consultant will have to review most policies and procedures at this time for their legality and appropriateness.

Step 7.   Once the draft policies and procedures are developed, the district's administrative team should assess them in order to ensure they will meet the operational needs of the district. The committee should meet at least several times with the administrative team for this purpose.

Step 8.   Once the draft policies and procedures have cleared the administrative team, legal consultants, and committees, they should be carefully typed and printed using a numerical system and perhaps different colors of paper for policies, procedures, and forms, which should also be included in the manual.

Step 9.   The policies should be presented to the board in small numbers. The board should not hurry through them, because this would imply to the public and staff that they are not important documents. In fact, it is suggested that once adopted, the policies most affecting employees be put in binders and distributed to them. They should also be recovered once a year for update.

Step 10.   The administrator appointed to develop the policy manual should be relieved, and another central office administrator should be given the task of continually updating the district's policy manual. Due to changes in legislation, district programs, and legal precedent, a district with a good policy manual probably will make ten to twenty updates per year.

Once a district has spent a lot of time and money on the development of a new manual or an update of an old one, it is very important that it is used properly. Certainly, the district's administrators are going to use many of the policies for management of school functions. Board members are going to refer to district policies to make sure they understand the broad guidelines under which the district is being managed. And, at times, teachers and community members are going to read specific policies that may affect them or the groups they represent, such as athletic teams or groups wishing to use school facilities. It is vitally important that all concerned have easy access to a district policy manual. Perhaps a copy should be placed in each school library, principal's office, city library, and, of course, in the hands of each board member. Many districts distribute copies to the teachers' association and other employee groups. Before distribution, however, it is desirable to put the policy manual out to review by the district's legal advisor or others qualified to make sure the policies are legal and do not violate state statutes or due process.

Another question that often comes up while a district is developing policies is whether or not policies need to be developed that parallel state or federal statutes. Legally, probably not; but can a district expect its administrators and other employees to be familiar with voluminous school code books and the many volumes of laws, rules, and regulations that apply to school districts by both state and federal agencies? Of course not! The purpose of the policy manual is to inform employees as to what the policies of their district might be. It is reasonable to expect them to be familiar with their local policy manual, and this can be important if a case for employee discipline ever arises from a violation of a state or federal statute. Therefore, it is only good sense to develop policies that parallel state and federal statutes when it is judged that employees should be aware of what they are expected to do and not to do.

A similar case can be made regarding employee-negotiated agreements. District policies should exist that parallel contract language. Thus, it is very important to update the policy manual each time a new agreement or contract is signed. Many times, there will be personnel policies in manuals that pertain to only one type of employee. Typically, the teachers will have a negotiated agreement and the support staff will not. This creates a bit of confusion, and care should be taken when developing separate sets of policies for different employee groups. Also, care should be taken to see there are no conflicts with language in district policies and statements made in employee or student handbooks. In some states, district policies and employee handbooks have sufficient power to legally bind the district to the included language.

In summary, the policy manual of the school district should be a living document that serves as the chief guide for district management and, therefore, is a signpost for administrators, board members, teachers, and other staff who are responsible for carrying out their duties. Unfortunately, in today's legalistic world, policy manuals have become far thicker and wordier than they should be, but still they are very necessary and important enough that a district should make time and resources available to do a good job on the initial and subsequent updates.

Many policies will need implementation procedures, and this is just as serious an endeavor as the development of the original policy itself. The procedure attached to a policy sometimes becomes even more important in a legal challenge, as many times due process of an employee or student is breached in the process of implementing a policy such as teacher evaluation. The procedures need not only legal review but also intensive input from the administrators who will be responsible for using them. Orientation sessions for all district administrators often are a good idea *before* procedures are attached to policies. The procedures attached to policies are often very complex and should be understood by the administrators who will implement them. Unfortunately, many districts never take the time to develop procedures for policies and wind up with a situation where past practice becomes not only the policy but the procedure.

ROSEMARY A. SALESI

Whole Language, Literacy, and School Policy

As literacy needs shift so have the instructional strategies needed to meet future issues. In the past, it was necessary for only a small number of individuals to be literate (Aaron, Chall, Durkin, Goodman, and Strickland, 1990). The current national goal is that "by the year 2000, every adult in America will be literate and will possess the skills necessary to compete in a global economy and to exercise the rights and responsibilities of citizenship (National Governor's Association, 1990). Therefore, since literacy expectations have greatly changed, school policies toward literacy issues must also change dramatically.

In the 1930s, my father and mother left school, he having graduated from the eighth grade and she after completing her sophomore year. They were viewed as having more than an adequate education. They could read and write better than the typical fifth- and sixth-grader. They were more than well prepared to assume jobs in factories where the amount and difficulty of reading and writing expected was completing simple forms and reading simple directions. They knew that in the event of a problem, the supervisor would interpret orally.

When I completed high school in 1960, the expected level of literacy had risen to about that of an eighth-grader. Occupational literacy needs were higher than those of my parents, and more middle and lower socioeconomic-level students continued on into postsecondary educational programs or received on-the-job training that allowed for advancement. By the year 2000, it is projected that many jobs will require at least a second-year-college reading level (Aaron et al., 1990) and the ability to think abstractly—both of which are considerably beyond the literacy expectations for blue-collar workers fifty years ago.

These changes in the expectations for literacy call for changes in instruction. Over the last fifteen to twenty years, perceptive teachers have recognized the shifts in literacy, society, and the workplace. Many of our new innovative instructional strategies were developed in response to these needs. Out of their classroom experiences, these teachers are continuing to identify new strategies. What is different about this paradigm is that it is tied to teachers and their classrooms rather than to commercial materials, policies, curriculum, assessment, or staff development. This new paradigm is aimed at meeting the

growing literacy demands of the twenty-first century, and school policies need to support both the teachers and their programs. To this end,
administrators face several challenges in setting literacy policies:

1. Institutionalizing whole language
2. Redefining and creating a flexible curriculum
3. Rethinking assessment
4. Funding classroom and school libraries
5. Facing the censorship issue: protecting students' right to learn
6. Creating a collaborative working environment

Whole Language: A New Paradigm

The key principles of whole language are not new, but their
combinations do create a new paradigm. Heald-Taylor (1989) states:

> In whole language it is believed that youngsters acquire lan-
> guage rather than learn through direct teaching; that language
> learning is child-centered, not teacher-dominated; that language
> is integrated rather than fragmented; that children learn by
> talking and doing rather than through passive listening; that
> they learn to read and write by engaging in experiences with
> literature and writing, as opposed to drills and workbook exer-
> cises; and that children learn best in interactive problem-solving
> situations rather than in isolated individual tasks. (pp. 15–16)

Whole language is a dynamic philosophy based on theory and
research as practiced in the classroom. It is this belief system that
separate whole-language teachers from teachers who use some of the
strategies found in whole-language classrooms. And it has the potential of meeting the growing literacy and educational demands we face
in the twenty-first century.

As I stated, whole language as held by many of today's classroom
teachers, reading specialists, special educators, speech specialists, administrators, and teacher educators is uniquely rooted in practice.
Over the years, teachers and teacher educators, frustrated like myself,
took what we knew about language, language learning, and learning
in general, and through practice and learning from and with children,
refined theory, which continues to be further refined.

Teacher educators have been there assisting and mentoring, but
like the classroom teachers who learn from the students, the college
faculty learn as much from the teachers as they offer in return. Thus,

unlike most innovations that often are instituted from the outside, the development of whole language has and will continue to come from classrooms at all levels. "It is the teacher's stated beliefs, the character of classroom interaction, and the teacher's and students' underlying intentions, the *deliberately* theory-driven practice—not simply the behaviors—that make a classroom whole language" (Edelsky, Altwerger, and Flores, 1991, p. 18).

Challenge 1: Institutionalizing Whole Language

Mandating a literature-based or whole-language curriculum may lead to confusion. Teachers, out of fear, lack of adequate preparation, or a differing belief system may sabotage the program. Policy regarding the institutionalizing of whole language may need to support and encourage teachers, but not force immediate change. It may include providing professional days for school visitation, outside consultants, money for graduate courses in reading, language arts, children's literature, and so on, and most importantly, time to grow professionally.

On the average, it takes three to five years for "traditional" teachers to become whole-language teachers. Keep in mind that this is not a new bag of tricks to be learned, but rather a body of knowledge about language, language learning, and possibly a different belief system, where teachers may need to rethink their roles in the classroom. Learning is a social process best achieved through direct engagement and experiences. The whole-language teacher recognizes that because the learners' purposes and intentions are what drive authentic learning, his or her roles in the classroom will change from authoritarian to serving as a model, mentor, or coach and even, sometimes, a learner.

Challenge 2: Flexibility in Redefining Curriculum

In this paradigm, the purpose of the instruction is to create critical readers and writers, those abstract thinking workers necessary for the twenty-first century. These students will know how to use language to learn about the world, past and present, as well as to hypothesize about its future. If learners' intentions are to be honored, the curriculum will shift to follow students' interests. Certainly, teachers are guiding that learning, but there will need to be flexibility in redefining the curriculum.

One cautionary note: I regularly come across cases where the administrator has encouraged teachers or agreed to allow teachers to establish a whole-language classroom and then has proceeded to put in place regulations such as using basal readers so many days per week or correcting and grading journals or requiring all desks be kept in rows, or not allowing teachers to have classroom libraries, and so forth. Such regulations are in direct conflict with the whole-language belief system and only lead to confusion and teacher frustration.

Challenge 3: Rethinking Assessment

During this period when teachers are shifting roles, assessment policies need to be rethought. Standardized tests are not practical or, for that matter, fair in this whole-language paradigm. The content of reading and writing is authentic and assessment needs to mirror that. Assessment needs to be detailed and sensitive, giving evidence of "*how* as well as *what* a child is learning across a range of different learning contexts" (Barrs, 1990, p. 244). Whole-language teachers need assessment strategies that profile students' strengths and needs. Assessment strategies need to shift to include such methods as structured observation, sampling of students' work, error analysis, in-depth interviews, checklists, portfolios, and cumulative records (Barrs, 1990; Au, Scheu, Kawakami, and Herman, 1990). An even more difficult aspect of this challenge is changing the entire report card system to reflect this assessment and gaining support of the community. Students' strengths and needs cannot and should not be reduced to a grade.

Challenge 4: Funding Classroom and School Libraries

The single most important characteristic of the whole-language classroom is the eclectic consumption of all types of resources, particularly children's literature. As schools shift from textbooks to tradebooks, administrators will have to ensure that there are sufficient funds to support both classroom libraries and a substantial school library collection across the years. Classrooms using the integrated approaches of whole language require collections that have up-to-date information in the content areas.

Today's school library also encompasses technology. Computers and software must be available for both large group instruction and individual use. Although word processing is not essential for writing instruction, when students are allowed to compose at the computer, fluency and revision are enhanced.

Challenge 5: Facing Censorship Issues—Protecting Students' Right to Learn

When we expose children to "real literature," we also expose them to values, controversy, and ideas. "Great literature by definition deals with profound human issues—with good and evil, war and peace, love and hate, patriotism and cowardice, sin and redemption" (Wolk, 1990, p. 7). It is not only parents who may object to many of the thought-provoking tradebooks, but also superintendents and school boards, who under the protection of the 1988 Supreme Court decision *Hazelwood School District* v. *Kuhlmeier*, have considerable power to strike books from the curriculum (Bjorklun, 1990). In politically adversarial times, schools may retreat from protecting students' right to read to actually promoting censorship. To avoid allowing ourselves to become the censors, it is essential that a materials selection and review policy be developed that ensures that books are thoughtfully and sanely considered so that we truly distinguish between values and orthodoxies. As we prepare students for the twenty-first century, public education has a responsibility to instruct students in the heritage that is common to all American groups and religions, a heritage of tolerance and diversity (Bjorklun, 1990). As a society we cannot afford censorship that limits and inhibits students' exposure to the thought-provoking materials and issues.

Challenge 6: Creating a Collaborative, Innovative Working Environment

The final challenge administrators face in working with teachers may be the most important. Just as children need a collaborative, learning-focused environment, so do teachers. As teachers, we cannot take children where we have not been ourselves. If teachers are to help children take risks and experiment in the learning process, teachers also need an environment that is safe for them to take risks. If that is to occur, administrators need to operate from a similar philosophical position, necessitating their also examining "their beliefs about learning and teaching and about teacher development" (Newman and Church, 1990, p. 24). I urge you to read and learn more about the whole-language paradigm. Highly recommended are *Becoming a Whole Language School: The Fair Oaks Story* (Bird, 1989), *The Administrator Guide to Whole Language,* and *Whole Language: What's the Difference* (Edelsky, Altwerger, and Flores, 1991). Visit whole-language classrooms or take a graduate course or workshop, keeping in mind the complexity of this paradigm. Whole language offers today's schools a new vision on how to meet tomorrow's literacy needs, but administrative leadership and school policies are keys to its successful implementation.

References

Aaron, I. E., Chall, J. S., Durkin, D., Goodman, K., & Strickland, D. S. (1990). The past, present, and future of literacy education: Comments from a panel of distinguished educators, Part I. *The Reading Teacher, 43,* 302–311.

Au, K. H., Scheu, J. A., Kawakami, A. J., & Herman, P. A. (1990). Assessment and accountability in a whole literacy curriculum. *The Reading Teacher, 43,* 574–578.

Barrs, M. (1990). The primary language record: Reflection of issues in evaluation. *Language Arts, 67,* 244–253.

Bird, L. (Ed.). (1989). *Becoming a whole language school: The Fair Oaks story.* Katonah, NY: Richard C. Owen.

Bjorklun, E. C. (1990). School book censorship and the first amendment. *The Educational Forum, 55,* 37–48.

Edelsky, C., Altwerger, B., and Flores, B. (1991). *Whole language: What's the difference?* Portsmouth, NH: Heinemann.

Heald-Taylor, G. (1989). *The administrator's guide to whole language.* Katonah, NY: Richard C. Owen.

National Governors' Association. (1990). *Educating America: State strategies for achieving national education goals.* Report adopted by members of the National Governors' Association. Washington, DC: National Governors' Association.

Newman, J. M., and Church, S. M. (1990). Myths of whole language. *The Reading Teacher, 44,* 20–26.

Wolk, R. A. (1990). Values, orthodoxies, and public schools. *Teacher Magazine, 2,* 7.

LAWRENCE F. ROSSOW

Policy Advice for Principals: Search and Seizure

Students do have privacy rights. This was established by the U.S. Supreme Court decision in *New Jersey* v. *TLO* (1986). In that decision, the court said that while students have privacy rights and, therefore, prior to being searched some constitutional standards need to be met, those constitutional standards need not be as high as those the police must have when searching adults. The probable cause standard is what is required when police are searching adults. Because of the special relationship between educators and students, school authorities should not be saddled with the same requirements as police. Therefore, the lesser standard, that is, the reasonableness standard, would be the appropriate standard for the school people to use.

The reasonableness standard can be understood by looking at its two major components. The first component is called reasonable suspicion. This means that, before starting the search, the searcher must have some basis for suspecting that the student is carrying contraband which, if produced, would show that the student broke a school rule or law. Second, the searcher must comply with reasonable scope. That is, the searcher must use a search method that is not extensively intrusive in light of the student's age and sex.

An examination of these two prongs of the reasonableness standard is necessary. How can the searcher meet this reasonable suspicion standard in the first instance? Reasonable suspicion can be established by answering two questions: (1) how is it that we know this contraband exists, and (2) what is our source of information? We should get our information that "John Doe" has contraband and that the contraband is located in a particular place from people such as teachers, several students, our own experience, or the student's own history of carrying contraband.

The concern is much less if searching an inanimate object versus a personal search. The reasonableness standard was developed by the Supreme Court for use in personal searches. The search of lockers or other school-owned containers need not be a primary concern for Fourth Amendment purposes. However, do not personalize these searches by not telling the students ahead of time that they should

For a fuller discussion of this topic, see Rossow, L. F. (1990). *Search and Seizure in the Public Schools*. Topeka, KS: National Organization for Legal Problems in Education.

have no expectations for privacy in these school-owned containers. As a matter of fact, some states such as Oklahoma have moved to stipulating by state statute that the school personnel must inform students, on a regular basis, that they should have no expectations of privacy for those school containers. Therefore, when school containers are searched, Fourth Amendment implications are not there because students should not have expectations for privacy.

Assuming that reasonable suspicion has been established, we now must concern ourselves with having reasonable scope. We must select a search method that fits the age and the sex of the student. On a continuum, there are search methods that are highly intrusive, such as strip searching, and search methods that are less intrusive, such as having the student themselves empty their pockets and placing the contents on the counter for us to examine. The closer we come to the body and the way in which the searcher touches the student's body are involved in any implication of the intrusiveness with which the courts are concerned in establishing the reasonable scope requirement. When dealing with elementary or junior high school students, we will need to use search methods that are less intrusive than when searching high school students.

The main concern here is the use of sniff dogs as part of our search method. Whether a sniff dog is a search method or an information-gathering device that helps us establish reasonable suspicion depends on how that dog is handled. If we are going to use the dog simply to help us establish suspicion to determine generally the whereabouts of drugs, the search-and-seizure method would be correct, for example, using the dog to identify which locker contains the contraband. It is when students are in the vicinity and when dogs and students come together in the same general area that there can be problems. As soon as the dog's nose, for example, comes in contact with the student's body, this could trigger a Fourth Amendment concern for the conduct of the search already underway. If the dog is in the presence of the student, this is no longer a simple matter of data collection. The dog then becomes a tool in the hands of the handler and must be considered a part of the specific search method the court considers extremely intrusive. The only more intrusive method would be the strip search.

While we are talking about search methods, we should point out that no court has yet sustained a school district's use of a strip search as a valid method. In all instances where the constitutionality of the search was challenged by the student when a strip search method was used, the students have won those cases. As a blanket policy, it is best to not use strip searching under any circumstances.

To summarize, in order to conduct a constitutional search, the searcher must have reasonable suspicion that the search is going to turn up evidence that the student has broken a school rule or law. The best way to make sure you have suspicion, if the search is challenged, is to be able to show that you had sufficient information coming from reliable sources that led you to believe that the contraband existed and existed on that person. Second, you must use a search method that is reasonable in scope. If the method selected is too highly intrusive given the age and sex of the student, then that standard can be difficult to establish as having been met. Therefore, we recommend that the sex of the searcher be the same as that of the student and that the appropriate search method be selected based on the age of the child. Use less intrusive methods for younger children than you would for older children.

If using sniff dogs, attempt to use those dogs when students are not present. Use the dogs in order to collect information, to narrow the field, and to help establish a suspicion that drugs exist in certain locales. As a general practice, never use a strip search as one of your methods.

CHARLES MCCORMICK

The Importance of Policy in the Role of the School Business Official

The work of the school business official employed in a local education agency is directly policy related much, if not most, of the time. There should be little debate about the extent to which policy is an important aspect of public education, given the policy directives received from the federal and state governments, in addition to the policy provided by the local board of education and board of control. Although the importance of a policy-oriented role for administrators is a major tenet of this book and although this tenet is confirmed by this author's professional experiences, it is interesting to note the lack of discussion of policy issues in school business management texts (e.g., Candoli, 1984; Hentschke, 1986; Wood, 1986). While policy courses have relatively recently been added to the curriculum in education administration programs, there is no guarantee that such a course is required for the future school business manager. Certainly, given this and the importance of policy in the business official's role, there ought to be at least an overview of policy as an important part of the official's professional responsibilities.

In contrast to the lack of content in the profession's preservice training texts, the profession itself recognizes and expects substantial involvement in policy-related matters by its members. Excerpts from "The Code of Ethics for School Administrators" (Figure 4.5) and from the "Standards of Conduct for the Association of School Business Officials" (Figure 4.6) (Richel, 1990) from the Association of School Business Officials, International, make clear directly and by implication some of the broader policy-related functions expected of the business official.

These items make it clear that to fulfill his or her professional responsibilities adequately, the business official must be more than merely a recipient and implementor of policy. The business official has a professional responsibility to assist with developing, operationalizing, implementing, interpreting, and evaluating policy, as well as to seek to change ineffective or bad policy. In addition, the business official should also be a consumer of policy research. Given the many facets of the business official's involvement with policy, how are they addressed or how can they occur in the typical operations of a school district or business official's department?

FIGURE 4.5 • *Excerpts from* **Code of Ethics for School Administrators**

The educational administrator:

- Makes the well-being of students the fundamental value in all decision making and actions.
- Fulfills professional responsibilities with honesty and integrity.
- Supports the principle of due process and protects the civil and human rights of all individuals.
- Obeys local, state, and national laws and does not knowingly join or support organizations that advocate, directly or indirectly, the overthrow of the government.
- Implements the governing board of education's policies and administrative rules and regulations.
- Pursues appropriate measures to correct those laws, policies, and regulations that are not consistent with sound educational goals.

FIGURE 4.6 • *Excerpts from* **Standards of Conduct for School Business Officials**

In relationships within the school district, it is expected that the school business official will:

- Interpret the policies and practices of the district to subordinates and to the community fairly and objectively.
- Implement, to the best of the official's ability, the policies and administrative regulations of the district.

The responsibilities of school business officials often include items such as budget, finance, and accounting; collective bargaining; support services including food service, transportation, and data processing; purchasing; risk management; liaison to the district's law firm; planning; buildings and grounds; construction; and others. The actual relationship the business official has to specific policies and policy functions will vary with the categories of work for which the official is responsible and the size and type of local education agency in which the official is employed. Such functions will vary greatly among different types of school districts (e.g., elementary versus high school districts) and among different types of local education agencies (e.g., school district versus intermediate unit; vocational education unit versus a special education unit). The discussion here cannot be applicable to all situations, nor can it be totally comprehensive. It is, however, illustrative of the primary policy functions with which a business official is likely to be involved in the typical school district.

Development of Policy

The business official is obviously in the key position for the development of those policies that address the business functions of the school district. While the conduct of many of the business functions may b dedicated by state law or regulations, federal law or regulations, ccounting standards, and other external regulatory sources, many olicies regarding the business affairs of a district remain under the ntrol of the board of education. Under what conditions can admistrators disburse cash prior to the board's approval? Can bills be p d prior to board approval to ensure receiving a discount for pro t payment? Can a cash advance be given to a staff member who is ng to attend a conference? What are the circumstances under wh the district's facilities may be rented to community organizatic or individuals? Can they be rented to organizations that want to u hem for profit-oriented activities? The business official should be a ely involved in the development of needed policies in the business a. Such involvement could include identifying the need for policy, ting policy language, and advising others as to the content of a cy.

Another aspect of policy development with which the business cial can assist is to help make the process of development itself cessful. Have those people who should be involved with the development of a policy in fact been properly involved? The constituencies to sider include students, faculty, custodial staff, secretarial staff, rents, administrators, personnel from other local governmental entites, parent/teacher organizations, booster clubs, and union representatives. Have the communications among those who are developing nd those who will be affected by the policy been sufficient and thorough? Has enough time been spent with people? Have things been educed to writing when needed? Have face-to-face meetings occurred where these are desirable? With the movement toward more collegial management/labor relationships within the workplace, it is crucial to allow input from the many audiences who will be affected by a policy prior to actually adopting and/or implementing it. It may very well be easier to interpret, implement, and evaluate a policy of a public entity if the various audiences have had some input and have accepted some ownership in the development and content of the policy. In some instances, the business official may be the most appropriate judge as to these aspects of the policy-development process.

Similarly, the official should assist with policy development in other arenas of the school district. While the official may not be the best source of policy about, for example, curriculum, he or she will likely be a good source regarding the potential costs a policy may incur. Are there implications of which others are not aware? Is there a need to review the intent or language of a policy with the district's attorney, architect/engineer, insurance carrier, or other external entity? The business official may be more aware of the need to consider such things given his or her daily involvement with legal, insurance, building, or other such matters.

Operationalizing Policy

Policy once written (or more preferably, before it is written and adopted) must be operationalized. That is, whatever is needed to actually implement and enforce a policy must be identified, developed, or located and put in place to be used. Administrative regulations and/or procedures may be needed in order to describe how the policy will be implemented and applied. Arrangements should be made to inform those people or audiences who need to know of the presence and content of the new policy. Perhaps a form must be developed, printed, and disseminated as a result of the policy. Or, perhaps resources (e.g., funding, staff, space, etc.) must be found or allocated in order to enact the policy. It is often at this point that a policy that otherwise appears to be desirable and potentially effective comes to be doubted. It is a situation that is analogous to the ability of groups to agree upon goals but disagree vehemently when it comes to deciding what is to be done to achieve those goals. (Remember the 1990 congressional budget process.) The business official must be prepared to address and assist with many aspects of operationalizing policy.

Implementing Policy

For the business official, the impact of the actual implementation of a policy can range from merely taking the time to inform a few staff members in the business office about the new policy to completely changing the manner in which a major business function within the school district is performed. It may be a policy with which the business official will have little to do on a day-to-day basis, or it may be something the official is given primary responsibility to implement and monitor. Perhaps the balanced perspective is to recognize that while, on the one hand, most affairs of a school district are ultimately business affairs, on the other hand, the degree of actual involvement the business official will have in those activities will vary greatly depending on what the policy is.

Interpreting Policy

Very often policies, especially new or changed ones, will need to be interpreted or explained to various audiences. It may be either necessary or desirable to explain a policy to administrative staff, union representatives, the public, community groups, parent-teacher organizations, and so on, depending on the nature of the policy. Policies in public schools affect people's pocketbooks, jobs, children, political interests, professional practices, and the like—important aspects of their lives. In a public entity funded with tax dollars within the context of a democratic society, it is certainly odd to think that the entity does not have a responsibility to explain its policies. People want to know why something is being done. What will it mean to them? Assuming that the process of explaining a policy is a dialogue, the audiences may have something to say about the burden or cost the policy is imposing on them.

Evaluation of Policy

Formal and/or informal evaluation should be done to measure the actual impacts, both intended or unintended, a policy is causing, as well as to assess the degree to which it should be maintained as is, changed, or voided. The business official may be asked to gather objective data or to provide expert opinion to assist with the evaluation of a policy. Indeed, the official has a professional responsibility to attempt to change policy that leads to inefficient use of the entity's resources and assets or that infringes on ethical standards or the tenets of a free society. Is the policy achieving its intended effect? Is that effect proper? Is it possible that a policy has been adopted that should not have been? Hopefully, what the policy was intended to achieve was articulated and debated at some point during the policy-development process. Ideally, some discussion occurred as to how this achievement or effect would be measured empirically. If not, there may be difficulties with objectively measuring the effects of the policy. Opinion may be all that is available as a basis to evaluate a policy. If it has not occurred previously, the evaluation will likely bring out discussion of the competing perspectives characteristic of most issues addressed by policy. Consider, for example, the area of special education, and the competing aspects of issues (e.g., cost, individual versus group rights, efficiency, etc.) become quite obvious.

Questions can arise at this point as to the effectiveness of the policy versus its implementation. Perhaps we have a policy in question that is basically a good policy but for which the procedures are highly inefficient. All aspects of a policy that do not lead to the desired impact should be reviewed, such as actual policy language, regulations, and communications to staff. For the lack of a single horse, an otherwise desirable and effectively written policy may be unsuccessful due to a minor flaw in the manner in which it was operationalized or implemented.

Policy Research

School business management is of necessity a pragmatic profession. However, it is one that is amenable to theoretical and research efforts in general but especially in the area of policy. The practicing business official is in a very good position to assist with field-based policy research, to benefit from the knowledge base and implications good policy research can offer to the profession, and to demonstrate the implications of theory and practice. As a profession, school business management is in its relative infancy and has not yet established a knowledge base, research agenda, or mechanism (e.g., research journals) necessary for the development of this aspect of a profession. Thus, policy research activities within school business management may not only be useful in improving administrative practices, but also may be an important contribution to the development of the profession itself.

References

Candoli, I. (1984). *School business administration: A planning approach* (3rd ed.). Boston, MA: Allyn and Bacon.

Hentschke, G. C. (1986). *School business administration.* Berkeley, CA: McCutchan.

Richel, F. M. (1990, September). "Professional ethics for school business officials." *School Business Affairs, 56*(9), 20–22.

Wood, R. C. (Ed.). (1986). *Principles of school business management.* Reston, VA: Association of School Business Management International.

Restructuring: Converting Public Policy into Real Practice

The notion of restructuring public schools has captured national attention and a position in public policy. In the goals statement adopted by the National Governors' Association at its meeting early in 1990, this body (with many other organizations and individuals before them) documented the need for dramatic change: "Our public education system must be fundamentally restructured in order to ensure that all students can meet higher standards. . . . Restructuring requires creating powerful incentives for performance and improvement, and real consequences for persistent failure (National Governors' Association, 1990, p. 16).

A push for fundamental change in the way schools function comes from numerous directions, reflecting public discontent and frustration with the way things are in education. Legislators, commissions, governors, and business people all are involved in attempting to resolve "the problem." Since the early 1980s, their involvement, from the National Policy Board to individual state legislatures, has resulted in the development of education policies mandating school reform, and now, at the beginning of the 1990s, favoring the restructuring of schools. The pressure for change on those directly responsible for operating schools has been enormous, unrelenting, and often accompanied with unforgiving criticism.

The coping strategies of educators swept into these waves of reform have been inventive, creative, resistant, and even desperate, dependent to some extent on their tolerance for change and their individual values and beliefs regarding education. School reform of most of the 1980s was not reform for which educators were given an integral leadership role. Task forces and commissions were appointed among the states to "answer the failings of the education system as outlined" (Lewis, 1989, p. 34) in the federal government's 1983 report, *A Nation at Risk.* As competency testing, career ladders, high school graduation requirements, homework, and no-pass, no-play rules were legislatively mandated, educators found themselves filling bureaucratic roles of responder and implementor. When alternative views about reform grew, through the studies of Adler, Boyer, Sizer, and Goodlad, and received increasingly more attention, policy making regarding school reform refocused in the later years of the 1980s. Deep structural changes that support "empowering leadership" (Lewis, 1989, pp. 34–40)–in short, restructuring–are now called for, encouraged, and in some places, prescribed.

However, what *restructuring* means, both in policy and in real practice, is not fully understood. Presently, it means different things to different educators. It threatens some; it is a panacea to others. Although it is still "a concept in flux," Lewis (1989, p. 14), in *Restructuring America's Schools,* says that "those who invited the elephant in, the nation's policymakers and many of its researchers, leaders, and practitioners, agree substantially on what it looks like" (p. 3). It would seem to include at least the three types of changes that Elmore (1990) describes: changes in teaching and learning in schools, in conditions of teachers' work in schools, and in the governance and incentive structures under which schools operate. It implies different roles and relationships for everyone involved in schooling and different uses of time and space. As David (1990) suggests, "pressure on school districts to restructure is mounting" (p. 209), from policy makers on down, to "decentralize authority, create more professional workplaces, and focus resources on teaching and learning" (p. 211). School administrators, district and school based, who operate for the most part in "highly centralized, tightly regulated bureaucratic structures" (p. 210) are those expected to work the magic that will transform the duckling into a beautiful swan. Some administrators would like to do it. Others are afraid, cautious, tired, mistrustful. Some are willing, but lacking the skill to take the first step toward a transformation; some are skilled, but without the motivation. Some think their schools are beautiful swans already.

Those who are attracted by the potential of restructuring for increasing quality in the classroom, open minded about its possibilities, placed in the position of responding to state or local policies regarding structural changes in schooling, or simply looking for strategies to make school a better place for all the players can use present policy developments to improve real practice without committing themselves to immediate Herculean tasks. Guided by the following principles, practitioners can work "with deliberate speed" toward change that will, in time, have a deep and solid foundation.

Principal 1: There Are No Quick Fixes in Restructuring Schools. Considering the time and energy required to make lasting change of any kind, TIME becomes a significant factor with which to reckon. Everyone connected with schools–principals, teachers, noninstructional personnel–operates on a treadmill, attempting to perform a full week's work in any given day. To ADD tasks, even professionally fulfilling tasks, will overburden an already weary staff. The time problem needs to be confronted directly (Tuthill, 1990), and all parties must be willing to stay the course. A suburban school superintendent in Florida, discussing initial attempts and learning about the concept of restructuring, said this:

> I began to understand what a problem restructuring was going to be. I had thought that all we'd have to do was go into districts and make these few changes and it would work. Soon after, I realized that this is a much more profound subject than we—at least I— have been giving it credit. . . . What does bother me is that some- times we get in too much of a hurry, and we don't take long enough time to work our way through all these situations. (A. Wiggins, Personal Communication, December 18, 1990)

Principal 2: Shared Visions Grow Out of Common Needs. Change in a school or district begins with a perceived need. Begin by talking with those involved about how things are and ask how they can be better. A place for leaders to begin developing a shared vision is by putting out their own vision for the organization to see and by develop- ing a clear mission for the organization, one that is both tied symbol- ically to the traditions of the system and imaginative enough to allow for significant change (Hines, 1990).

Principal 3: Change Begins with a First (Small) Step. Invite in a small nucleus of the staff, or a cross-section of key stakeholders to talk about some problem or desired change

> and just see what happens out there. . . . Don't . . . say "whatever we decide here is going to be." Say, "the problem is so-and-so, and I'd like your input; and they can start working from there. . . . But all they need to do is get this different way of looking at the problem. Start that way with it, get comfortable with it, and then work your way down [the organizational pyramid]. . . . It's going to take a long time. . . . The first three or four months, everybody gets *gung ho.* They think once an individual plan comes to fruition, the whole concept does. But it doesn't work that way. At least take the first year to figure out what you want to do. Try one of your experiments (projects). . . . Take that whole year, and pay attention to what people have to say. (A. Wiggins, Per- sonal Communication, December 18, 1990)

Principal 4: In Schools, Everyone Deserves an Opportunity to Lead (Barth, 1988). In organizations where teachers and staff members are not valued for their professional capabilities, where the most capable are overburdened and the less capable receive assistance in professional growth inconsistently, where they work in isolation, where recognition is competitive and decisions are made at the top, things cannot get better. Share the leadership tasks and not just with a trusted elite. "Schools can help all the adults and youngsters within their walls learn how to earn and enjoy the recognition, satisfaction, and influence that come from serving the common good" (Barth, 1988, p. 640). On a district level, one school superintendent invited principals and their staffs to share in leading and decision making by seeking their own solutions to problems and by giving them the resources to do it.

> We allowed each one of them to set it (the solutions) up. . . . We gave them money they asked for . . . we did the research. What [one school] . . . wanted to do was close down school once a month or even once a week to do home visits and [have] relationships with parents. . . . Another school . . . set up the idea that their teachers would be paid to stay late at night to keep the library open for research, so that kids could come back later or stay longer. . . . These are some of the kinds of projects we set up under restructuring. Very superficial projects, but we had to start some place. (A. Wiggins, Personal Communication, December 15, 1990)

When leaders share in decision-making, some issues will have to be negotiated. The important points are to "start some place," and then train the team.

Principal 5: Power-Sharing Requires Training in New Skills (Carrano, 1990). If there is going to be any change within a school or within a district in the way in which decisions are made or in who is involved in the decision-making process, training must accompany the changes. Teachers particularly have been programmed to play a minor role in the operation of schools; parents and students have not been invited regularly to collaborate in shared responsibility. Taking a first step in these new waters would be to develop and implement training in team dynamics, while setting up the opportunity for a voluntary team to begin assuming some responsibility for the operation of the school. "School restructuring thus becomes a real option" (Carrano, 1990, p. 40).

Principal 6: Restructuring Implies New Partnerships and Coalitions of Support (Lewis, 1989, p. 144). Schools and school districts actively involved in creating structures for school improvement welcome new alliances, coalitions, and partnerships, sometimes even "bringing former adversaries together. They do this by focusing on the educational goals of restructuring and by developing a shared set of expectations among superintendents, school boards, teacher unions, and their communities" (Lewis, 1989, p. 144). Superintendent Ann Wiggins, Florida's 1991 Superintendent of the Year, refers to her district's relationship with the teachers' union that supported her in her election to the position.

> We meet approximately once a month at their headquarters and sit down with their president and vice president, and we talk informally about things we want to do and potential problems we might have. . . . Keeping that door to communication open has helped immensely. . . . We want their input and they usually give it. . . . We go together [to restructuring conferences] and try to present [ourselves] to the community as a group so they understand that we don't have an adversarial relationship. (A. Wiggins, Personal Communication, December 1990)

The parent community can also be a partner in the process of restructuring, and recognizing and encouraging the increased participation of parents and the community (Lieberman & Miller, 1990) is a valid step for a school administrator to take. Parents, generally, welcome an increased voice in the affairs of the school. Before they can be a positive force for change, however, they need attention, First, "you have to get parents communicating and comfortable with the school, . . . then they'll learn its structure and how they can help support it, and then you can get to advocacy" (Snider, 1990, p. 13).

If new partnerships and coalitions within the school environment are to be more than just window dressing, then the school leader will have to facilitate their development by sharing information. The ease with which information flows up, down, and throughout the school organization distinguishes a vital system from one hardened into a "top-down" bureaucratic structure.

Principal 7: School Administrators Cannot Carry Out Steps toward Restructuring Unless They Have Been Given the Authentic Power and Responsibility.

Principal 8: The Purpose of Restructuring Is to Ensure a Quality Education for All Students. "Schools must be able to effectively educate children when they arrive at the school house door, regardless of variations in students' interests, capacities, or learning styles. . . . As steps are taken to better prepare children for schools, we must also better prepare schools for children" (National Governors' Association, March 7, 1990, p. 16).

Groups of policy makers, such as the National Governors' Association (1990), believe that better preparing schools for children includes deep structural changes in the organization and operation of schools in order to serve the total range of students and resolve the complex problems associated with that range. Policy makers know, also, that real change can only be effected by professional school leaders—the practitioners. The changing of "the old order" into real practice, however slowly or swiftly, is in those hands. The first step is to "start some place."

References

Barth, R. S. (1988, May). Principals, teachers, and school leadership. *Phi Delta Kappan,* 640.

Carrano, F. (1990, December 12). Training the players for power sharing. *Education Week,* 40.

David, J. L. (1990). Restructuring in progress: Lessons from pioneering districts. In R. F. Elmore and Associates, *Restructuring schools. The next generation of educational reform* (pp. 209–211). San Francisco: Jossey-Bass.

Elmore, R. F. (1990). Introduction: On changing the structure of public schools. In R. F. Elmore and Associates, *Restructuring schools. The next generation of educational reform* (p. 5). San Francisco: Jossey-Bass.

Hines, T. (1990, December). Restructuring in YOUR school: Ten steps for principals. Unpublished manuscript, University of Florida.

Lewis, A. (1989). *Restructuring America's schools.* Arlington, VA: American Association of School Administrators.

Lieberman, A., & Miller, L. (1990, June). Restructuring schools: What matters and what works. *Phi Delta Kappan, 71*(10), 761.

National Governors' Association. (1990, March 7). Text of statement of education goals adopted by governors. *Education Week,* 16.

Snider, W. (1990, November 21). Parents as partners: Adding their voices to decisions on how schools are run. *Education Week,* 13.

Tuthill, D. (1990, June). Expanding the union contract: One teacher's perspective. *Phi Delta Kappan, 71*(10), 775–780.

IRA BOGOTCH

Managerial Virtues of Necessity and Choice

In education, there is hardly a policy directive that is so routine that its implementation does not cause some concern or frustration for school principals. This tends to be especially true within states and districts that call out loudly for reform. It is precisely within these reform-pressure locales, however, that the voices of school principals may be least heard. The voices you will hear shortly are those of a few principals from Dade County, Florida, a school district with a continuing reputation for reform efforts.

Their statements illustrate their perception that external policies and directives actually make their jobs more difficult. In some instances, no doubt, such policies have prevented them from doing what they believe would be best for their schools. The problem is not just that the state or district mandates programs without providing adequate resources. That reality is well known. The greater obstacle is that mandated programs have created educational conflicts, particularly in the predominant school domain of curriculum. Let's listen as principals describe some of these conflicts.

[The state] keeps adding content to us. It just takes away basic time we could spend in reading and writing and math when they put a lot of other objectives in there, even though they may be important. They have put things into the curriculum without giving us budgetary monies to fund properly. It has weakened our total curriculum when they keep adding in all kinds of objectives that must be taught.... They may all be wonderful, but something is giving every time you put more objectives in.—(Elementary School Principal)

The district in some instances will go beyond what the state requirements are. Problems are created as a result of that. For example, I believe firmly that electives are important. I think kids need to enjoy coming to school. Based on the state and district requirements, it is very, very difficult. (Middle School Principal)

I used to have some discretion in separating what a college board curriculum was from what a general curriculum was. I have none of that anymore. I am told specifically what to do by the state. There are core standards. The district has taken it a step further and has developed in-house testing, subject area testing, which takes the state objectives and then sees the degree to which teachers are teaching them. They've developed a whole normative thing that holds constant socioeconomic factors. Then we are put back and asked what is going on in terms of individual performance of kids.–(High School Principal)

We've made the classic mistake and that is we think we can give everybody the same thing. But what about the kid whose own priorities, own needs are so great that they don't need [what the state requires.] It's not within my power and I have to sit here and answer to parents and to everyone else and watch what it does to the students.–(High School Principal)

Stroh, Kustra, and Smith (1990), in another reform context, Illinois, have similarly concluded that state policies "confounded their [principals'] ability to function effectively" (p. 174). As adjunct or non-participants in the external policy-making process, the role of school principals as leaders is blunted. For all practical purposes, principals manage schools as best they can. That is, they follow policy directives and structural requirements even when they disagree.

Yet, for many school principals, the mismatch between policy and reality creates opportunities to negotiate and implement choices. Although a few within this group, those who capture the headlines, may be labeled risk takers and mavericks, our primary concern ought to be concentrated on principals whose managerial behaviors emphasize discretion, choice, and negotiated orders within the school's organizational structure. But, it is here where we can differentiate the quality of school managerial performance. Here is where principals combine their knowledge of education and managerial skills on a daily basis with heuristic qualities. As a result, some principals' behaviors are admirable, even virtuous.

What permits us to call managerial performance virtuous is that, on one level, principals have chosen deliberately to integrate qualitative behaviors within the required school structure. And, on a second level, they knowingly use qualitative behaviors in order to make people work better. The first level of managerial behaviors, to paraphrase Shakespeare, makes a virtue of necessity; the second level encompasses virtues of discretion. On this dual level of action, managerial behaviors need to be seen by both principals and policy makers as practical and worthwhile.

Managerial virtues of necessity and discretion can offer school principals specific behavioral guidelines. The starting point is the school's structure, that is, what principals are required to do on a regular or frequent basis. Principals devote the majority of their long work week to the necessary managerial tasks. These actions in practice provide teachers and students with a basic understanding of the school's structure. The regular or frequent actions create a visible presence (Andrews and Smith, 1989), help others to recognize that daily activities are necessary for the school to function properly, and therefore, are perceived as what is structurally important.

External policy directives currently operate on only one level of reality: structure. Even when defining the qualitative goal of "school excellence," structure and quantity dictate how it is to be measured. Even since *A Nation at Risk*, "excellence" has been defined by higher student achievement test scores, increased graduation requirements, exit criteria tests, longer school days, more required courses in elementary school, elaborate teacher evaluation systems, teacher certification tests, higher teacher salaries, increased teacher decision-making responsibilities, and greater parental and community involvement. The list is certainly not complete, but the nature and meaning of excellence is evident. Excellence means everyone—principals, teachers, and students—needs to do more.

For the school professional, these policies are to be implemented as best they can, given the circumstances. To date, the reform measures have ignored the qualitative dimension, namely, how to do better. A principal's ability to comprehend the local political dynamics of policy making and to remain committed to quality education is remarkable because (a) practical understanding of management itself is limited and (b) the reality of school management is filled with contradictions (Clark and Astuto, 1988; Counts, 1930/1971; Miles, 1971). When the pace of policy making is accelerated, as it is in every reform state, the inclusion of quality into external directives becomes problematic. These policies add extraneous and conflicting values to schools, rather than having a value-added effect. The conflict is readily apparent in this principal's words:

> We were identified by the Ford Foundation as one of the top 50 urban high schools in the country. They gave us $21,000 for a curriculum project. We designed a critical thinking project. We freed teachers to write and find curriculum and put it together. Then we set up an inservice schedule. All of the inservice was done in social studies, science and English. We did it. We did a pre and post test and used two other high schools as the control and

what we found was that we did increase critical thinking significantly. But the problem was that it didn't improve the state assessment scores, so we dropped it. . . . [But] I'm not giving you enough information. We were doing it not to improve critical thinking, but after we had analyzed our state assessment test scores, we realized the kids had trouble with thinking-type problems. So by teaching critical thinking we might get them to pass the test.—(High School Principal)

Here, the quantified "more" that was chosen was the standardized test scores, while the qualitative "better" that was rejected was the successful critical-thinking program.

The line between daily necessities and discretion is not straightforward. This simply means that school principals exercise judgment and discretion in all of their behaviors, whether or not they are aware of it. Even in areas where state and district funding dictate how resources are to be allocated, a principal may use discretionary dollars consistent with policy and practice in order to supplement funds. Similarly, in hiring teachers, a principal's preference and criteria have been known to mediate central office hiring policy. Other examples indicate how principals negotiate mutually agreeable solutions with faculties regarding collective bargaining restrictions, meetings, discipline, released time, and noninstructional responsibilities. Again, the voices of principals are most articulate in drawing the line between structure and discretion.

[In teacher evaluation,] I have very little control of the system that is used and I must do it by a certain procedure. [But] in terms of information evaluation, how I work with teachers and help them improve, I have a great deal of latitude here.—(Elementary School Principal)

[In staff development,] I think that almost anything I would want teachers to become involved in, I can probably also get credit for them if we are interested in doing it a certain number of hours and writing up a plan. . . . I can use every faculty meeting for an inservice opportunity, and they [teachers] must come to faculty meetings.—(Middle School Principal)

The effect of collective bargaining is sometimes a hindrance in terms of doing the things that need to be done. One of the things I wanted to do was to develop team leaders in the school, which I was able to do. Teachers were willing to volunteer to do this. I wanted to compensate them. I couldn't do it because of the collective bargaining contract because there was such thing as "team leader." The impact of that was negative because we have teachers who we are not able to recognize.–(Middle School Principal)

Most policy makers, whether legislators or government and corporate officials, still assume that schools can be controlled by pressing buttons and turning switches. They have offered no insights on how to make schools better. Moreover, their knowledge of daily school interactions is extremely limited. As a result, they concern themselves with relatively simple ideas that can be translated into broad, uniform directives (Bogotch, 1988; Darling-Hammond and Wise, 1985). Ultimately, it is up to school professionals to develop educational and managerial models that address quality directly.

Beyond school structure, principals can choose to make a virtue of necessity by integrating qualities into the regular, structural patterns of managerial behaviors. There is no recipe dictating how qualities are combined with required behaviors. The managerial tasks and situations facing principals are far too numerous for such a precise calculus model of when to do this or how to do that. The same, of course, may be said of great works of literature and music. How the writer applies the elements of plot to create tragedy or comedy defies any single formula. And, all the notes are already there for the composer to arrange and the conductor to interpret. Why should it be any different for the human dramas [or comedies] that are being lived within our schools? The integration of discretionary behaviors with the existing school structure is a function of managerial knowledge and skills. The art is to systematically arrange managerial behaviors to improve the performance of others. It is in this fundamental human endeavor that managerial activities are deemed virtuous.

The real plot of any school drama is more likely to be found within the notion of school managerial virtues rather than within pushbutton, mechanical models of schools. The managerial virtues described here do not exist on some higher, moral plane. Not at all. We find them right on the conventional field of action where work is done. Managerial virtues create choices for others and ourselves, give meaning, complete actions, and result in harmony. In short, virtue is that specific knowledge that helps us to realize the best in ourselves and in others.

The question that remains is how to convince more school practitioners and policy makers of this reality. As more and more educational policies originate at the state level, the distance between policy makers and school building principals increases. Yet, if we ever expect to establish quality within schools, all of us had better look and listen more closely to practitioners who can provide us with the best available evidence of what works.

We must not assume that anyone really wants the matter to rest at the present level of noncommunication between policy makers and school professionals. By articulating the managerial virtues, we offer a sense of what principals can do within schools. But how can principals attract the attention of policy makers when the primary responsibility of the former is to implement policy as best they can? We have seen here that, too often, this reality has meant that principals try to make the best of an inappropriate situation. As a result, their public posture appears obedient, if not submissive. Whereas within schools principals seek to be perceived as open, understanding, and fair minded, in policy-making forums, principals may need to demonstrate professionalism by expressing a passion for excellence (standards), a pride in their schools' educational achievements (information), and an intolerance of school injustices (assessments). Any or all of these public behaviors come with a price, namely, a personal responsibility for failure (incentives) (Bogotch, 1990).

Conversely, we must ask what can policy makers do to support managerial virtues? First, they need to put a moratorium (their word!) on policy directives mandating schools to implement programs unsystematically, thereby causing educational value conflicts. Second, in order to foster a more professional school environment, they need to shift their governmental and business incentive programs from a national focus to local forums. Meaningful rewards and recognition ought to come from school clients and local participants.

The national (presidential!) and state school recognition programs are fraught with opportunities to mislead the public about the real meaning of educational quality. We have no national system of education in the United States, nor a single standard by which all schools can be judged fairly. Having national or even statewide awards ignores what thousands of schools and hundreds of thousands of teachers are accomplishing every day. I am afraid that the standardized criteria for national recognition have already led to some serious abuses. Recent cases of test score erasures and false reporting of grades may be only aberrant behavior stemming from character flaws. But if plot remains the essential element, we cannot permit the system to continue to place daily, conflicting pressures on individuals. Rewards from afar create too many opportunities to cheat.

Policy makers need to be educated about the daily realities within schools. Only then will they begin to introduce policies that facilitate the necessary work of school principals. But, neither policies nor policy making should be blamed for all the wrongs in education. Policies reflect political values, not professional educational behaviors. Whatever the gap between the two, principals and school administrators are not helpless. School administrators have shown themselves to be intelligent and resourceful; but, they alone have not transformed schools into joyful places of learning for children or teachers. What the debate between leadership and management has ignored is that within the daily managerial role lies matters of substance, necessity, and choice. As with so many enterprises, success depends upon attention to the daily, little things that matter most.

Virtuous practices of necessity and choice are expected of all professionals, regardless of the plot. But, when they occur in the midst of educational conflict, the practice is even more virtuous, for it is these behaviors that have the power to make schools better places in which to work and learn.

References

Andrews, R., & Smith, R. (1989). *Instructional Leadership: How Principals Make a Difference.* Alexandria, VA: ASCD.

Bogotch, I. (1988). Good law, good practice, good sense: Using legal guidelines for drafting educational policies. *Planning & Changing, 19*(2), 86–95.

Clark, D., & Astuto, T. (1988). Paradoxical choice options in organizations. In D. Grifiths, R. Stout, & P. Forsyth (Eds.), *Leaders for America's schools: The report and papers of the National Commission on Excellence in Educational Administration* (pp. 112–130). Berkeley, CA: McCutchan.

Counts, G. (1930/1971). *The American road to cultures: A social interpretation of education in the United States* (Reprint edition). New York: Arno Press and The New York Times.

Darling-Hammond, L., & Wise, A. (1985). State standards and school improvement. *The Elementary School Journal, 85*(3), 315–336.

Miles, M. (1981). Mapping the common properties of schools. In R. Lehming & M. Kane (Eds.), *Improving schools: Using what we know* (pp. 42–114). Beverly Hills, CA: Sage Publications.

Stroh, L., Kustra, R., & Smith, R. (1990). State policy: The impact on principals' management of their role and responsibilities. *Illinois School Research and Development, 26*(3), 156–174.

JOHN MADDAUS

Parental Choice Plans
at the Local Level

Administrators, school board members, parents, and others considering whether and how to increase parental choice of schools (or educational programs within schools) at the local level face a complex task. Among the questions that will need to be addressed are the following:

1. What educational goals might increasing parental choice achieve?
2. How much choice already exists, and how might such choices affect parental response to the proposed changes?
3. What do we know about how parents already behave with the existing range of choices, and what can we predict they might do if that range of choices is expanded?
4. What program changes would actually be required to achieve the proposed goals?
5. What are the implications of such changes for administrators, teachers, and others in the school system?
6. Are the benefits of expanding parental choice worth the costs that can be anticipated?

Goals of Choice

Advocates of parental choice believe that choice will promote both excellence and equity in education (see Section One). Some proponents of choice, especially conservatives such as Milton Friedman, argue that free-market competition could result in greater variety and quality to meet the desires of consumers. Advocates, in particular liberals such as John Coons, also believe that choice will empower especially those parents with limited resources to act on behalf of their children. Goals such as promoting variety in education and empowering parents are thus intermediate goals to the ultimate end of achieving excellence and equity.

One major problem is the possibility of conflicts between parents, administrators, teachers, school board members, and others about what the fundamental purposes of schooling ought to be. Perhaps the most obvious example is the commitment of fundamentalist Christian

parents to their conception of religious education, a purpose incompat-
ible with present constitutional interpretation and with some concep-
tions of education for individual freedom and citizenship in a pluralist
society (Peshkin, 1986). In addition, there are potential conflicts aris-
ing out of a variety of other educational philosophies in U.S. schools,
including social efficiency, humanism, social meliorism, and develop-
mentalism (Kliebard, 1986). This diversity of philosophies suggests the
possibility that no single measure of excellence, such as tests of basic
skills, will be acceptable to all. Indeed, choice assumes that parents
should be free to pursue their own visions of excellence for their
children.

Equity is also a concept about which conflicting views exist.
There is no clear consensus on what group characteristics (race, language, gender, socioeconomic status, disability, etc.) require attention,
what outcomes would be acceptable, what methods are legitimate, or
even whether schools should be responsible for achieving an equitable
society at all. Parents can be expected to focus on the needs of their
own children rather than of children in general. Thus, their views of
equity issues would be largely dependent on their social position relative to others with whom they might be compared.

Existing Choice Opportunities

Even in a district that has never consciously addressed the issue
of parental choice of school, some school enrollment options certainly
exist. The most basic option exists with relation to housing choice.
Depending on their family resources and other personal circumstances, parents who are moving their families from one home to
another may take schools into account in deciding where to move. Two
major surveys of parents have reported that between 50 and 60 percent
of parents say that they considered schools in making decisions about
housing (Williams, Hancher, and Hutner, 1983; Darling-Hammond
and Kirby, 1985). Less frequently, due in part to the costs involved,
parents may move their families primarily for the purpose of enrolling
them in a different school. For example, parents who believe that their
children are academically gifted may be attracted to school systems
that have developed and implemented innovative gifted and talented
programs. Other school enrollment choices that exist in most parts of
the country involve opting out of public education entirely, either
through enrollment in private schools or home schooling. Approximately 10 percent of all elementary and secondary school students are
enrolled in private schools. The number of home-schooled students

nationwide is subject to much dispute, with estimates in the late 1980s ranging from 150,000 to 1,000,000 or more. Few would dispute, however, that the number of such students is growing rapidly (Lines, 1990).

Within public education, opportunities for parents to influence their children's school (or within-school) enrollment have existed for decades without ever being labeled as parental choice programs. One urban school administrator, when asked about the voluntary transfer program he administered, responded that his district didn't have a parental choice program, only a racial balance program. Parental (or sometimes, at the secondary level, student) choice may exist, to greater or lesser degrees, in many programs that go by other names. These include alternative schools described as dropout prevention programs, vocational educational programs, parental consent in special education programs, magnet school programs, town tuitioning arrangements in rural Maine and Vermont, statutory or customary agreements among administrators that may be prompted by parent requests, and so forth. Some schools allow parents to express their preferences (usually honored) for certain teachers, while other schools let parents choose between graded and ungraded classrooms.

In summary, parental choice already exists, at least to some degree, virtually everywhere in the United States, although in many cases it exists under some other name or is an informal practice without any name. Unfortunately, the existence of such programs and practices may give rise to serious equity problems. Not everyone can afford to live in the relatively affluent districts that are most likely to support outstanding programs or to send their children to private schools. Not everyone knows that they can (in some districts) request a transfer to another school or make a request for a particular teacher. Parents are not equal in their financial resources or their access to information networks, and this frequently has real implications for the education of their children.

What Parents Think and Do

The reasons that parents (or students) choose schools are quite likely to be an element of local school folklore. Educators opposed to expanding parental choice, for example, may cite cases in support of their view that choices would be made for all the wrong reasons, leading to harmful effects on school programs. Thus, observers of the local education scene in central New York not too many years ago were likely to have been aware of a certain outstanding high school athlete.

According to a major story in the sports section of a local newspaper, this young man switched high schools by moving in with relatives in order to finish his high school athletic career with the best team in that part of the state. Such an incident may make more of an impression than the hundreds of anonymous black families each year who, in pursuit of higher quality instruction for their children, request voluntary transfers to schools in more affluent sections of the major city in that region.

Numerous research studies have surveyed parents about the criteria they use in selecting schools for their children. In addition to participation on athletic teams, these include academic quality (teacher knowledge, skills and attitudes, curriculum, administrative leadership, academic standards, instructional methods, etc.); student outcomes (grades or test scores, achievements of graduates); school atmosphere (discipline, values, climate); school/class size (individual attention); extracurricular activities, parental involvement; physical condition of the building; safety; location (distance from home, transportation arrangements, neighborhood characteristics, etc.); student characteristics (race/ethnicity, socioeconomic status), financial cost; before- and after-school child care arrangements; preschool enrollment; religious instruction, religious training, and commitment of staff; prior enrollment by family members or friends; parental employment on school staff, and child's preferences (Maddaus, 1990). The 1990 Gallup poll, like several earlier surveys addressing this issue, found that the most important considerations were teacher quality, student discipline, and curriculum, each of which were considered very important by over 70 percent of those surveyed (Elam, 1990).

The major controversy with respect to parental criteria concerns the impact of using certain criteria on the prospects of achieving the goals of excellence and equity. Evaluators of the Alum Rock public school voucher demonstration project (see Section One) assumed that academic quality related to preparation for employment should be the primary criterion for parental choice of school. Instead, their survey revealed that 70 percent of parents cited location as a consideration, whereas only 32 percent cited program features, 30 percent cited family/friends/prior enrollment, 18 percent cited school quality, and 18 percent cited staff. This project is especially significant because the parents involved were predominantly poor and minority (55 percent Mexican American, 10 percent black)—in other words, precisely those people for whom academic excellence is presumed to be most important and problematic (Weiler, 1974; Bridge, 1978; Bridge and Blackman, 1978).

The Alum Rock study suggests the importance of examining the significance of neighborhood schools. Those parents who find what they want in their neighborhood schools are unlikely to pursue other options. Research on the school choices of white parents in Syracuse, New York, found that parents seek to manage the moral and social environment in which their children grow up. Good schools in good neighborhoods, in this moral and social sense, offer a cohesive environment that is both caring and controlling. Bad neighborhoods with bad schools, in this same sense, are a threat to children's well-being and may cause parents to look elsewhere for schools. Parents will focus on the academic quality of schools only after they are satisfied with the moral and social environment of the schools under consideration and their surrounding neighborhoods (Maddaus, 1988b).

The researchers at Alum Rock, however, focused on a different explanation for the preponderance of responses citing location as a criterion for choice. They concluded that parents had inadequate information on which to base a choice and, therefore, that choice programs should not be instituted until adequate information systems had been developed and implemented successfully. They cited data from their surveys indicating that some parents were not even aware that their children were participants in the voucher demonstration project. Coons and Sugarman's regulated voucher proposal (see Section One) places major emphasis on providing parents with the information they need to make informed decisions. Special attention must be given to outreach efforts directed at parents with limited education, who may have limited access to the usual printed materials and/or may be uncomfortable about visiting schools to gather information. Also, minority group parents may have limited contact with school professionals who are most frequently white. Providing equal access to necessary information is crucial to guaranteeing equity in parental choice programs, even if some parents (informed or not) will still prefer neighborhood schools for the reasons suggested previously.

While one can never be certain of the consequences of instituting a new parental choice program, a prediction that seems relatively safe is that those parents who have been successful in enrolling their children in the schools they desire under the existing options may not be especially interested in utilizing new options, at least in the short term. A Gallup poll in 1986 found that while 68 percent of public school parents would like to have the right to choose which public school their children attend, only 24 percent of these parents would actually send their children to other schools if they had that opportunity (Gallup, 1986). While 24 percent represents a significant number of students, this finding could be reassuring to those fearing massive upheaval if a majority of parents were to seek schools other than the ones in their own neighborhoods. Subsequent Gallup polls indicate that support for choice among public schools remains stable at over 60 percent, but the survey regarding how many parents would actually transfer their children to other schools has not been repeated (Elam, 1990).

What might happen in the long term is of course less certain. On the one hand, some parents might become hostile to the changes that could result in their children's schools as a consequence of providing expanded options for other parents and their children, leading to a decline in the overall percentage of parents supporting choice. Maddaus (1988a) interviewed white parents in Syracuse, New York, eight years after a voluntary transfer program, including magnet schools, was instituted in that city in a successful effort to achieve elementary school desegregation. He found that these parents, especially those in middle-income neighborhoods, strongly supported neighborhood schools and had very mixed feelings about the voluntary transfer program. These parents also voiced varying degrees of opposition to several other types of choice programs. Thus, the expansion of choice that accompanied desegregation has not had the effect of popularizing the concept of choice, but rather of highlighting its potential drawbacks, at least for some families. The details of the program adopted clearly make a significant difference.

On the other hand, while parents at present seem to like the idea of having a choice, it is less clear that they think of themselves as active consumers of educational services in the sense that Friedman suggests (see Section One). Rather, they perceive choice as a last resort option if problems develop with their children's education in neighborhood schools. A recent survey of parents in England, where the Thatcher government introduced open enrollment as part of the Education Reform Act 1988, found that only 11 percent of the parents interviewed clearly thought of themselves as consumers (Hughes, Wikeley, and Nash, 1990). If this perception were to change significantly, it could result in major changes in behavior.

Implications for School Programs

In thinking about parental choice programs, it is not enough to consider the parents alone. There is much more to establishing a parental choice program than hiring someone to dispense informational brochures and process parents' applications. Parental choice has a supply side as well as a demand side. Offering parents the right to choose, without simultaneously diversifying the range of school program options from which to choose, may be a recipe for parental frustration (Elmore, 1986). In his analogy between selling schools and selling groceries (see Section One), Friedman argues that giving competition and free enterprise greater scope compels providers to work more efficiently in order to provide improved quality and a greater variety of products. Coons and Sugarman (see Section One), in their hypothetical case illustrating how choice would work, suggest that allowing choice would also permit teachers to specialize in what they enjoy most and do best. In his report on the first year of the Alum Rock public school voucher demonstration, Weiler (1974) notes that Alum Rock's superintendent of schools was attempting to decentralize the district's program. Weiler devotes a great deal of attention to the development of a wide range of mini-school programs which were the real source of diversity in the Alum Rock project. While some diversity within a school district may occur naturally, as each neighborhood school responds to its own clientele and their interests, the establishment of a parental choice program such as the one at Alum Rock would give added impetus to diversifying curriculum and programs at the building level or below. This diversity, however, may produce little change without an active and varied set of information-dissemination strategies to contact parents of diverse backgrounds and interests.

Parental choice programs also have a wide range of other implications for school districts. The movement of students from one school to another may result in significant changes in the composition of the student bodies of the various schools. In some cases, such as magnet schools for desegregation, this is the primary intent of the program. (If parental choice is not instituted as a strategy for achieving desegregation, any such plan in a racially diverse community will still need to take racial balance into account.) Secondary schools might retain and attract more at-risk students by instituting or expanding programs to meet their needs, such as improved vocational programs and flexible scheduling. Changes in public schools resulting from a parental choice program may have the effect of attracting some private school children into the public schools. Such changes will have multiple implications for facilities, staffing, staff development, and other aspects of school programming.

One major area that will need to be addressed at the local level is transportation. In the absence of new or expanded arrangements for busing students, parental choice may result in a low response and/or may be accessible only to those relatively affluent families that can provide their own transportation, leading to serious equity problems.

While some advocates have suggested that choice will save money in the long run by promoting efficiency, the available evidence in the short run suggests that choice programs can require significant and continuing financial investments. A school district may have to pick up the expense of additional busing, including, in some states, busing of students to private schools if access to such schools is expanded by the choice plan in question. Other aspects of choice programs with significant budget implications include parent information programs, additional staff for new or improved programs, staff training, time spent on program planning and curriculum revision, extended hours of operation, and new equipment and supplies. In short, parental choice could have many implications for virtually every aspect of a school district's operations and budget.

Implications for School Staff and Community

The implementation of any new program requires a period of adjustment for all involved. Despite the best efforts in planning before a new program goes into effect, there will be unforeseen changes and delays in implementation. The best staff training in the world will not anticipate every problem or convince everyone with a role in the new arrangements. A good deal of patience on the part of all concerned will be necessary while the transition takes place.

Of the long-term changes, perhaps the most important is a subtle shift in relationships among all those concerned: administrators, teachers, parents, and even students. The old hierarchical model of authority from school board to administrators to teachers to students, with the parents mostly on the outside looking in, will no longer apply. In its place, a new, more collaborative set of relationships must be developed, requiring an opening of two-way lines of communication that were once either one-way or largely closed. For example, people accustomed to the notion that classroom and home were the exclusive turf of teacher and parent respectively will need to get used to the reality of parents visiting classrooms and teachers making home visits. Collaborative decision making has important implications for leadership and management styles, and even for who exercises leadership and participates in management. For members of school boards, overseeing a system that encourages diversity will be a very different experience from making policies designed to be applied uniformly in all schools.

Finally, there will be some difficult ethical dilemmas to be faced in dealing with both overall program features and individual cases. One question decision makers will have to face involves the question of access to programs. On what basis will students be assigned to schools or programs that are overenrolled? Should entrance into particular schools be selective and therefore competitive (e.g., should a magnet schools program include a gifted and talented school, or screen students applying for a fine arts school on the basis of talent)? Selective schools may enhance the performance of the students who are admitted to them, but at the expense of removing successful role models from other schools and thus perhaps lowering the performance of those students who remain. Other program features with ethical implications include the details of transportation, program selection and development, and staff assignment.

Ethical decisions will also arise in relation to individual students. In the past, residence dictated enrollment, and school building staff were left to cope with the consequences of geography. But under a parental choice program, building-level administrators (and teachers) will have to decide to what extent to recruit desirable students (based on academic ability, behavior, athletic talent, etc.) and to discourage less desirable students from applying. Pupil personnel directors will have to decide which schools to recommend when parents ask which schools are available. In short, to the extent that school staff are in a position to influence parental requests either before these are made or to act on them after the application is received, they will face difficult ethical issues in doing so.

Is Choice Worthwhile?

School board members, parents, administrators, teachers, and others in any given community should decide whether expanding parental choice of school is desirable in their own community (Association for Supervision and Curriculum Development, 1990). Both the benefits and the costs will vary greatly from one community to another. Well-planned parental choice programs have clearly proven to be effective as a means of achieving school desegregation. Other significant positive effects, justifying the costs involved, may well exist. However, definitive and widely generalizable studies of the effects of parental choice programs on student achievement (for both those who choose nonneighborhood schools as well as those who do not), socioeconomic integration, parental involvement, school improvement, and other desired outcomes have yet to be produced. A single definitive answer to these questions may be impossible, since so much depends on the characteristics of the particular community and the details of the program adopted. The best we may be able to hope for from research may be the identification of characteristics of programs that produce desired outcomes in relation to the characteristics of the communities in which these programs are found. Rhetoric aside (and there is a great deal of it from both sides), it will still be the responsibility of local decision makers to decide what will work in their communities.

References

Association for Supervision and Curriculum Development. (1990). *Public schools of choice.* Alexandria, VA: Author.

Bridge, R. G. (1978, May). Information imperfections: The Achilles' heel of entitlement plans. *School Review, 86*(3), 504–529.

Bridge, R. G., & Blackman, J. (1978, April). *A study of alternatives in American education, Vol. IV: Family choice in schooling* (Report R-2170/4-NIE). Santa Monica, CA: Rand.

Darling-Hammond, L., & Kirby, S. N. (1985, December). *Tuition tax deductions and parent school choice: A case study of Minnesota* (Report R-3294-NIE). Santa Monica, CA: Rand. ERIC Document No. ED 273 047.

Elam, S. M. (1990, September). The 22nd Annual Gallup Poll of the public's attitudes toward the public schools. *Phi Delta Kappan, 72*(1), 41–55.

Elmore, R. F. (1986, December). *Choice in public education.* Santa Monica, CA: Center for Policy Research in Education.

Gallup, A. M. (1986, September). The 18th annual Gallup poll of the public's attitudes toward the public schools. *Phi Delta Kappan, 68*(1), 43–59.

Hughes, M., Wikeley, F., & Nash, T. (1990, July). *Parents and the national curriculum: An interim report.* Exeter, England: School of Education, University of Exeter.

Kliebard, H. M. (1986). *The struggle for the American curriculum, 1893–1958.* Urbana: University of Illinois Press.

Lines, P. M. (1990). Home instruction: Characteristics, size, and growth. In Van Galen & Pitman (Eds.), *Home Schooling: Political, historical, and pedagogical perspectives.* Norwood, NJ: Ablex Publishing.

Maddaus, J. (1988a, September). Families, neighborhoods and schools: Parental perspectives and actions regarding choice in elementary school enrollment. *Dissertation Abstracts International, 49,* 477-A (University Microfilms No. 8806952).

Maddaus, J. (1988b, November). *Parents perceptions of the moral environment in choosing their children's elementary schools.* Paper presented at the annual meeting of the Association for Moral Education, Pittsburgh, PA.

Maddaus, J. (1990). Parental choice of school: What parents think and do. *Review of Research in Education, 16,* 267–295.

Peshkin, A. (1986). *God's choice: The total world of a fundamentalist Christian school.* Chicago: University of Chicago Press.

Weiler, D. (1974, June). *A public school voucher demonstration: The first year at Alum Rock* (Report R-1495-NIE). Santa Monica, CA: Rand.

Williams, M. F., Hancher, K. S., & Hutner, A. (1983, December). *Parents and school choice: A household survey.* Washington, DC: U.S. Department of Education. ERIC Document No. ED 240 739.

SECTION FOUR REFERENCES

Campbell, P. F., Cunningham, L. L., Nystrand, R. O., & Usdan, M. D. (1985). *The organization and control of American schools* (5th ed.). Columbus, OH: Charles E. Merrill.

Ehrenreich, B. (1990). *The worst years of our lives: Irreverent notes from a decade of greed.* New York: Pantheon.

First, P. F., & Nowakowski, J. (1986). *Research report: School district response to Senate Joint Resolution #25.* Springfield, IL: State Board of Education.

First, P. F. (in press). Evaluating school boards: Looking through next generation lenses. In P. First & H. Walberg (Eds.), *School boards: Changing local control.* Berkeley, CA: McCutchan.

Hickrod, G. A., Franklin, D., Hubbard, B., Hines, E., Polite, M., & Pruyne, G. (1989). *Guilty governments: The problem of inadequate educational funding in Illinois and other states.* Normal, IL: Center for the Study of Educational Finance, Illinois State University.

Hudgins, H. C., & Vacca, R. (1985). *Law and education: Contemporary issues and court decisions* (2nd ed.). Charlottesville, VA: The Michie Co.

Institute for Educational Leadership (IEL). (1986). *School boards: Strengthening grass roots leadership.* Washington, DC: Author.

Kimbrough, R., & Nunnery, M. (1976). *Educational administration.* New York: Macmillan.

Lewis, A. C. (1988). Presidential politics and the schools. *Phi Delta Kappan, 69,* 324–325.

McCormick, C., & First, P. F. (1991). Police your business policies. *The American School Board Journal, 178*(1), 30–31.

Nowakowski, J., & First, P. F. (1989). School board minutes: Records of reform. *Educational Evaluation and Policy Analysis, 11*(4), 389–404.

National School Boards Association (NSBA). (1982). *Becoming a better board member: A guide to effective school board service.* Alexandria, VA: Author.

National School Boards Association (NSBA). (1987). *American school boards: The positive power.* Alexandria, VA: Author.

Peterson, P. E. (1976). *School politics Chicago style.* Chicago: The University of Chicago Press.

Reecer, M. (1989). Yes, boards are under fire, but reports of your death are greatly exaggerated. *The American School Board Journal, 176*(3), 31–34.

Reutter, E. E., Jr. (1985). *The law of public education* (3rd ed.). Mineola, NY: Foundation Press.

Roosevelt, F. D. (1936). Speech, Syracuse, NY, Sept. 29.

Shanker, A. (1989). Pressures on local control. *American School Board Journal, 176*(3), 31–34.

Soltis, J. (1988). Reform or reformation? *Educational Administration Quarterly, 24,* 241–245.

U.S. Bureau of the Census. (1987). 1987 Census of Governments, Vol. 1, Government Organization Number 2, Popularly Elected Officials. Washington, DC: Author.

Index